940.
McW

s L.
Ont.

4-
es,
R. J.
ard)

Gas!
The Battle for Ypres, 1915

Gas!
The Battle for Ypres, 1915

by
James L. McWilliams
and
R. James Steel

"Thou shalt ascend and come like a storm,
thou shalt be like a cloud to cover the land."
Isaiah XXXVIII, 9

Vanwell Publishing Limited
St. Catharines, Ontario

Canadian Cataloguing in Publication Data

McWilliams, James L.
  Gas! The Battle for Ypres, 1915

Bibliography: p.
Includes index.
ISBN 0-920277-01-2

1. Ypres, 2nd Battle of, 1915.   2. World War,
1914-1918 - Campaigns - Belgium - Ieper.
3. Gases, Asphyxiating and poisonous - War
use. I. Steel, R. J. II. Title.

D542.Y7M29   1985   940.4'24   C85-098222-7

ISBN 0-920277-01-2
Printed and bound in Canada by John Deyell Company

Contents

From the Authors
to the Readers

We have made use of three types of source in compiling this account of events of 70-odd years ago. First there are the memories of survivors; though valuable, these are coloured by subsequent events and are often fragmentary. Secondly there are the accounts (both published and unpublished) written by participants shortly after or even during the event; these are generally vivid but uncritical, often incorrect in detail. Thirdly there are the official documents — War Diaries, reports, and the various Official Histories of the war; these record in cold statistical terms the factual (or what were thought to be factual) aspects of the event.

If our readers also consider the emotional, almost panic-stricken nature of those far-off days, the vast number of participants of several nationalities, and their lack of experience with the major factor — chlorine gas — they can begin to understand the problem of the researchers. At this stage of the Great War even the official records were rather haphazard affairs. It was, for instance, quite common to find a major event occurring at different times according to different reports. Therefore historical judgement had to be rendered on such seemingly simple facts as the time a barrage began, or the number of troops holding a particular trench. We have attempted to present an absolutely true account. If we have failed on any point we beg our readers' indulgence and request that they contact us if they have information which will enable us to rectify any such errors.

All dialogue is taken from interviews with survivors, their letters to us or other written accounts. Quotations taken from published works are, with one exception, acknowledged individually. The exception is Colonel Mordacq's comments, all of which are here acknowledged as being quoted from his fascinating book, *Le drame sur l'Yser*. Reports by many of the Canadian officers were quoted from the 1920 publication, *Canadian War Records*.

7

We would like to acknowledge our indebtedness to the work of Colonel A. Fortescue Duguid whose *Official History of the Canadian Forces in the Great War 1914-1919* (Volume 1 plus Appendices and Maps) proved of inestimable value in ordering events. In cases of conflicting evidence we nearly always accepted Duguid's impeccably researched version. All messages, official documents or histories not otherwise acknowledged are taken from Colonel Duguid's superb account.

Several unpublished manuscripts were also of special significance: George S. Tuxford's "Memoirs" (housed in the Saskatchewan Archives, Regina); George S. Bell's manuscript held by the Public Archives of Canada; Tom Drummond's memoirs held by his family, and A.W. Bennett's unpublished memoirs.

We would like to express our gratitude to the following who assisted in the research for this book in a variety of ways: Dr. D.W. Larson (University of Regina) for his valuable advice regarding the nature of chlorine gas; Mrs. Bertha I. Tuxford (Victoria) for her kind permission to quote from the unpublished memoirs of George S. Tuxford; to A.W. Bennett for kind permission to quote from his manuscript; to Alice Gordon (Regina) for kind permission to use the memoirs of her father, Tom Drummond; and Mr. Stan Lovelace for kind permission to quote from his private wartime diary.

We would specially like to thank Mrs. Jeanette Metka of Moose Jaw who so willingly gave of her time to assist us in translating various French sources. Others who deserve special thanks are the ladies of the Moose Jaw Public Library for their enthusiastic assistance in many matters, and Mr. Douglas S. MacGowan of St. Catharines for his untiring assistance.

A special thanks must go out to Mr. Hilaire C. Vandermeersch of Tillsonburg, Ontario for taking time out of his Belgium holiday to root out facts and figures from the Ypres battlefields.

We would like to thank the Public Archives of Canada for permission to reproduce material from Divisional, Brigade, and Battalion War Diaries held in Ottawa and the C.B.C. for permission to quote from the radio series "Flanders Fields" produced by J. Frank Willis.

Thanks must go also across the Atlantic to the Public Records Office, London, England and Service Historique de l'Armée, Vincennes, France for permission to reproduce material from their respective war records.

We must also express our gratitude to our wives and families who proved to be so understanding during the long hours of research and writing.

To everyone who assisted us in any way we would like to express our most sincere thanks. We must also say that while no effort has been spared to ensure that the facts in these pages are correct in every detail, the responsibility for error is ours alone. Every effort has been made to credit accurately all sources used in this book, but we shall welcome any information which will enable us to correct any errors or omissions.

J. McW. & R.J.S.

To the following veterans who provided information by way of letters, tape recordings, interviews, and questionnaires, we offer our most humble thanks: John Bell Armstrong (Victoria, B.C.), Bert Baines (Cambridge, Ont.), G.M. Beaton (Victoria, B.C.), A.W. Bennett (Calgary, Alta.), Charlie Brown (Vancouver, B.C.), J.J. Brown (Sudbury, Ont.), Lachie Campbell (Glasgow, Scotland), Ernest Cave (Colchester, England), Godfrey Cochrane (London, England), D.C. Cooper (Victoria, B.C.), A.D. Corker (Victoria, B.C.), Bryce Cozens (Victoria, B.C.), Herbert Crosbie (Regina, Sask.), W. Draper (Glasgow, Scotland), Harold Fuller (Bexhill-on-Sea, England), W.W. Gale (London, Ont.), Robert C. Glegg (Santa Rosa, Calif.), Jim Gray (Chatham, Ont.), C.R. Hobby (Stirlingshire, Scotland), H. Jones (Lethbridge, Alta.), Harold Kempling (Hamilton, Ont.), James Kennedy (Toronto, Ont.), Stan Lovelace (Victoria, B.C.), A. Lukeman (Conway, Ont.), Willard MacCallum (Charlottetown, P.E.I.), K.W. McLean (Victoria, P.E.I.), Sandy Mitchell (Falkirk, Scotland), David Ogilvie (Bedford, England), Joseph Rees (Hamilton, Ont.), J.A. Rigby (Smith Falls, Ont.), Tom Running (Grand Island, N.Y.), Perley Smith (Port Hood, N.S.), Linden Somerville (Niagara Falls, Ont.), J.R. Tomlinson (St. Paul, Alta.), Richard Watts (Thorold, Ont.), Leonard Wernham (Dumfries, Scotland), Robert West (St. Catharines, Ont.), James Whittaker (Arundel, England), C.S. Williams (Drayton Valley, Alta.), Albert Young (Long Island, N.Y.), Tom Young (Tarbert, Scotland).

Chapter One

Ye Blind Guides
(April, 1915)

*"Ye blind guides, which strain at a gnat and
swallow a camel."*

Matthew XXIII, 24

On the night of 13 April, 1915, on the Ypres Salient, a figure
slipped over the parapets of the German trenches north of
Langemarck. The moonlight revealed a German soldier, Private
August Jaeger, an automobile driver attached to the 234th Reserve
Infantry Regiment. Jaeger, perhaps disillusioned by a soldier's life,
was deserting.

The French trenches lay several hundred yards away across the
corpse-littered expanse of no man's land. Neither the French nor the
Germans had been sending out many patrols during these balmy
spring nights, and both sides had assiduously avoided causing any
commotion. In fact, on many occasions the common soldiers had
fraternized in no man's land, so there seemed little likelihood of running into trouble on the journey across. Jaeger crossed without incident, and before midnight he had turned himself over to men of the
4th Battalion of Chasseurs. In no time at all he found himself
marching away from the hated western front escorted by several
cheery *poilus*.* But first he was to be interrogated at the headquarters of the French 11th Division. This interrogation should have
changed history.

The deserter talked freely, giving detailed information regarding trench strengths and routines. Jaeger even pointed out his
own commanding officer's report centre, on the road north from
Poelcappelle, "the last house in red brick on the left of the exit." But

---

* *Poilus* (literally "the hairy ones") French nickname for the common soldier.

11

what really startled the interrogator was the last portion of the ex-chauffeur's statement:

"An attack is planned for the near future against the French trenches . . . With this object in view four batteries have been placed in position in the first line trenches; these batteries each have 20 bottles of asphyxiating gas . . . At a given signal — 3 red rockets fired by the artillery — the bottles are uncorked, and the gas on escaping, is carried by a favourable wind towards the French trenches. This gas is intended to asphyxiate the men who occupy the trenches and to allow the Germans to occupy them without losses. In order to prevent the men being themselves intoxicated by the gas, each man is provided with a packet of tow steeped in oxygen."

When General Edmond Ferry commanding the French 11th Division read the prisoner's statement he was shocked. The idea of "asphyxiating gas" boggled the mind. Yet there seemed no reason to doubt Jaeger. Despicable as his actions may have been, he certainly appeared to be telling all he knew. If he was making up the story, then to what end? Ferry decided to act at once. He ordered the forward lines thinned out to avoid casualties, and instructed his artillery to attempt to rupture the buried gas cylinders. Ferry then sent an officer to warn the 28th Imperial Division* on his right and advise the Canadian brigade which was due to relieve some of his own troops that night "to exercise the greatest vigilance and to seek suitable means to prevent inhalation of gas."[1] These reports plus copies for his own Corps, and Army headquarters were sent at noon, 14 April. "We thus thought we had done, as quickly as possible, everything necessary to avoid *surprise*, the effect of terror, and the heavy losses which the Germans counted on inflicting with this new and abominable weapon of war."[2]

In this manner Ferry's information regarding this new threat was introduced into the maze of command structures responsible for the Ypres Salient. The French divisions, including Ferry's 11th, came under General Henri Gabriel Putz who, though French, was in turn subordinate to Albert, King of the Belgians. These French forces were also part of the *Groupe Provisoire du Nord* under the Command of General Ferdinand Foch at Cassel. As representative of General Joffre, Commander-in-Chief of the French Army, Foch

---

* Most British divisions were named "Imperial" Divisions.

was responsible for co-ordinating operations with the British and Belgians. Thus at this crucial sector on the north side of the Salient the command structure was an amazing conglomeration of British, Canadian, French and Belgian generals.

The Salient was garrisoned by both British and French troops. The southern half of the arc was held by the British — three divisions of General Plumer's V Corps. In the southwest corner was the 5th Imperial Division. Beside them the 27th Imperial Division stood watch. Facing due east were the 28th Imperials. Next came troops of the French XX Corps under General Balfourier. The French High Command was anxious to turn over their portion of the Salient to the British. As a result, the 1st Canadian Division was scheduled to take over from one of the French Divisions, General Ferry's 11th.

The Canadians, and the 27th and 28th Imperial Divisons were part of the British V Corps under Sir Herbert Plumer. In appearance a perfect replica of the red-faced, white-mustachioed Colonel Blimp, Plumer was a very able soldier. His V Corps was a new formation, but "Fussy" or "Daddy" as he was known would soon have things in perfect running order. His immediate superior was the commander of the Second Army, Sir Horace Smith-Dorrien. He was described by a later historian thusly: "Smith-Dorrien was a clever, sensitive and rational man. No other officer of equivalent seniority — with the possible exception of Sir Ian Hamilton, bound for Gallipoli — was his equal intellectually, and none could rival his ability in handling large numbers of men with economy and decision."[3] Sir Horace had already saved the British Expeditionary Force by disobeying instructions to retire from Le Cateau in the first month of the war. His decision to stand and fight had enabled the bulk of the clumsily handled British force to escape almost certain defeat. But unfortunately for all, Smith-Dorrien had incurred the enmity of his superior.

At the top of the chain of command was the Commander-in-Chief of the B.E.F., Field Marshal Sir John French. "Weak-willed yet cunningly stubborn" was the verdict of one historian.[4] Events were to prove this assessment only too clearly.

Ferry's information was received with scepticism. His immediate superior, General Putz, sent the information on but confided to a British liaison officer that he did not believe it himself, "For the prisoner, on further examination, had exhibited such great knowledge of the German position and defence arrangements, that he had come to the conclusion that the man had been primed and sent over with the intention to deceive."[5]

Certainly it was difficult for anyone in April, 1915 to express any logical ideas on "asphyxiating gas". What was it? Tear gas? Probably, if it existed at all, it was something rather trivial and ridiculous — certainly only effective locally. The only precedents for such ideas were the complaints by unsophisticated South African burghers during the Boer War almost fifteen years earlier. Their protest had eventually been traced to the smell of bursting High Explosive shells. Besides, the use of any form of poison had been outlawed by the Geneva Convention years ago.

The next morning, 15 April, "Daddy" Plumer's V Corps headquarters received a field message from his 28th Imperial Division. This added more information to that received from Ferry the day before. It described how the gas cylinders worked, and enclosed a sample of the tow or cotton waste from Jaeger's gas mask for analysis. "Prisoner said a dress rehearsal of attack, but without gas, was to have taken place on the thirteenth. French 11th Division report having seen three red lights in German lines on night of thirteenth-fourteenth about one a.m. French Division announces capture of another prisoner today who confirms above on general lines."

The second deserter was Julius Rapsahl former N.C.O. of the 4th Landwehr Regiment (52nd Reserve Division, XXVI Reserve Corps). Rapsahl had been reduced to the ranks for striking an officer and this probably accounted for his decision to desert. He too carried a package of cotton waste to be used as a mouth protector, though he claimed it was to protect him against French gas. This disgruntled ex-N.C.O. had surrendered to the 69th Regiment, 11th (French) Division at 7 a.m. on Thursday.

At 1:50 that afternoon a dispatch arrived at Plumer's V Corps from Smith-Dorrien's Second Army Headquarters advising that the German attack was expected that very night. This startling information had come from a Belgian agent "confirmed from other sources." The dispatch was specific:

"Passages have been prepared across old trenches to facilitate bringing up of artillery. Germans intend making use of tubes with asphyxiating gas. They are placed in batteries of 20 tubes per 40 metres along front of XXIV (sic XXVI) Corps. *A favourable wind necessary.*"*[6]

A key clause was the fact that "a favourable wind" was necessary. If the wind was unfavourable—that is from the wrong direction or too light to carry the gas forward—there could be no attack for the moment. This clause seemed to have been overlooked with dire consequences.

It can however be understood from this message that the three British divisional commanders—Alderson (1st Canadian Division), Snow (27th), and Bulfin (28th)—realized the nature of the threat. Indeed the War Diary of the Canadian Assistant Director of Medical Services for that day states: "Attended consultation of Officers at V Corps with Director of Medical Services, 2nd Army, presiding. Rumour that this evening the enemy will attack our lines using an asphyxiating gas to overcome our men in the trenches. Arrangements made for the handling of 1,000 wounded tonight in the V Corps."

The choice of the word "rumour" in the ADMS War Diary suggests that the warning was not taken seriously by senior officers. Also there was no mention of any special attention for victims of the "asphyxiating gas," although particular arrangements had been made for extra wounded.

There is no record that this information was passed down below Divisional level except for General Ferry's warning to the 2nd Canadian Brigade which had already relieved some of his troops. However, the information must have percolated down, though no Brigade war diary makes mention of orders concerning asphyxiating gas.

Nevertheless, some mild precautions were taken. During the afternoon a British air reconnaissance was carried out. Two years later when the Americans entered the war the British General Staff supplied them with all of their information on gas warfare. In that account it was stated that British airmen saw gas cylinders in the German trenches at the crossroads of Broodseinde. Were these discovered on 15 April? It is known that one plane at least stayed out till 7 p.m. It reported all roads clear for three miles behind the German lines with no unusual movements detected on the front.

---

* Authors' italics

Perhaps this report added to the sense of security enjoyed by the allied high command.

That same night the gigantic Canadian Brigadier, Arthur Currie, recorded in his personal diary, "Attack expected at night, to be preceded by sending of poisonous gases to our lines and the sending up of three red lights (reported by prisoner who came into French lines)." He ordered his own 2nd Canadian Brigade to take several precautions. The brigade artillery was ordered to fire on the German breastworks, placing a shell every twenty yards, although the battery commanders were not told why. For Major "Andy" McNaughton of the 7th Battery, this was "one of the best days I had had in the war." At this date British artillery was allotted an incredible three rounds per gun per day! To McNaughton, formerly a lecturer at McGill University, the chance to fire 90 rounds demanding pinpoint accuracy was a welcome challenge. Despite McNaughton's scientific and accurate gunnery there was no sign of any "gas cylinders" rupturing in the German front line.

That afternoon the British also ordered a stand-to, and from five o'clock till midnight the troops waited for the expected attack. After midnight all battalions slept by their arms and equipment.

The French XX Corps, under whose command Currie's 2nd Brigade came, ordered no special precautions. Nevertheless, the Canadians' reserve battalion, the 5th, 'stood to' like its British counterparts.

The next morning a young officer at 2nd Brigade Headquarters wrote home. "Last night we got ready to receive a German attack. Divisional Headquarters notified us that the Germans intended to attack with tubes of poisonous gas; but it didn't materialize . . . Today is quite normal. The air is quite smoky and not good for artillery observation."[7] There had been no wind.

And so the expected attack had not taken place and Friday dawned uneventfully. By now General Ferry had received a belated reply to his urgent message to XX Corps, Army, and French General Headquarters. The latter warned him "(i) all this gas business cannot be taken seriously . . . (ii) a divisional commander has not the right to communicate direct with allied troops, but only by the channel through Army Corps (iii) the distribution of troops in the trenches . . . has been fixed, *ne varietur*, by the instructions of the French General Headquarters."[8] G.H.Q. had certainly put Ferry in his place, and his presumptuousness had been noted. Daily life could go back to normal in Ypres and the infamous Salient surrounding it.

The Ypres Salient had become legend back in the autumn of 1914. During the months of October and early November the Germans had desperately sought to break the deadlock in Flanders by successive massed attacks on a thin line of British regulars — the "Old Contemptibles." Despite fearful losses, the attacks had failed and a seventeen mile salient around the ancient town of Ypres had been the result. The courageous tenacity with which it had been held had created the legend. The Ypres Salient had taken on an emotional and spiritual significance which its strategic value never for a moment warranted. Withdrawal to a more defensible line was never again seriously considered by the Allies.

Ypres itself was a typical 14th century town encircled by a medieval moat. Before the war, 17,000 citizens had gone quietly about their occupations in this picturesque backwater of Flanders. The town's two significant features were St. Martin's Cathedral and the Guild Hall of the Cloth Merchants, two of the finest examples of Gothic architecture in the world.

The majority of Ypres' inhabitants had stayed on despite the proximity of the front. Though the "Cloth Hall" had been gutted, men on scaffolding worked to repair its famous tower. The town's excellent restaurants remained open and the small shops, especially the pastry shops, did a good trade with soldiers from many lands.

Around Ypres the Salient extended in an arc from Steenstraat, five miles north of the town, to St. Eloi, less than three miles south of the town. Forming the diameter of this semicircle were two canals, the Yser Canal running north from Ypres, and the Ypres-Comines Canal leading southwards.

The countryside around Ypres was fertile and densely populated. Several small creeks or *beeks* drained the area inadequately and the inhabitants had long ago built a network of drainage ditches to carry off the surplus water. The rural population of this portion of Belgium had not vacated their homes despite the war. True, some had fled during the First Battle of Ypres in the preceding autumn, but most had stayed on. In the countryside the farms, villages, and hamlets were almost untouched by the war, and within two miles of the firing line plans were afoot for spring planting. There seemed no reason to believe that the almost tranquil conditions of the past months would change in the spring of 1915. After all, the Germans had been held off before, and nothing had changed since, had it?

General Ferry's intelligence report of 14 April was *not* the Allies' first warning of poison gas. Charles Lucieto, the outstanding French spy, had reported from the Ruhr and the Rhineland that the Germans had been producing poison gas at the Mannheim factories of *Badische Anilin und Soda Fabrik*.[9] Despite Lucieto's reputation for accuracy his report had been ignored by the French High Command.

The British too had been warned. During the early hours of 28 March, German trenches east of Zillebeke had been raided. "I captured a German officer who spoke English very well," reported the Sergeant in charge. "He wrote a statement in my carbon book to the effect that gas cylinders were in No Man's Land, to be used on us at the first favourable wind." The Sergeant was dispatched at the head of a small patrol to test the truth of the German's statement. "We found gas cylinders in dozens over a space of some hundred yards exactly as he said. This further information was passed to headquarters."[10] No more was heard of this incident until eighteen years later when the Sergeant wrote a letter to the *Daily Express*. This information had, however, been confirmed that same day by the Bulletin of the French Tenth Army which had just vacated the salient in front of Zillebeke. Unfortunately, the Bulletin had never been forwarded to the British troops who had taken over the area.

Evidence, or at least clues, continued to trickle in after Ferry's report. On Friday, 16 April, the morning after the expected attack had failed to materialize, a Belgian agent's report was circulated as a bulletin to allied headquarters. It told of a German rush order for 10,000 "mouth protectors" made in Ghent and to be carried in cloth bags 10cm. by 17cm. "The mouth protectors, soaked with a suitable liquid, will serve to protect the men against the heavy asphyxiating gas which the Germans intend to discharge towards the enemy lines, notably on the front of the XXVI Reserve Corps."

The next day, 17 April, the 5th Imperial Division suddenly seized Hill 60, the famous refuse dump facing the southeastern face of the Salient. When the British mines went off, blasting apart the German trenches and parapets, an exceptional panic was noted. "In the midst of this inferno could be seen German soldiers, some in their shirtsleeves and without weapons, falling over one another in their struggle to escape into the communication trenches, others in their terror forcing their way through their comrades at the bayonet's point."[11] Consequently, the 13th Brigade seized Hill 60 without opposition. Holding it, however, became a nightmare as the Germans made tremendous efforts to retake the pulverized refuse pile and British casualties mounted. In their local reports the hard-pressed British repeatedly mentioned strange "gas vapours" which produced tears and temporary incapacitating effects. Where were these vapours coming from? By Tuesday, 20 April, it had been decided that the enemy was employing harmless "lachrymatory shells" (Tear Gas).

A day later at the other end of the Salient British air reconnaissance noted a marked increase in rolling stock at Wervicq, behind the German line. There was no evidence of reinforcements, but it was obvious that something had been delivered in bulk to the German forces facing the French and Canadians there.

For those who understood the German mind and had an eye for recent history there were further disquieting suggestions — from the Germans' own official communiques. On 14 April — "Yesterday week, northwest of Verdun the French employed mines emitting yellow asphyxiating gases:" on 17 April the following, "Yesterday, east of Ypres, the British employed shells and bombs with asphyxiating gas." It had been the practice for the Germans to prepare their people at home for some ruthless breach of conduct by accusing the Allies of it beforehand. Supposedly this added an aura of moral rectitude to their own actions. Yet in spite of such evidence from Germany's past conduct, this curious window on their intentions was ignored.

During these last few days a German document had been captured which should have made shocking reading for Allied intelligence. It was a copy of the German Second Army's memorandum of 16 October, 1914, and it listed among "the arms at the disposal of the pioneers . . . flame or asphyxiating gas projectors."

No one had pieced together these various interlocking clues. At that time Allied intelligence was unable to assemble all of these separate reports, and no individual officer except Ferry had taken seriously the fragments he had seen. Armies which still sent their men into battle in kilts or in blue jackets and red *pantalons* were apparently unable to imagine concepts so unchivalrous as poison gas.

The Generals' almost universal attitude towards innovation is typified by an entry in the diary of Douglas Haig, commanding the British First Army.

"Lord Dundonald arrived from England. He is studying the conditions of War in hopes of being able to apply to modern conditions an invention of his great-grandfather for driving a garrison out of a fort by using sulphur fumes. I asked him how he arranged to have a favourable wind!"

The date of this rare joke by Sir Douglas was 8 April, just two weeks before many of his countrymen were to die from the enemy's poison gas propelled by "a favourable wind."

Meanwhile, on the same night that the British had seized Hill 60, the Canadian Division had completed its relief of the French 11th Division. It was a very relieved General Ferry who bade farewell to the Salient. In those last hours of the changeover men of the 10th Canadian Battalion were told by their Gallic comrades that their battalion had suffered less than thirty casualties since Christmas. One company, it was claimed, had not lost a man. The *poilus* maintained that this was due to keeping totally out of sight. Unfortunately, fate decreed that the 10th Canadians would not duplicate this feat, for within a week 500 of those bronzed westerners would not answer the roll call.

Chapter Two

Covenant with Death
(January – April, 1915)

"We have made a covenant with death,
And with Sheol we have an agreement;
When the overwhelming scourge passes through
It will not come to us."
                              Isaiah XXVIII, 15

Although the Allies did not know it, they had already been "attacked" by poison gas on three separate occasions. These had taken place long before the "lachrymatory shells" were first noticed at Hill 60. The earliest, in fact, had occurred nearly six months ago, before the war was three months old.

At that time Erich von Falkenhayn, the German Minister of War, had been given the added responsibilities of Chief of the General Staff. This ambitious fifty-three year old soldier had succeeded the discredited von Moltke after the German invasion of Belgium and France had broken down. General Staff planners had assured the Kaiser of victory within four months, but the juggernaut had come untracked within one. Von Falkenhayn had been given the task of seizing that elusive victory.

Now he had begun searching for the means to launch the decisive blow and thereby snatch victory from a situation which could only grow worse. From his position of supreme power von Falkenhayn, remaining aloof and reserved, saw the German empire as a beleaguered fortress. He believed that he must hold onto every inch of ground and yet handle his forces with the utmost economy since the siege had no end in sight. Yet it was always possible that a new weapon might alter the balance of power so drastically that Germany could break the deadly stalemate.

One of the first acts of the new warlord was an order to reopen research on chemical munitions. This had been carried on secretly in the years before the war. As a result of von Falkenhayn's order, Major Max Bauer, Chief of Heavy Artillery and the Fortress Section of Operations Branch had convened a group of scientists to develop a chemical shell of incendiary, smoke, irritant, or stink type to drive enemy troops from inaccessible places.   The result was the "Ni-shell." The "Ni" stood for *Niespulver*—sneezing powder. Professor Nernst of Kaiser Wilhelm Institute had developed the idea of placing an irritant among the balls of standard shrapnel shell.

On 27 October—less than a month later—three thousand of these non-toxic shrapnel shells had been fired at Neuve Chapelle. The unsuspecting victims had been British and Indian troops in that sector. It speaks volumes for the shells' effectiveness that the victims did not realize that they had been victimized till they read about it after the war. Legend has it that Professor Nernst's 'Ni shells' were abandoned after von Falkenhayn's son had won a case of champagne by wagering that he could stand unprotected in a cloud of the professor's irritant for five minutes and emerge unharmed.

Meanwhile another type of gas weapon had been developed and was about to be tested. This was the "T Shell" named for Hans Tappen. Tappen was one of the chemists who designed the new weapon, an explosive shell filled with xylyl bromide, a liquid irritant. It would be tested against the Russians.

The Battle of Bolimos began on Sunday, 30 January, 1915, when the Germans fired 18,000 of these T Shells into the Russian positions along the Bzura and Rawka Rivers in Poland. The gas went almost unnoticed by the Russians and the Germans met a fierce resistance. Incredibly, it was only later that the German scientists realized that the volatility of xylyl bromide had been reduced to almost nil by the extreme cold.

By March the T Shell had been modified by the addition of bromoacetone to counteract low temperature. This time the Germans tried out their gas shell at Nieuport against the French. Once more the gas went unnoticed. In the army confidence in gas warfare had sunk even lower.

Meanwhile the French too had indulged in some ineffective gas warfare. They had developed *cartouches suffocantes*, half pound projectiles fired by special 26 calibre rifles. These cartridges were filled with ethyl bromo-acetate in liquid form. The French had also produced *grenades suffocantes* which appear to have been used as early as February, 1915. These were filled with irritants to the nose, eyes, and throats, but only in extreme doses could they prove lethal.[1]

While these attempts to employ poison gas had been unfolding, another type of asphyxiant had been proposed to Falkenhayn. In January of 1915 the German warlord had decided to try the new gas. The only question was where and against whom.

"On 25 January, 1915, with my chief of staff, I was summoned to Mézières to the General Headquarters to confer with Falkenhayn," wrote General Bertold von Deimling.[2] This "ultra Prussian militarist," as he was known, actually hailed from Baden, and he commanded the XV Corps now stationed along the Ypres Salient. Deimling's command was part of Duke Albrecht of Württemberg's Fourth Army.

After von Deimling had been ushered in von Falkenhayn had come right to the point. "He confided to us that they were going to put into service a new weapon of war, toxic gas, that it was in my sector that they had thought to make the first attempts." Deimling's XV Corps held the southwestern arc of the Salient opposite Zillebeke.

The method was simplicity itself. "They would deliver these toxic gases in steel bottles which they would install in the trenches, and they would release the gas when a favourable wind blew." The gas to be used was the deadly chlorine gas.

Deimling's superior, the commander of Fourth Army, was Duke Albrecht of Württemberg. He had already been informed of von Falkenhayn's plans and had sent his Chief of Staff to attend the conference. Of course, even among German militarists there had been some initial repugnance to the use of chlorine gas. "I must admit that the mission to poison the enemy like one poisons rats had the same effect on me as it would on all honest soldiers: *it disgusted me*," wrote von Deimling, certainly no sentimentalist. "But if this poisonous gas made possible the capture of Ypres, perhaps it would gain us a victory which would decide the whole campaign. Before such a grand objective one must put aside personal objections. Let us get on with it come what may. This war is a case of legitimate defense and knows no law."

The decision to employ asphyxiating chlorine gas had come at the urging of Dr. Fritz Haber, the director of the Kaiser Wilhelm Institute for physical chemistry. Haber was a Breslauer who had recently been appointed head of a new section of the war ministry. Formerly an N.C.O. in the Landwehr, or militia, Haber had been promoted to the rank of Captain by special patent. His argument for the use of such a deadly chemical as chlorine gas hinged on three claims. First was that Germany was justified in using gas warfare because the French had already tried it albeit in an "inefficient manner." Secondly, "countless lives would be saved if the war could be ended more quickly this way." Thirdly, Haber assured the doubtful von Falkenhayn that the Allies "did not have the technical capability to respond very quickly with cloud gas discharges of their own."[3]

Dr. Haber had pointed out that chlorine gas was a potent lung irritant; was heavy and therefore not easily dissipated; and that it left no noticeable residue. Germany had already been producing 37 tons per day (compared to Britain's 1 ton) for her dye industry. It would take less than a week's supply at the pre-war rate to launch a full scale gas attack. Germany, like the Allies, had been struggling to overcome a severe shortage of artillery shells. This, plus the German generals' distrust of gas, convinced Haber that he would not be successful in obtaining shells to deliver his chlorine gas. Therefore he had decided that a gas cloud projected from commercial cylinders fitted with special screw-on "domes" to protect the discharge valves would be adequate to the task—if wind conditions were suitable.

Once the decision had been made it became obvious that special engineer units would have to be formed to project the gas cloud. Colonel Peterson of the engineers had therefore been ordered to form *Pionierregiment 35* from regular combat engineers and assorted scientists.

Dr. Haber had meanwhile supervised the technical work and had recruited the scientists. The latter included three future Nobel Prize winners, physicists James Franck and Gustav Hertz, and Otto Hahn, the chemist.

Misleading codenames had been given to the various components. The heavy steel gas cylinders were 'F Batteries' while the entire chlorine gas cloud system was codenamed 'Disinfection.' It was hoped that in this way the secret weapon would remain unnoticed by Allied intelligence.

By late February the first of the chlorine gas cylinders or 'F Batteries' had been installed along von Deimling's front near the village of Gheluvelt in the Ypres Salient. Front line troops were repeatedly placed in readiness to assault, but each time lack of a suitable wind aborted the attack. Early in March two cylinders were burst by British artillery fire. Several German infantrymen were badly gassed and one died coughing blood from his tortured lungs.

Shortly afterwards, the accident was repeated, only this time it was caused by rifle shots. Three men died before their terror-stricken comrades, and fifty others became gravely ill. "I saw them at the ambulance," wrote von Deimling. "They were suffering horribly. These accidents had gravely lowered the troops' confidence in these new weapons. They distributed to the soldiers some primitive protective devices with which, in case of danger of asphyxiation, they must cover their noses and mouths."

Nevertheless, the laborious night work went on until 10 March when all 6,000 cylinders had been embedded in the front line. But the elusive "suitable" wind failed to materialize in the weeks that followed. Thus on 25 March a change of venue was recommended by the Fourth Army Commander, Duke Albrecht of Württemberg. An "alternate gas front" was to be established on the north side of the Salient between the villages of Steenstraat and Poelcappelle. A new supply of cylinders was assembled for this alternate gas front. Meanwhile, the original 'F Batteries' stayed in position on the southwestern curve of the Salient.

For the Germans this delay was nerve-wracking. What if a British attack or raid revealed the hidden cylinders in the Zillebeke sector? In the northern sector especially there was a distinct lack of aggressive spirit. In fact, nearly every night, von Kathen's reservists slipped out into no man's land to fraternize with the French, and desertion had become a problem. There was always the chance that a prisoner or a deserter would give away the secret.

Nevertheless, on 5 April, *Pionierregiment 35* began installing F Batteries in the front line trenches of this alternate gas front on the north of the Salient. The infantrymen of the XXIII and XXVI Reserve Corps were hardly delighted to see these deadly cylinders being buried amongst them. By 11 April, Colonel Peterson of *Pionierregiment 35* was able to report that 5,730 of the F Batteries had been installed between Steenstraat and Poelcappelle. 'Disinfection' was ready for action.

The overall plan was as follows: The XXIII and XXVI Reserve Corps were to follow up the release of the gas cloud with assaults on the Allied positions north of Ypres. On the western end of the Salient the 45th and 46th Reserve Divisions (XXIII Reserve Corps) were to attack south then swing west and cross the Yser Canal at Steenstraat. Immediately to the east of the 46th were the 52nd and 51st Reserve Divisions (XXVI Reserve Corps). They were to follow the gas cloud and capture the high ground known as Pilckem Ridge which ran parallel to the front line. Later objectives included "the securing of the Yser Canal up to and including Ypres." Reserves were few—the 51st Division had a brigade as did the XXVI Corps. Fourth Army reserve included two infantry divisions plus the Guard Cavalry Division.

This rather simple plan was tested with a dress rehearsal (minus the star performer—chlorine gas) on Tuesday 13 March. Three red flares early in the morning signalled the start of the exercise. This was the exercise described by the two deserters and the flares reported by the French 11th Division.

From the start it appears that the German High Command expected only limited results from the gas cloud. Indeed, the *Reichsarchiv* states, "The battles of Ypres . . . had their origin on the German side solely in the desire to try the new weapon, gas, thoroughly at the front."[4]

The events of April, 1915 appear confusing at first glance. But if it is kept in mind that von Falkenhayn had decided to switch his main effort to Galicia for a major blow against the Russians, the train of events falls into perspective. The proposed gas attack had become of secondary importance. Only his impatience to test 'Disinfection' under battle conditions had kept von Falkenhayn interested. Fourth Army was informed that it was more important to launch the gas cloud as soon as possible than it was to obtain deep penetration, and Duke Albrecht's request for a division to exploit a possible break-through was rejected.

On 5 April, the XXVIII Corps immediately to the east of the proposed area of attack, reduced its trench garrison "so that battalions not in line might undergo special training in the attack on trenches and in open warfare."[5] The support and reserve battalions of this Corps were then temporarily brigaded as a unit called

'*Sturmbrigade Schmieden*.' The men of this 'stormbrigade' must have realized that something was afoot when the Kaiser visited them at Dadizeele on the 15th "and stood each man a litre of beer out of his own private purse."[6]

Three days after the installation of the gas cylinders began, von Hugel commanding the XXVI Reserve Corps, notified his subordinates that the objective of the forthcoming attack was simply to seize the "ridge along the road Boesinghe Pilckem-Langemarck-Poelcappelle." Once this limited objective had been secured all units were to "dig in immediately and establish mutually covering strong points."[7] This would entail an advance of only one and a half miles. Evidently the old Württemburger was not expecting too much from the newfangled gas cloud.

Two days later, on Saturday, 10 April, von Falkenhayn ordered General Ilse, the Chief of Staff for Duke Albrecht's Fourth Army, to visit him at headquarters. There he impressed upon Ilse the necessity for carrying out 'Disinfection' as soon as possible. He finished by pointing out that the XXVI Reserve Corps might soon be needed elsewhere. Thus one day before the installation of the F Batteries was completed Ilse hurried back to the Fourth Army with word to get moving.

Duke Albrecht therefore ordered the attack to take place on Thursday, 15 April. The fateful day passed without a breath of wind, and as their comrades on the southeastern side of the Salient had done so many times, the infantry stood down after a day of tension. A few yards away, across no man's land, the Canadians, warned of the impending attack, continued their stand-to till midnight.

This failure did nothing to convince von Hugel of the value of 'Disinfection.' The next day he cautioned his heavy artillery and his Divisional Commanders that the effects of the cloud gas might prove insufficient to get the infantry onto Pilckem Ridge without heavy losses. If this happened the attackers were to halt and dig in until the enemy's resistance had been softened up by a bombardment of T Shells. This seems to have been a rather forlorn hope considering the absolute failure of the T Shells at Bolimow and Nieuport.

The next day, Saturday, 17 April, the first German troops began moving out of the Salient. It was the long-awaited move to Galicia on the Eastern Front. Railway yards in the rear began to bustle with activity as troop trains carried away Duke Albrecht's reserves.

That same evening disaster struck opposite Zillebeke on the southern arc of the Salient. Deimling's line included the previously mentioned 60-meter high pile of refuse known as 'Hill 60.' It will be remembered that this was a section of XV Corps line where hundreds of the 'F Batteries' had been buried a month earlier. After a month waiting for a favourable wind, they were still there, unused and deadly. When the British mines exploded, blowing the top off Hill 60 there was absolute pandemonium in the German trenches. Mines had a terrible effect on morale at the best of times, but the ensuing panic was unheard of. No *feldgrau* wanted to die the hideous death inflicted by chlorine gas, and the survivors stampeded to the rear to escape from the ruptured cylinders.

This feeling of sheer panic must have been shared by von Deimling, and by his superiors right up to von Falkenhayn. It would be almost impossible for the British not to discover some of the 'F Batteries.' Incredibly, the steel cylinders appeared to have escaped almost intact. There were no obvious ruptures, only a faint, irritating odor which lurked about Hill 60. Von Deimling ordered prompt counterattacks with massive artillery barrages. Still the dogged British held on to their impossible little salient within the Salient. On Tuesday, 20 April, the German artillery began employing T Shells filled with tear gas, but with no noticeable effect.

On Monday, the nineteenth, a diversionary tactic began — the long range shelling of Ypres. To do this, Duke Albrecht's Fourth Army had been given two of the enormous 17" guns called "Big Berthas" by the Allies (in honour of Bertha Krupp, daughter of the manufacturer). However only one gun was ready to fire its monstrous one-ton shells into the doomed city. The other in the Houthulst Forest would have to sit idle for an entire week because its cement platform had not yet hardened.

Duke Albrecht and Ilse were now being hounded to launch their gas attack on the northern arc of the Salient before the enemy had time to react to their assumed discovery of the F Batteries on Hill 60. At the same time they were threatened with the loss of their XXVI Reserve Corps which was needed in Galicia. Thus 20 April was set for the unveiling of 'Disinfection.'

Tuesday, the fateful day, dawned bright and calm. There was

no breeze to carry the asphyxiating gas over the enemy's line. The attack was postponed. Meanwhile to the south on Hill 60, T Shells had begun to fall on the British "Tommies." Surely the secret was now out.

This was too much for von Falkenhayn. The next day he and his Chief of Operations Colonel von Tappen, descended upon Duke Albrecht's headquarters at Thielt. There they made it clear that the oft-postponed cloud gas attack was to be launched at the first possible opportunity. Albrecht was encouraged not to set his goals too high by expecting a great advance; he was merely to try out the gas cloud immediately. No more delays could be tolerated. As a result, Duke Albrecht issued orders scheduling 'Disinfection' for early the next day—5 o'clock on the morning of Thursday, 22 April, 1915.

Chapter Three

In a Place
Called Armageddon
(14 April - 21 April, 1915)

"And he gathered them together in a
place called in the Hebrew tongue Armageddon."
Revelation XVI, 16

The Canadian relief of Ferry's 11 Division had begun on Wednesday, 14 April. The first battalions in the front line were, from the right, the 10th and 7th Battalions of the 2nd Canadian Infantry Brigade. This brigade was led by Brigadier General Arthur Currie, a future commanding officer of the Canadian Corps. He stood out in any crowd due to his immense size, towering over all the generals and staff officers. Born in Napperton, Ontario, Currie had gone to Vancouver Island as a young man. There he tried teaching, selling insurance, and real estate broking. He had developed an interest in the Militia and had served several years in the ranks. By 1914 he was the thirty-nine year old lieutenant-colonel of the 50th Gordon Highlanders. Now he was leading an entire brigade of westerners into the Salient.

Next to Currie's Brigade came two of 3rd Brigade's four battalions—the 16th on the right and the 14th forming the junction with the French. The first morning in their new trenches shocked the Canadian volunteers. Private J.E. Lockerby of the 16th Canadian Scottish wrote a letter home. "When day dawned it presented a gruesome sight. Hundreds of dead Germans were lying between our lines with all their equipment on, just as they fell in a charge made several months ago. Many of the French who were killed in these trenches during the winter are buried right here, some have hardly enough earth over them to conceal their clothing."[1]

Perley Smith of the 7th British Columbians remarked, "They

31

were not very sanitary in their mode of living and they left their dead on top of the ground and the dirt and filth was terrible. We had used the water that the French were using, but when it was baled down we found there was a number of dead Frechmen at the bottom of it."

The Canadians took formal possession of this macabre area at 10:00 a.m. on Saturday, 17 April, when Lieutenant-General E.A.H. Alderson took command of the sector. Alderson was a fifty-six year old English career officer. He had served with the British Army since 1878 in such campaigns as the First and Second Boer Wars and Wolseley's Nile Expedition of 1884-5. In 1906 he had been promoted Major General and given command of the 6th Division, Southern Army, in India. Now he found himself in command of the 1st Canadian Division, an army of raw but eager volunteers.

When he had been appointed to command the Canadians Alderson had been assured that it was just another British Division, but he was soon bewildered to discover that he owed some vague allegiance to the Canadian government in Ottawa. As far as the troops were concerned, the Division was not British nor were they colonials; they were *Canadians*.

This nationalistic attitude extended even to equipping the Division. Alderson was soon to find that the Canadians were armed, not with the excellent Lee-Enfield, but with the Ross rifle. This weapon was a Canadian weapon produced by Sir Charles Ross, a friend of the Minister of Defense, Sir Sam Hughes. The latter hotly defended the rifle and Alderson was eventually compelled to publish the following Routine Order:

"Rifles: It is to be noted that with the exception of the Divisional Mounted Troops men are not permitted to be in possession of M.L.E. (Lee-Enfield) rifles."[2] The fact that such an unusual order had to be considered at all speaks volumes for the reputation of the Ross rifle.

Brigadier General Currie had reported in March concerning the Ross, "They find after firing a few rounds, that the shells seem to stick in the bore and are not easily extracted, in fact, more than ordinary pressure must be applied . . . This seems to me to be a point where the most rigid investigation is necessary, as a serious interference with rapid firing may prove fatal on occasions."[3]

There were many other reasons for distrusting the Ross: It was too heavy; it was too long; the magazine was difficult to load and only held five rounds besides being easily damaged; the Ross was sensitive to dirt; the sight was easily bent; the bayonet was short and — horrors of horrors — it was prone to flop off while firing, thus leaving the owner without a bayonet until nightfall when he must slip out over the parapet and attempt to retrieve it.

The trenches these green Canadian volunteers took over were incredible. They were scattered, unconnected, with no traverses or parados, and with parapets so flimsy they were not even bullet-proof. The barbed wire defences were so meagre that the 10th Canadians reported on the night of 15 April (the date of aborted first gas attack) that a soldier had walked right through the line without noticing, and had been halted by a German sentry. The 10th summed up their position: "We did not see how it could possibly be held if a determined effort was made to take it by a strong force."

Canadian Artillery batteries found no dug-in emplacements or sheltered battery sites. The 'gun positions' were merely spots behind hedges or on an open field with several branches stuck in the ground as camouflage. Wagon lines and Brigade Ammunition Columns were a mile or more to the rear while the railhead was back at Vlamertinghe, two miles the other side of Ypres.

The Canadians were not the only newcomers to the northern arc of the Salient. The same night that they took over (14-15 April), the sector to their left was also changing hands. Here the 45th Algerian Division took over with its 91st Brigade going into the line and the 90th staying in reserve near Boesinghe.

These Algerian *zouaves* and *tirailleurs* were an easygoing lot. Reliefs at night were sheer pandemonium with frequent breakdowns of transport (mostly farm wagons) and constant smoking and laughing. Yet it was difficult to become angry with them especially when they lounged along the banks of the Steenbeek fishing in their picturesque red and blue uniforms. Fishing was their passion and when one would get a bite they all laughed uproariously.

Their own initiation to the trenches of the Salient was as disillusioning as was the Canadians'. On 17 April Captain Louis Botti of the 7th Zouaves wrote in his diary: "I wanted to entrench. Impossible, it is a cemetery; at certain places booted sock feet stick out of the ground and at a spot where we pass a hundred times a day, a red *pantalon* appears.

"Everywhere that we look we discover out-stretched corpses which we can only think of burying . . . They sleep where normally the parados should stand, nameless, meaning nothing to anyone."[4]

To the left of the Algerians was the 87th Territorial Division which held the line as far as the village of Steenstraat on the canal. These territorials were elderly men by military standards. Frenchmen all served three years in the Active Army then eleven with the Reserves followed by seven in the Territorial Army. This meant that the latter were men between the ages of thirty-six and forty-three. Their replacements were even older, some being over fifty.

For some time now the men of this division had been fraternizing with the enemy. Many of these territorials had been meeting the Germans in no man's land to exchange tobacco, wine, bread, and of course, news. As a result security and surveillance had become very lax.

There was no second line of fortifications in the French sector of the Salient. Despite the fact that trenches appeared on headquarters maps, the newly arrived 45th Division found only a scattering of isolated positions located along the Yser Canal and Pilckem Ridge. Behind the British and Canadian sector there was a similar situation except that there was a more-or-less last ditch defensive position partially completed less than half a mile from Ypres. This was shown on maps as 'The General Headquarters Line' for some obscure reason. It consisted of several well-sited redoubts connected only by a belt of wire eighteen feet across and three feet high. There were no trenches in the G.H.Q. Line.

During those early spring days, as long as supplies of sandbags permitted, the infantry laboured to shore up their feeble defences. The artillery, on the other hand, was given something more challenging to do. The batteries were ordered to pound the German breastworks in hopes of drawing attention away from the imminent attack on Hill 60. This meant close shooting over the flimsy front line trenches, unprotected from the rear by parados. However, much to the satisfaction of all but the nervous *feldgrau*,* not one shell fell short. Nevertheless there were no noticeable results to the

---

* German nickname for their own troops, from the "Field Gray" color of their uniforms.

German front line till dawn on 20 April.

On that morning Captain Rae of the 16th Canadian Scottish reported that the enemy's parapets had been changed around during the night. Now openings appeared at regular intervals. Something seemed to be afoot across no man's land.

Later that day Brigadier Currie's 2nd Brigade forwarded a message to Divisional Headquarters. One item read as follows: "Trenches shelled yesterday 6 p.m. by shells giving heavy fumes which caused stupifying and sick feeling followed by heat. Only three or four such shells." The message was sent at 5:15 p.m. — almost twenty-four hours after the fact.

Shelling had been on the increase everywhere, and all ranks had noticed it. On Monday roads and bridges to the north and east of Ypres had begun to receive attention. Now on Tuesday Ypres itself was being pounded. Enormous one-ton shells from the Germans' 42 cm. howitzers had begun crashing into the old town. These 'Big Berthas' fired at the rate of ten rounds per hour and caused horrendous damage. A shell landing in the open blew a crater 15 feet deep and 40 feet wide.

A trickle of refugees began to leave the town. The bombardment continued without abatement and by Wednesday the five-century old Cloth Hall would be utterly destroyed. The work of centuries of genius took only hours to destroy. Ypres was doomed.

At 4.00 p.m. on the 21st Colonel Jean J. Mordacq rode out to reconnoitre the positions his troops were to take over that night. Mordacq, a twenty-six year veteran who had begun his career with the 2nd Zouaves, now commanded the 90th Brigade of the 45th Algerian Division. In Elverdinghe he met General Putz doing the same thing in an automobile. The Colonel went as far as Pilckem where officers of the 1st Battalion d'Afrique advised him to stay, as any movement forward of that point drew instant heavy fire. So from the crest of Pilckem Ridge Mordacq surveyed the scene. It was panoramic: "To the south one could see very distinctly the Yser Canal (joined in the faint distance by a stream, the Yperle), bordered by trees already much damaged by the bombardment but which adequately masked the trenches established along the canal. Steenstraat, Langemarck, Poelcappelle, St. Julien were similarly visi-

ble as were the Belgian, French and English trenches which marked
that line. Finally, to the north, one could see very distinctly about
three kilometers away the famous forest of Houthulst.''[5] Unknown to
the French veteran this forest at that moment sheltered thousands of
German infantry who would be filing forward to trenches opposite
his own position that night.

By late afternoon Mordacq had reached the junction of the line
with the Canadians. There he saw men of the 14th Royal Montreals
who were to be relieved that night. The veteran of numerous
French-colonial campaigns was impressed with his first Canadians.
"All, . . . were magnificent men, giving an impression of strength,
endurance and ability, very stylish in their practical tight-fitting
uniforms and their smart hats which they wore with such dash.

"All were very young as well, with a frank expression, happy
and a little youthful, being very different from the English Tommies, and by contrast — was it an illusion on my part? — more like our
poilus.''[6]

That night the planned relief of the 91st Brigade took place. It
was the usual tumultuous, disorganized affair, but when it was completed almost everyone was in the right place. Next to the Canadians were the 1st Tirailleurs in two sections, the right half under
Major Villevaleix, the left under Major de Fabry. The next sector
was held by the 1st African Battalion under Major Trousson. On
their left were units of the 87th Territorial Division — the 74th and
73rd Territorial Battalions.

The Canadian battalion now on the immediate right of Mordacq's Algerians was the 13th Royal Highlanders of Canada, part of
the 3rd Canadian Infantry Brigade. The 13 were a sister regiment of
the famous Black Watch of the British Army. These highlanders
from Montreal wore a uniform almost identical to their sister regiment. The 13th Battalion's front line lay in low ground facing the
Germans' 2nd Reserve Ersatz Brigade before Poelcappelle Ridge.
Their left flank lay on the St. Julien-Poelcappelle Road with the 1st
Tirailleurs of the 45th Algerian Division on the other side of the
road.

To the right of the 13th lay the 15th Battalion. This was also a
kilted unit composed primarily of militiamen from Toronto's 48th
Highlanders of Canada, although, there was also a number of men
of the 97th Algonquin Rifles from the mining towns of northern On-

tario. Their front trenches swung up from the 13th Battalion's onto Stroombeek Ridge where it joined with the trenches held by the 8th Canadian Infantry Battalion.

The 8th hailed from Winnipeg and was made up of 90th Winnipeg Rifles. This regiment had served in the Northwest Rebellion of 1885, and had been known by the rebels as "The Little Black Devils." That was the title they still preferred.

The last Canadian battalion in the line was the 5th (Western Cavalry) Battalion, an infantry unit formed from eight western cavalry regiments. "Tuxford's Dandies" as they were known, were under the command of Lt. Col. George Tuxford, a Moose Jaw district farmer. A noted athlete and member of several Northwest Championship teams, Tuxford held the distinction of having organized and led the longest cattle-drive in history—from Moose Jaw to Dawson City during the Klondike Gold Rush of '98. The 5th held a position on the south side of a creek named the Stroombeek. Their "Trench" continued to the Ypres-Passchendaele Road then resumed on the southern side of it for another 400 yards. There it joined up with a trench held by the 3rd Battalion, Royal Fusiliers of the 28th Imperial Division.

Observers during the night of 21-22 April noted two rather unusual occurrences. At 2:50 in the morning those on duty at Turner's 3rd Brigade Headquarters heard a zeppelin fly northwest over the front lines. Somewhat earlier Colonel Currie of the 15th Battalion (48th Highlanders of Canada) had noted, "While I was doing the rounds of the forward trenches I could not help noting the roar of wagons and limbers along the whole German line in front of us. The night was very calm, and whilst it was quite usual to hear a lot of wagons about rationing time, still on this occasion the whole German line seemed to be in motion. I had never heard anything like it before. Something extraordinary was certainly happening . . . I reported the occurrence to headquarters that night."[7]

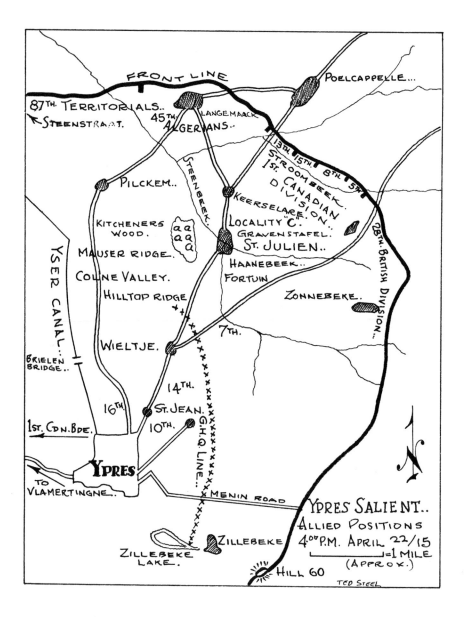

FRONT LINE

POELCAPPELLE...

87TH. TERRITORIALS..

←STEENSTRAAT.

45TH.

LANGEMARCK

ALGERIANS..

13TH. 15TH. 8TH. 5TH

STROOMBEEK

1ST. CANADIAN DIVISION..

PILCKEM..

STEENBEEK..

KEERSELARE..

KITCHENERS WOOD.

LOCALITY "C".

GRAVENSTAFEL.

ST. JULIEN..

28TH. BRITISH DIVISION...

MAUSER RIDGE.

HAANEBEEK..

COLNE VALLEY.

FORTUIN

HILLTOP RIDGE

ZONNEBEKE..

YSER CANAL..

7TH.

WIELTJE.

BRIELEN BRIDGE..

14TH.

16TH.

ST. JEAN.

GHQ.LINE..

10TH.

1ST. CDN. BDE.

YPRES

TO VLAMERTINGNE..

MENIN ROAD

YPRES SALIENT..

ALLIED POSITIONS

4.00 P.M. APRIL 22/15

ZILLEBEKE

=1 MILE

(APPROX.)

ZILLEBEKE LAKE.

HILL 60

TED STEEL

38

Chapter Four

Disaster Shall Fall Upon You
(1:00 a.m. - 5:00 p.m., 22 April, 1915)

"But evil shall come upon you,
  for which you cannot atone;
disaster shall fall upon you
  which you shall not be able to expiate
and rain shall come on you suddenly
  of which you know nothing."
                              Isaiah XLVII, 11

Thursday, 22 April, dawned warm and sunny. It was one of a series of beautiful spring days. The temperature soared into the seventies, and signs of spring were everywhere. Green shoots edged up through the war-torn landscape and made every man recall home and other sunny spring days of his youth. The swollen *beeks* and drainage ditches glinted like bands of silver in the welcome sunshine, and the blue skies were almost cloudless.

In the Canadian trenches the renovations continued. On the left, or western end of their sector, the 13th and 15th Battalions noted changes across no man's land. Both reported that "pipes" were now projecting through the German parapets. This information was duly passed to Divisional Headquarters.

Those in the front lines noticed considerable enemy air reconnaissance during the morning and afternoon, but no allied planes were seen. All the while, the unfortunate town of Ypres continued to suffer under bombardment. By afternoon the French to the left began to receive heavy shelling which eventually shifted onto the Canadian lines. But by late afternoon all firing had died out and there was almost complete silence. Even the enemy aircraft had gone home.

The peace and serenity were emphasized by the message received at Brigadier General Turner's 3rd Brigade Headquarters just before 3:00 p.m. It advised that one hundred mouth organs had arrived and were waiting to be picked up at Divisional Headquarters six miles away at the Château des Trois Tours west of Brielen.

The surrounding countryside as far forward as the reserve line was a hive of springtime activity. Everywhere farmers were on the land despite the artillery fire. If ever there was a determined attempt to ignore reality this was it.

In the French sector the sunny day was appreciated although the condition of the trenches was not. The general attitude in the Algerian Division was summed up by Major de Metz of the 2nd Zouaves who confirmed that while his men's morale was excellent they were disappointed about the deplorable condition of their trenches. They were not enthused by all the pick and shovel work which lay ahead and, "they would have preferred a hundred times more to have a sector where they were fighting."[1]

The relief the night before had come off reasonably well despite the noise and confusion, and there had been no casualties. Colonel Mordacq was worried about the relief of a company of the previous brigade's 7th Zouaves. Thus he sent a staff officer off at 7:00 a.m. to investigate. Captain de Veulle eventually returned to report a complete muddle. Due to a lack of correct maps, Major Gougne's half battalion of 2nd Zouaves had been able to find neither the entrenchments they were to occupy nor the company of the 7th which they were to relieve. Thus the men of the 7th Zouaves were forced to remain in their position north of Mortelje Farm* for one more day. They would be relieved that night. In the meantime the 7th came under the command of Mordacq's 90th Brigade.

Across no man's land the suspense and the dread could almost be tasted. The trenches were packed with troops who had been there for over twelve hours. Twenty-four hours earlier they had been huddled in Houthulst Forest waiting to move into these trenches. They had been there, well hidden, at the moment that Colonel Mordacq of the 45th Algerian Division had scrutinized the wood from Pilckem

---

* Known to the British and Canadians as Turco Farm, the name which will be used throughout this narrative.

Ridge three miles to the south. According to the plans, the suspense should have been over hours ago.

At midnight orders had been received to release the gas at 5:00* that morning. The men were to carry unloaded rifles with bayonets fixed. Respirators had been checked to insure they were damp, while steps and ladders had been put in readiness to climb over the parapets. In pitch black the engineers had gone out to cut passages through their wire. Finally, the sandbags had been removed from the F Batteries and their tubes laid over the parapets.

But a northeast wind had not risen. After several short postponements word had been received at 5:30 cancelling the operation until a suitable breeze should spring up. All through the warm day thousands of *feldgrau* had sat impatiently, alert for the first hint of motion in the warm air.

Meanwhile, 5,730 ominous cylinders lurked beneath the parapets. When the orders came to open the valves they would spew out 149,000 kilograms of chlorine gas in a greenish-yellow cloud. It would only take from six to eight minutes to empty the F Batteries. Of these, 1,600 were the standard commercial type, and 4,130 were smaller ones specially designed for gas warfare.

At about 3 o'clock the one sight that every man in the German forward position was dreading appeared. In the skies above Langemarck a French reconnaissance plane droned into sight. If the pilot spotted the packed trenches a barrage would be the result. Casualties would be terrible in the crowded trenches. But worse would happen if those ominous cylinders were holed by shell fire. Everyone waited with bated breath. Then the German artillery took up the challenge. A tremendous storm of fire followed the lone plane. Never before had one aircraft attracted such a concentration of fire power. The pilot struggled to gain altitude and manoeuvered vainly. Abruptly he turned and headed back to safety behind his own lines. The German infantry waited in dread. Had he seen them? But the April afternoon continued without incident.

---

* British time will be used throughout this work. German time was one hour later.

In the meantime behind the allied lines different scenes were being enacted. There were eight Canadian battalions in reserve. At Vlamertinghe, on the main road west of Ypres, the 1st and 4th Canadian battalions were playing a spirited game of football. George Bell of the 1st (Western Ontario) Battalion later recalled, "As we cheered our favourite athletes we heard the thunder of artillery increasing in intensity, and we stopped for a few minutes to watch shells bursting in the distance, flecking the sky with fleecy smoke. 'Our 2nd Brigade must be giving Fritzie an extra dose of iron rations,' I said to myself and turned my attention to sports."[2]

At that moment the entire 1st Brigade was playing football—except for seventeen men of the 3rd Toronto Battalion who had just been taken away to serve stretches of Field Punishment No. 1. This involved being tied spreadeagled to a wagon wheel, but these seventeen would turn out to be the luckiest men in their battalion.

Also in reserve were two battalions each from the 2nd and 3rd Brigades. Stretched out in companies from Ypres to Gravenstafel was the 7th British Columbia Battalion commanded by the "World's Champion Rifle Shot", Lt. Col. Hart-McHarg who had won that title at the Palma Match at Camp Perry, Ohio, in 1913. In divisional reserve in Ypres was the 10th Canadians, an "outfit" (as westerners referred to their battalions) made up of Albertans—ranchers, homesteaders, cowboys, railroaders, and small town clerks.

The 3rd Brigade, under Brigadier General R.E.W. Turner V.C., had in divisional reserve the 16th Canadian Scottish, a composite battalion collected from across 2,000 miles. 'A' Company was supplied by the 50th Gordon Highlanders from Victoria, 'B' from Vancouver's Seaforth Highlanders, 'C' from the 91st Argylls of Hamilton, and 'D' from Winnipeg's Camerons. No common uniform had yet been devised, so each company would go into battle wearing its own tartan. Stretched along the Ypres-Gravenstafel Road were the companies of the 14th Battalion, a bilingual unit from Montreal.

Eight miles to the northeast the men of General von Kathen's XXIII Reserve Corps and von Hugel's XXVI Reserve Corps were still packed in their trenches. It was a short time after four o'clock when someone first noticed the breeze springing up. Those with their helmets off felt the tell-tale cool sensation on their scalps as a slight northeast breeze wafted over their trenches. Wisps of last year's grass swayed in the wind before them in no man's land, and on the wire the red and blue tatters of a French officer's uniform began to stir. At 4:40 the word came: the valves on the deadly F Batteries were to be opened at five o'clock.

Approximately a mile and a half behind the junction of the French and Canadian lines stood the battered village of St. Julien. On 22 April it housed two battalion headquarters, the 13th (Royal Highlanders) and the 15th (48th Highlanders) plus three companies—one each of the 13th, 14th, and 15th. Just 500 yards to the north of St. Julien on the right side of Poelcappelle Road stood the 10th Battery, Canadian Field Artillery. The battery's limbers were sheltered further south in a large shellhole beside the Haanebeek.

It was now five o'clock. The Canadian Divisional Commander, General Alderson, was five miles from his headquarters, the Château des Trois Tours. Alderson was accompanied by only one man, his artillery commander, Brigadier-General Burstall, and they were on foot. Slightly over a mile from the front trenches and one thousand yards in front of St. Julien, they had taken this afternoon to familiarize themselves with the division's northwestern sector. Their horses were miles behind, sheltered in the village of Wieltje along with a company of the 7th British Columbians.

One other general was at that moment on foot in the Salient. Sir Horace Smith-Dorrien, commanding the British Second Army, was returning from a visit to Hill 60. There he had personally congratulated the survivors of the gallant 13th Brigade which had suffered such heavy casualties in holding on to the famous refuse heap. Now Sir Horace was walking towards Ypres where shells could be seen falling. Before him stretched a panorama including the French and German lines on the other side of the old city.

At the same moment, above, in the cloudless evening sky, the drone of an approaching plane could be heard. Many heads were raised, as with eyes shielded by hands, the curious attempted to identify the aircraft. It was a British machine, one of No. 6 Squadron's two-seater BE2c's. This scout, piloted by Lieutenant L.A. Strange, cruised towards the German lines, intent on locating the enemy battery flashes. In the failing light, neither Strange nor his observer noticed a second intruder. All at once, from the other craft, which bore the black Maltese Cross of the German Empire, three small objects dropped. Almost silently, like crimson flowers, they burst into bloom — three red flares.

At that moment Lt. Col. J.A. Currie of the 15th was a few yards northeast of St. Julien, returning from an inspection of his battalion's trenches. "A heavy cannonade and rifle fire broke out along the northeastern face of the salient along a sector held by the French troops. The rifle fire seemed to grow heavier every minute," wrote Currie, "and a strange yellow haze grew over the distant line of French trenches."[3]

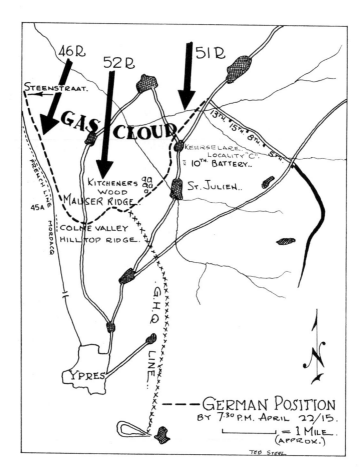

Chapter Five

The King of Terrors
(5:00 p.m. - 7:30 p.m., 22 April, 1915)

"He is torn from the tent in which he trusted,
and is brought to the king of terrors."
                                                    Job XVIII, 14

The strange yellow-green cloud had been spotted by the French front-line troops. The sentries' first glimpse of it was a series of "smoke puffs" which appeared at regular intervals along the German trenches. By the time these puffs had billowed into sizeable patches of dirty fog hundreds of curious were peering out into no man's land.

The pale green cloud continued to grow and to roll silently and inexorably towards them. "What can compare for mysterious terror with this uncanny, greenish wall?" a German professor enthused. "Airmen who followed events from above have told how extraordinary it looked when the clouds came up to the enemy trenches, then rose, and after as it were peeping curiously for a moment over the edge of the trenches, sank down into them like some living thing."[1]

The *joyeux** were engulfed by the mysterious cloud. "I had the impression that I was looking through green glasses," wrote the M.O. of the 1st African Battalion. "At the same time, I felt the action of the gas upon my respiratory system; it burned in my throat, caused pains in my chest, and made breathing all but impossible. I spat blood and suffered from dizziness. We all thought we were lost. It grieved us to see poor Cordier. He was purple, incapable of walking."[2]

---

* Popular French nickname for their African infantry meaning "the happy ones." The British nickname for them was "Turcos."

Shrieks of fear and uncontrolled coughing filled the poisonous air. Terrified soldiers clutched at their throats, their eyes starting out in terror and pain. Many collapsed in the bottom of their trenches and others clambered out and staggered to the rear in attempts to escape the deadly cloud. Those left in the trenches writhed with agony unspeakable, their faces plum-coloured, while they coughed blood from their tortured lungs.

Moments after the greenish vapours had engulfed the French trenches, the German field artillery opened up with a shattering roar. It was 5:10, and a rain of shrapnel descended on the *poilus* and *joyeux*. Then at 5:20 the German infantry appeared, climbing over their own parapets into no man's land. The faces of some were partially concealed by small gauze and cotton masks similar to those worn by surgeons. Many had disobeyed the orders to carry unloaded rifles, and had stood upon their parapets firing into the tormented territorials and Algerians. Now they advanced cautiously, hounded by their officers to keep closer to the dreaded gas. All along the French sector they advanced with little opposition. On the left they swept through the 87th Territorial Division's positions without meeting resistance. The men with whom they had traded tobacco a few nights previously now lay dead or dying in the trenches. The 1st African Battalion and the Tirailleurs put up a short resistance on the 45th Division's front, but were almost immediately asphyxiated.

From behind these positions the French 75's and 120's were still firing steadily in reply to the German barrage. A few minutes after six the artillerymen spotted the green cloud, now dispersed somewhat, and behind it waves of masked Germans. "Despite the gas, the gunners had immediately opened fire with shrapnel until the ammunition was exhausted — and this was quickly done," an artillery officer related. "By a lucky chance the chlorine fumes had passed a little north of the batteries. The Germans, their faces covered with a type of mask, had suffered great losses and had stopped for a moment.

"But soon we heard distinctly the cries of their officers, 'Forward! Forward!' and the rolling artillery barrage which preceded them intensified more and more. Finally groups of the enemy surged to the right and to the left. It therefore became necessary to hastily extricate the guns, or to abandon them. A great number of the gunners were not able to escape in time, and were made prisoners."[3]

Colonel Mordacq's 90th Brigade lost every one of its guns — three batteries of 75's and two of 120's in those few minutes. By seven o'clock the guns were silent.

This was to be a devastating blow to the French in the days to come. *Groupement d'Elverdinghe* had been very short of artillery even before this. Its only heavy artillery had been this handful of ancient 120's with the 87th Territorial Division.

Farther south in Kitcheners' Wood sat a battery of heavy British guns, 4.7's belonging to the 2nd London Battery, Royal Garrison Artillery. This unit, having only seven rifles with which to defend itself, fought a stubborn rearguard action as the first Germans entered the wood. This enabled the gunners to remove the firing pins and the breechblocks which the survivors carried back with them.

It was 5:20 when news of the catastrophe first reached the rear echelons. Colonel Mordacq's telephone rang. It was Major Villevaleix of the 1st Tirailleurs. "In a gasping voice, between coughs, barely audible, he announced to me that he was violently attacked, that immense columns of yellow smoke projected from the German trenches now extended across all of his front, that the Tirailleurs were beginning to evacuate the trenches and beat a retreat. Many were falling asphyxiated.

"I confess," wrote Mordacq, "that upon hearing such words, and especially in such a voice, I wondered for a moment if the major had not lost his head a little or was suffering from a blow on the skull."

Then the phone rang for the second time; De Fabry of the Tirailleurs was on the line. His men were being asphyxiated and shelled, and he and the survivors were about to pull back although they were trapped between the gas and the barrage.

When the phone rang a third time Mordacq lifted the receiver with dread. Villevaleix gasped out, "Everyone is falling around me, I am quitting my Command Post." Then the line went dead.

Colonel Mordacq rushed outside, mounted his horse, and rode towards Boesinghe accompanied by a handful of his colourful Spahis. When they arrived they could distinguish wisps of "yellow smoke" beside the canal. "We were seized by a violent tingling in the nose and throat, the ears commenced to buzz, breathing became painful, an overwhelming odour of chlorine surrounded us."

The horses wisely baulked, so the Colonel and his escort dismounted and entered Boesinghe. "In the outskirts of the village the scene was more than sad; it was tragic. Everywhere were fugitives — territorials, *joyeux, tirailleurs, zouaves*, artillerymen, — without weapons, haggard, greatcoats thrown away or wide open, running around like madmen, begging for water in loud cries, spitting blood, some even rolling on the ground making desperate efforts to breathe.

"I shall see for a long time, in particular, a staggering *joyeux* who with loud cries demanded milk and noticing me, called, 'My colonel, these . . . have poisoned us . . . .'

"No effort was made to stop the bewildered fugitives. We soon gave that up. It was no longer soldiers who were escaping but poor souls who had become suddenly insane.

"All along the canal was the same scene: without noticing bullets or shells, a crowd of unfortunate sufferers on both banks had come to beg for water to relieve their horrible sufferings."

Appalled, Mordacq pressed through Boesinghe to the all-important bridges, expecting the worst. However, two companies of Gougne's half-battalion of Zouaves were there. They, it will be remembered, had been unable to locate their counterparts of the 91st Brigade during the relief of the night before. By this time they had efficiently organized the defense of the bridges and were serving as a rallying point for the fugitives from the front. They had also been joined by a platoon of 7th Zouaves and a section of Engineers.

Somewhat reassured, the Colonel sent a staff officer to his Command Post at Elverdinghe with instructions to direct all available reinforcements to the Boesinghe area and to beg assistance from the Division. Then Mordacq toured the sector. He was beseiged by artillery officers who pleaded that he launch an immediate counterattack to retake their guns. But Mordacq could only reply, "With whom and with what?" He had not one artillery piece left to support an attack and only a handful of *zouaves* and fugitives to make an assault.

It was now only 6:45 p.m. In one and three quarter hours the enemy had been able to seize the Het-Sas region and advance as far as the bridges at Boesinghe. Although there was now less than an hour of daylight, most of the 87th and 45th Divisions were already fugitives or casualties.

By this time large numbers of Mordacq's men were prisoners of war. The Medical Officer of the 1st African Battalion had been ordered to withdraw to Pilckem. "I was able, under a hail of bullets, to go as far as the railroad line. The latter however was being shelled with terrific precision. I tried to follow the road, but it too was being heavily shelled. I then decided to retreat across the fields, but after less than a hundred meters my route was blocked by barbed wire. I was able to cross the barbed wire network by creeping along a ditch, but I had lost a lot of time and suddenly saw the Boches only fifteen meters ahead of me. They were calmly marching along, rifles slung over their shoulders. One of them saw me and took aim, but even at that short distance missed me. What luck! Other Boches motioned me to move to the rear. Damn, I was a prisoner!

"I passed German columns moving up to the attack. In their midst they carried huge panels with various inscriptions which probably served to signal the infantry's positions to their artillery. Following the soldiers about to attack I also saw men carrying gas cylinders. All of them wore protective masks over their noses. Together with a group of prisoners we were herded into the forest of Houthults."[4]

There were only three places where 'Disinfection' did not yield complete success. One was Langemarck, a village just behind the trenches of the 1st African Battalion. Here the gas rolled forward clearing the ground of birds and hares, but somehow missing the garrison of the village. Thus when the men of the 51st Reserve Division whose first task was to capture the village, arrived in front of Langemarck they met a torrent of bullets. Into the ruins they plunged, and a long-drawn, vicious struggle resulted. By six o'clock — well behind schedule — Langemarck had fallen and the 51st Reserve Division moved on across the Haanebeek expecting to capture St. Julien. This they could not do for another two days.

Farther east across the Poelcappelle Road, the gas was to have enveloped the flank of the 3rd Canadian Brigade. For reasons never ascertained, the F Batteries here were not opened and the Canadian line was virtually untouched.

On the extreme western end of the German line there had been a third hitch in the plans. Here, near Steenstraat, the F Batteries had not released their deadly fumes. This meant that the Belgian grenadiers who held this important junction escaped the most deadly effects of the fumes.

The garrison on the Belgians' right flank was Colonel Lodz's Grenadier Regiment. These soldiers in their long blue greatcoats and white belts had established a nine-man listening post off to their right in Steenstraat's brewery. One of these grenadiers described the events of the late afternoon.

"All was so calm that we no longer thought about the war, so to speak, when suddenly around 5:30 p.m. (sic) that afternoon we saw a thick cloud rising above the German trenches opposite ours. Surprise and curiosity riveted us to the ground. None of us at that moment suspected what was going on. As the cloud of smoke grew thicker we thought that the German trench had caught fire. The cloud moved slowly towards us, but because of the wind we saw it was being carried towards our right flank onto the French line. Only the edge of the wave of gas reached us. It was less thick here but gave off a singular odour and seized me and affected my throat with such severity that for a moment I believed I was going to suffocate. Suddenly I heard cries around me, 'An attack! The Boches are there!'

"I looked in direction of the cries. There were French soldiers who occupied the area around Steenstraat bridge running towards our trenches. Several fell on the way. To our Corporal who asked what had happened I heard them answer, 'We are being poisoned!'

"We received the order to leave the listening post and to return to the front line trench. There all my comrades, silent but amazingly calm, waited quietly, their eyes fixed on the German line, rifles ready to fire.

"The major and the lieutenant were going, revolver in hand, from one to another, insuring that everyone was at his post. I can still hear the voice of the major, 'Let's go, my brave fellows, this is the moment to show the Boches that we are here, and that Belgians will not retreat. I am counting on you, that each of you will fight to the death.'

"By this time the cloud of smoke around us had almost dissipated. We then saw four or five Germans heading for the bridge. The rifles fired all together and two Boches fell. Beside me a man shouted, 'Perhaps they are French,' but no, ahead and to our right, were whole ranks of the enemy, bayonets fixed, advancing behind the cloud of smoke. They had reached the French line. I could distinctly see German officers striking their men with the flats of their swords to make them advance faster. All hell broke loose from our trenches. We opened rapid fire. The barrel of my rifle burned my fingers, but those damned Boches kept advancing, crossing the French lines. It was about 6 o'clock when, fearing to be outflanked, our major gave the order for half of the company to build a barricade at a right angle with our trench."[5]

To the right of Mordacq's brigade of Algerians was the 13th Royal Highlanders of Canada. An uneventful afternoon for those in the front line had been shattered at 5:00 when there was a sudden burst of rapid fire from the French 75's to their left and rear. Then someone spotted the slowly moving gas cloud.

"At first we thought it was just the intense musketry was creating this yellow haze," Ian Sinclair recalled, "and then it began to come into us, and the French on the left . . . started pouring into our trench, coughing and bleeding and dying all over the place."[6]

Major McCuaig of A Company rushed to the left into the French position to find out what was happening. He saw that the advancing Germans would soon outflank his battalion's position so he took matters into his own hands. Number 1 Platoon was ordered to double to the left into the *tirailleurs'* trenches.

"The remains of the Algerians were holding a sort of natural breastwork running back about 100 yards from the trenches and about 100 yards distant from the Poelcappelle Road and were exchanging brisk fire with the Germans, who after breaking through, had occupied a hedge about 150 yards from the French and running back a considerable distance. As there was not sufficient cover to permit of prolonging the French line further to the rear, I instructed Captain H.G. Walker to withdraw his platoon, which had just come up, and take a position in echelon to the Algerian line in the ditch of the Poelcappelle Road. As the withdrawal of this platoon almost caused a panic among the Algerians I was compelled to compromise by withdrawing only two sections."[7]

Thus the 13th had, in military parlance, "refused its flank" by lining the Poelcappelle-St. Julien Road which ran at right angles to their front line. At first the three thousand yard stretch was held by only McCuaig's two sections, but the *tirailleurs* and *zouaves* later fell back to this road-ditch position, and other odds and ends were rushed in to prolong the line south through Keerselaere to St. Julien. Runners were sent that way with request for assistance from Battalion Headquarters which was situated in the latter town, but all were killed or captured and the messages never got through.

The men of the 13th Royal Highlanders began to suffer both from the gas and from infiltrating fire from left and rear. Their flimsy trenches, unprotected by traverses or parados, were being blown to pieces. Ian Sinclair later recalled, "Our line of trenches promptly disappeared so we had nothing except a foot or eighteen inches of cover and so we fought from that."[8]

Six hundred yards to the rear of the front line two platoons of C Company were moving to block the tide. Major F.C. Norsworthy had moved this tiny force, the 13th's local reserve, to the left to line the ditch of the Poelcappelle-St. Julien Road. What deeds of sublime courage were enacted there will never be known for Major Norsworthy and his two platoons were wiped out to the last man. This valiant little band of Highlanders fought on through the evening to stem the rolling gray waves. No one knows when they were eventually over-run, but their sacrifice gained time for the dispatch of reinforcements which later that evening took their place.

Lt.Col. Currie of the 15th Battalion (48th Highlanders) was hurrying back to his Battalion Headquarters there when he saw the "yellow haze" on the French trenches. He arrived in time to meet a mob of Algerians pouring through in terror, without equipment or weapons. When his Adjutant, Captain Dansereau, attempted to question them in French he found himself ignored in the rush to the rear.

The Commandant of St. Julien was Lt. Col. F.O.W. Loomis of the 13th Battalion. It was obvious to him that disaster had befallen the French and that it threatened his own command, but no concrete information was available. So patrols were sent out, and runners tried to contact the detached companies as most telephone communications had been cut by shell fire. Loomis, who had been a general contractor in civilian life and had begun his military career as a Private in the Canadian Militia, concentrated his efforts on securing reinforcements and connecting up with the left end of the Canadian line almost two miles to the north.

All the while St. Julien was taking a severe pounding. "The air was thick with spent particles of steel and lead that rattled on the pavement and tiles as my Adjutant, Sergeant Miller and I made our way out of the burning shattered buildings through dense clouds of asphyxiating gasses,"[9] Colonel Currie wrote.

Currie moved up the line being formed by odds and ends of units in the immediate area—B Company of the 14th Battalion (Royal Montreal Regiment), his own B Company, plus individual *tirailleurs* and *zouaves* who had decided to stick it out with the Canadians.

Despite these efforts there was a gap of over a mile. Almost in the middle of this great hole stood the 10th Battery, Canadian Field Artillery near the village of Keerselaere. When the attack had begun, this battery, commanded by Major W.B. King, had opened up on the German front line in absence of any other orders, for their telephone had gone dead.

The men in the battery were affected by the gas cloud which had been released only one and a half miles from their position, but the firing went on like clockwork despite the swarms of Algerians in their blue jackets and white *pantalons* who struggled by on their left. Soon the 10th Battery was alone.

At about seven, a French sergeant who had stayed with the battery suddenly pointed beyond a hedge to the west of the road. *"Allemands,"* he said, and Major King looking that way could see hundreds of German helmets bobbing above the intervening hedge, less than 200 yards away. He quickly ordered two of his guns reversed and opened up rapid gun-fire over open sights.

"We had no idea what had happened," one gunner related. "It came right out of the blue. In the gun pit we had one of our men hit by a bullet." The other two guns remained on their allotted target despite the bullets pinging off the protective shields of the guns. A shower of leaves fell upon guns and crews as the willow trees above them were cut down by German machine gun bullets. In a few minutes, according to all logic, the 10th Battery would be wiped out. But no, the enemy fire dwindled and the Germans backed off to look for easier prey.

Assistance was on the way. Private Palin of the 14th Royal Montreals had been sitting in the dying sunlight cleaning his gear with his chums in St. Julien when the 'Stand-to' had been ordered. "I remember one Lance Corporal, Fred Fisher, of the 13th Battalion.

He came down looking for eight volunteers to carry up a machine gun, so eight of us stepped out. Well he set up his gun and we got in front of the graveyard of St. Julien village in kind of a sunken road or something. But all these Turco troops came through us. All they could say was, '*Allemain*, come plenty.' And they were coming plenty too."[10]

Fisher was in charge of the 13th Royal Highlanders' Colt machine gun and was one of a party of sixty men brought forward by Lieutenant Stairs from St. Julien. A member of the Toronto Public Schools Cadet Corps at the outbreak of the war, Fisher was now a Lance Corporal. With great courage and the skill of a veteran he worked his gun forward to an isolated building which commanded the ground to the north and west. Thus the German advance was checked and both sides began to dig in. Fisher was posthumously awarded the Victoria Cross.

Just south of beleaguered St. Julien was the 9th Battery, Canadian Field Artillery. Its C.O., Major MacDougall, was far away in the Forward Observation Post 1,200 yards from the German trenches. For the men of the 9th Battery the attack had been heralded by a cannonade. Then a yellowish cloud had become visible in the distance. It rolled closer and everyone was curious. "One fellow in our battery had been a chemist and when he smelled it he knew what it was," Gunner Lindon Somerville related. "He told us to urinate in our hankies and hang them over our noses. We had very few casualties from the gas.

"We were down in a little valley near a little creek. When the Germans attacked, two of our guns — A and B — pulled up the slope behind us and fired over the top of us at the Germans coming down the slope.

"There was one of our fellows got shot in the stomach. He was bleeding pretty good from the wound so I got a twig off a shrub, wrapped a bandage around it and shoved it in the hole. I took him down to a house they were using for casualties and laid him down beside some steps in one of the rooms. I left and went back to the guns. Years later he told me that when the Germans took the house they started bayonetting the wounded. He pulled a man that had died earlier on top of him and the Germans passed him by."

The swarms of *feldgrau* surged closer. By this time the officers were also sweating over the guns and the best shots were sniping away with their Ross rifles. "The Germans were coming down the slope and we were using shrapnel, firing over open sights. We were firing so fast that the breech of our 18 pounder seized and we couldn't get it open. I took a hammer and belted the handle several times and it finally opened. We then poured water on it and continued firing. You could see the waves of Germans coming over and then there'd be an opening in their line where our shrapnel had burst overhead." Orders were received for the 9th Battery to withdraw.

Major McNaughton's 7th Battery was set up 1,000 yards south of St. Julien. Suddenly a flood of Algerians "came running back as if the devil was after them, their eyeballs showing white, and coughing their lungs out — they literally were coughing their lungs out; glue was coming out of their mouths. It was a very disturbing, very distressing sight."[11] The raw Canadians remained where they were, pounding away, far above their three rounds per gun per day. Then from the rear and the flanks snipers began to pick off McNaughton's gunners. "Somehow we felt it was the normal course of war. It was unpleasant, it's true, but nobody got very excited about it."[12]

Behind the lines disaster was heralded first by the sudden outburst of artillery fire. Watchers then noted the dirty yellow smoke or haze which clouded the distant sunset. But most chilling was the dull, confused murmuring which grew ever louder and nearer. Its source soon appeared in the shape of panic-stricken fugitives in exotic blue and red garb, some collapsing in the throes of death. Football games came to a standstill as the Canadians gaped at the ever-increasing mobs of "Turcos" who streamed by without weapons.

Within minutes battalions were formed up to receive ammunition and rations. Meanwhile the sounds of the distant artillery duel grew steadily louder. Then around seven o'clock there was a sudden ominous lessening in the din. For a moment everyone paused in what he was doing. Then it was understood — the French 75's had abruptly ceased their hoarse barking.

Despite the growing awareness of the situation among the rank and file, above battalion level there was no inkling of what was going on. At 5:13 the 2nd Canadian Brigade had sent its daily Situation Report to Divisional Headquarters.

Section 1 situation normal. Section 2 fairly heavily shelled after 2:15 p.m. some shells melinite. Heavy bombardment and rapid rifle fire heard on our left at 5 p.m. Shells bursting near report centre 5:15 p.m.

At 5:25 the 3rd Canadian Brigade, some of whose men had already been gassed, had reported:

Situation quiet. Left Section reports observing at 5:00 p.m. a cloud of green vapour several hundred yards in length between the French trenches to our left and these of the Enemy. Firing is very heavy at that place also.

In actual fact the situation was now critical. An enormous rent had been torn in the allied line. Two small islands of resistance which threatened to be engulfed at any moment stood within the breach. One was Mordacq's Zouaves at Boesinghe on the Yser Canal; the other was St. Julien's small garrison of Canadians. The situation was well described by the German Official History: "The XXIII Reserve Corps had thrown the enemy back across the Canal between Steenstraat and Het Sas; the XXVI Reserve Corps had thrust forward as far as a line south of Pilcken and north west of St. Julien. The booty comprised unwounded prisoners to the number of 1,800 French and 10 British, more than 51 guns, of which four were heavy, and about 70 machine guns."[13]

German reports indicated that few French dead were found although approximately two hundred of those taken prisoner were "seriously incapacitated" by the chlorine gas and were hospitalized. Of these, ten per cent died. A casualty report submitted by the Medical Inspector of the French Army reported 625 gassed. Three of these men died.[14] Thus it seems that the chlorine cloud gas had been effective more as a psychological weapon than as a physical weapon. The greatest damage inflicted had been the panic induced by the approaching gas cloud.

What would the Germans do next? They were in position to seize the five bridges over the Yser Canal between Boesinghe and Het Sas. They already held a bridgehead at Het Sas plus the vital northern hinge of Steenstraat (with its bridge intact). From Zwaanhof Farm, held by the Zouaves, to St. Julien held by the Canadians lay a gap of 5,000 yards. Only 4,000 yards in front of the most advanced German infantry lay the shattered symbol of Ypres. From St. Julien to the end of the Canadian front line lay another gap of almost 2,500 yards. Here the Canadians had only a handful of miscellaneous companies, platoons, and individuals.

Von Kathen had before him one of the greatest opportunities a commander has ever been given. His XXIII Corps held two bridgeheads across the canal six miles behind four enemy divisions which still faced an aggressive foe. On his side he had momentum, surprise, numbers, a preponderance of artillery, plus the new terror weapon, to face a terribly demoralized and disorganized army frantically trying to regroup in the dark. The unguarded Channel ports were only a few days' march away.

On the eastern side of the breach von Hugel of XXVI Corps had an equally heady opportunity. His troops had merely to cross 4,000 yards of almost empty terrain to seize Ypres, the hub of the Salient. Alternatively he could swing to his left and roll up the enemy line. Either way, one Canadian and two Imperial divisions would be trapped.

As darkness began to close in on that spring day in 1915 limitless possibilities appeared to lie open to the German leaders. Which would they choose, and what could the Allies possibly do to prevent total disaster?

Meanwhile the 1st Canadian Division, in the absence of General Alderson who had still not returned from his reconnaissance, had compiled its Situation Report in a leisurely twenty-five minutes. At 5:50 it wired to V Corps, the 28th Imperial Division, and the 45th Algerian Division the following message:

No. 2 Brigade report trenches shelled during day. No. 3 Brigade report all quiet on their immediate front.

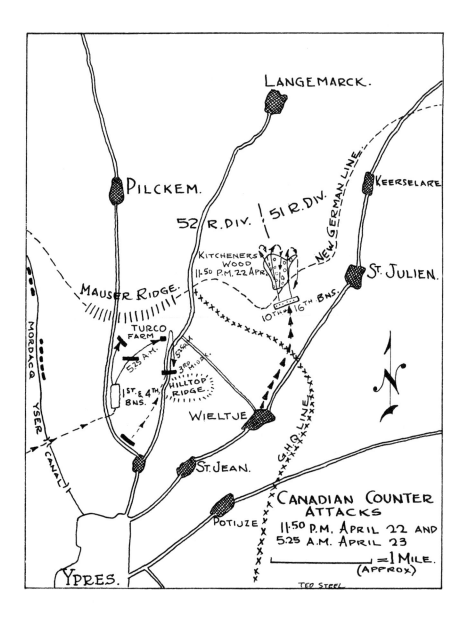

LANGEMARCK.

PILCKEM.

KEERSELARE

52 R.DIV. | 51 R.DIV.

NEW GERMAN LINE

KITCHENERS WOOD
11.50 P.M. 22 APR.

ST. JULIEN.

MAUSER RIDGE.

10TH & 16TH BNS.

MORDACQ

TURCO FARM

5.25 A.M.

5.25 A.M.

3RD MID BK.

1ST & 4TH BNS.

HILLTOP RIDGE.

WIELTJE.

G.H.Q. LINE

YSER CANAL.

ST. JEAN.

POTIJZE

N

CANADIAN COUNTER
ATTACKS
11.50 P.M. APRIL 22 AND
5.25 A.M. APRIL 23

=1 MILE.
(APPROX)

YPRES.

TED STEEL

58

Chapter Six

The Valley
of the Shadow of Death
(7:30 p.m., 22 April - 4:00 a.m., 23 April, 1915)

*"Yea, though I walk through the valley of the
shadow of death, I will fear no evil."*

23 Psalm

By 7:30 that evening the sun had set and darkness had
replaced dusk. A long terrifying night lay ahead for the shattered forces of the Allies — Belgian, French, Algerian, Canadian,
and British.

On the northern outskirts of Steenstraat the Belgian grenadiers
had already built a hook at the end of their trench which now
dangled 'in the air.' The bridge across the canal was in German
hands, and the main problem was to somehow make contact with
the French who were, it was hoped, on the other side of the village.

In the meantime, however, the task was simply to hang on.
Grenadier Defraeys wrote, "We were arranging a searchlight and a
good supply of ammunition. With three of my comrades I had been
assigned to man the searchlight. All had been prepared to receive an
attack. No one feared it. The first surprise had passed and we
wanted only to send down as many Boches as possible. Soon we
heard the sound of the approaching enemy in the rubble of the
houses demolished by the artillery. The searchlight was turned on
and its beam immediately revealed the enemy who had advanced to
within 30 or 40 meters. Our men fired without delay; the machine
gunners, for their part, emptying their belts of ammunition. They
fired accurately, for the cries and groans of the wounded rose from
the ranks of the enemy who soon about-turned, pursued by our fire.
At this moment German flares, red and green, shot up into the sky.

59

"It was a signal, doubtless, calling for artillery support, because several moments later, shells began to burst upon our trenches. The bombardment grew progressively more violent and at the same time a barrage swept the ground behind the first line. *The enemy was firing asphyxiating shells.* A good number of men were affected more or less gravely, but we held on all the same."[1]

These "asphyxiating shells" were more than likely T-Shells, but their effect was minimized by the Belgian defenders' prompt action. "Luckily we had made masks for ourselves," wrote machine gunner Henri Regard, "handkerchiefs and pieces of linen which we soaked with Yperlee and put over our noses and mouths."[2]

The Germans tried more attacks that night but failed to enlarge their bridgehead or seize any of the footbridges they hoped to capture.

On the other side of Steenstraat the line had, until two hours previously, jutted at right angles to the Yser Canal. Now it had been driven back parallel with the canal and on the *west* side of it to a spot midway between Steenstraat and Ypres. Into this area came two regiments of the 87th Territorial Division, the 76th and the 80th.

The 80th Territorial Regiment went for Steenstraat but ran into German machine gunners in Lizerne, 700 yards west of the canal. They fought on towards the village, but eventually bogged down before reaching its outskirts. It was not until three o'clock next morning that a Belgian patrol entering Lizerne from the north made contact with the 80th Territorial Regiment. One breach had been closed.

The 76th Territorial Regiment arrived quite late and headed rather hesitantly for Het Sas, a tiny hamlet farther south on the west bank of the Yser. Before reaching it they ran into Germans and their movement stopped, "hypnotized," according to Mordacq, "by several German patrols which had crossed to Het Sas." Eventually this unit linked up with the 80th to the north but made no attempt to link up with Mordacq's 90th Brigade to the south.

Meanwhile at Boesinghe Colonel Mordacq was attempting to stretch his thin line of troops to cover the gap. Fortunately for his peace of mind he had no idea how enormous the hole was. First he ordered the 7th Zouaves to cross to the east via the footbridges near the Zwaanhof Farm and "to execute, as soon as possible, a counterattack in the direction of Pilckem." Next, he ordered the 2nd half-battalion of Zouaves to replace the 7th on the west bank and ordered Major Gougne to prevent the Germans from crossing the canal at all costs and to establish contact to the north. Thus in Mordacq's view he would be closing the breach in the line. Little did he realize how far he would have to extend to the north and to the east to achieve this aim.

One reassuring figure was seen amongst all the confusion and heartbreak. It was *abbé* Gaillot, the 90th Brigade's padre. When the war had broken out this Dominican from Bretagne had been serving as a missionary in Canada. He had rushed home to France to mobilize with a front line unit, and his courage had since made him popular with the troops. He had not asked Mordacq for permission to come to Boesinghe, knowing that it would have been refused. However, on meeting the Colonel there he said simply, "Excuse me, my colonel, but I was unable to resist the temptation."

Before leaving Boesinghe for his chateau-headquarters at Elverdinghe the colonel met a lieutenant engineer and ordered him to blow up the bridges in the area. Only the Commander-in-Chief was authorized to issue such an order so Mordacq offered to put it in writing for the young officer. Lieutenant Hardelay merely replied, "Not necessary, my colonel, your word is good enough for me." Then both left, never to meet again.

Mordacq returned to his Command Post where he spent half an hour on the telephone attempting to glean a true picture of the situation. The results were depressing. Little solid information was forthcoming regarding troop strengths, positions, or plans, but he did learn for the first time of his precarious position in the five mile breach.

During this time the *zouaves* and assorted fugitives at Boesinghe were fighting off at bayonet point several German assaults on the bridges. These attacks eventually died down, but constant rifle fire between the defenders and the Germans kept everyone alert all night. So too did the delirious cries of the wounded on the east side of the canal. The padre, *abbé* Gaillot, asked for permission to go across the bridge with stretcher bearers to look for the victims of the gas attack. The captain replied, "That would be folly, father; you certainly would not return. You would be killed uselessly as would those who would accompany you."[3] The padre then crossed the bridge alone and vanished into the night around ten o'clock.

In the hour that followed the little garrison laboured under fire to build a barricade at the end of the bridge. Suddenly out of the darkness loomed first one figure, then several others. An officer of the Territorial Division was with the *zouaves* and without challenging, he fired his pistol into the group. At that moment a fusillade of rifle fire and a barrage of shells hit the defenders who quickly took cover. Some time later a body was discovered in front of the barricade. It was the *abbé* Gaillot, dead from a pistol shot in the chest.

While these tragic events were unfolding at embattled Boesinghe Colonel Mordacq was receiving a guest in the chateau at Elverdinghe. General Quiquandon, his divisional commander, had arrived for a council of war. Both felt that the only hope of preventing disaster was to counterattack. The problems here were two-fold—an acute shortage of available troops, and the total absence of artillery. Quiquandon informed Mordacq that he had arranged to borrow several British batteries and that two would be given to him. The general would also order a counterattack towards Steenstraat on Mordacq's left.

One other crucial act remained to be carried out. This was the destruction of the bridges near Boesinghe—a large railroad bridge south of the town, and a swing bridge on the main road through Boesinghe. Lieutenant Hardelay had been hard at work with a crew of volunteers attaching charges to the girders of the railroad bridge. Twice during the incessant bombardment he was knocked off the bridge into the canal, but he only left this work when he assured himself that the charges were ready. Then around three o'clock in the morning, Hardelay went over the road bridge. This was an easier proposition for it could be swung only by operating machinery on the west bank. Thus it was swung out from the banks to its position parallel with and in the centre of the canal. Hardelay then prepared to return to the railway bridge to fire the charges.

By this time Colonel Mordacq had moved his Command Post to the east bank of the canal near Zwaanhof Farm in a small cluster of buildings known from then on as "Mordacq Farm." He was reluctantly forced to evict its inhabitants, but despite the bombardment they merely moved to a neighbouring farm a short distance away.

Here at Mordacq Farm the Colonel would try to organize the proposed counterattack and to meet whatever dawn would bring.

It will be remembered that at five o'clock that evening when the gas attack burst upon the Allies, the Canadian commander, Lt. Gen. E.A.H. Alderson and his Artillery Commander were on reconnaissance northeast of St. Julien. After a long walk followed by a gallop through the milling crowds of fugitives, they had arrived back at the Chateau des Trois Tours, the Canadian Divisional Headquarters. By 5:55 the first message had been sent out ordering the 3rd Infantry Brigade to support the battered 45th Algerian Division and the reserve battalion to stand by. This message went out only five minutes after the situation report to V Corps (mentioned earlier) describing the 3rd Brigade's front as "all quiet." Evidently Alderson had arrived during the intervening five minutes.

Reliable intelligence was scarce, and all levels of command were isolated by lack of information. At 7:30 p.m. Alderson had received a telephone message from V Corps monumentally understating the case. He was advised that the French right "had been slightly turned," and that they were organizing a counterattack. This optimistic view was encouraged by the French Liaison Officer who assured Alderson that his countrymen were about to counterattack. Alderson in turn ordered his 3rd Brigade under Brigadier General Turner V.C. to attack the enemy in Kitcheners' Wood. As early as 8:16 Alderson notified V Corps of both these developments.

At nine the 5th Imperial Division reported to V Corps that the Germans had taken St. Julien, and that Mouse Trap Farm, where 3rd Brigade Headquarters was situated, had been captured. This sounded plausible enough, but was entirely false. Rumours and reports of this sort deluged headquarters at all levels during the night and made decisive action difficult, if not impossible.

Most of the night of 22-23 April was spent desperately trying to find reinforcements. This was true of all levels of command. Aside from these pleas and demands for situation reports there were few messages. One of the latter was received at 10:20 at Alderson's headquarters: it was sent by the division's Engineer officer informing Alderson that all the Canadian bridges were ready to be destroyed if necessary. This also included two bridges in the French sector. The more northerly of the two French bridges was a barrel bridge, and it was now rigged so that it could be swung to the west bank. The other was Bridge No. 4, best known as "the Brielen Bridge." It was prepared with charges, but would not be blown until absolutely essential.

Alderson's search for reinforcements began to bear fruit at eight when Smith-Dorrien at V Corps advised him that two Canadian battalions were being placed at his disposal. These were the 2nd and 3rd Battalions of his own 1st Brigade which had been on stand-by to move to Hill 60. Later in the evening the 1st and 4th battalions also were returned to Alderson.

British battalions were on the way as well. The first of thirty-three to eventually come under Alderson's command was the 2nd East Yorkshire Regiment from the 28th Imperial Division's reserve. Also from the 28th came the 2nd Battalion, The Buffs (The East Kent Regiment) and the 3rd Battalion, The Middlesex Regiment. They moved into line stretching from the Yser Canal to the village of St. Jean, halfway between Ypres and Wieltje. Also on the way was the 4th Battalion, The Rifle Brigade from the 27th Imperial Division.

Artillery was the other great weakness. The 45th Algerian Division on the left had lost every one of its artillery pieces and the Canadians' thirty-two 18 pounders and eight 4.5 howitzers were now covering a front of over 12,000 yards. This meant a frontage of 300 yards per gun!

One young staff officer motored up from Divisional Headquarters in search of information. Near Fusilier Farm (over 1,000 yards east of the canal) he found a lone French machine gun crew. They told him that they were the front line and that the enemy was 600 yards to the north on Mauser Ridge, a statement which was constantly verified by the enemy who shot up flares from along the ridge during the night. This solitary machine gun and its crew was the only allied force between the Canal and Hampshire Farm — a gap of over 3,000 yards.

All through the night crowds of civilian refugees continued to struggle westward out of the Salient, the vast majority making for

Ypres. There the sounds of continual wailing and crying, of crashing buildings, and the screaming roar of heavy shells mingled with the steady crackling of flames. Through this the pitiful procession jostled along the road and the railway tracks to Vlamertinghe. The goal was the railway station where all hoped to board one of the crowded trains. Shouting and clamouring, the frantic crowd of refugees swelled as the night of anguish lengthened. "Women, children, and badly wounded and gassed soldiers were placed on board the waiting train, the brute rush of the frenzied townsmen beaten back, discipline and some semblance of order preserved," wrote Hugh Pollard. "At midnight the last train left the shell shattered ruins of Vlamertinghe crowded with women and wounded and with white-coifed Sisters from the Convent of the Poor Clares crouching upon the floor boards. Shells wailed and wept over the village, and the permanent way behind the train was hit again and again by a dozen long-range shells."[4] The remaining refugees now turned reluctantly to the road west, on to Poperinghe.

Meanwhile, Canadian troops were going the other way. The 16th Canadian Scottish, each man wearing two extra bandoliers of ammunition, was striding through the fiery chaos of Ypres. No one seemed to know why or where, and one major was heard to rage, "Damn this staff! We are only two days out of the trenches and now they are . . . us around on night maneuvers."[5]

By ten o'clock the men were halted in an open field north of Wieltje while Lt. Col. Leckie reported to Brigadier Turner V.C. at Shell Trap Farm.* Here all ranks noticed a curious drying and tightening of the throat, and eyes began to water. Presently the C.O. returned, and the battalion lined up in four waves behind the 10th Canadians who were a few yards ahead in the darkness.

Soon the advance recommenced, and word was passed—the two battalions were about to attack the Germans in Kitcheners' Wood at the northern end of Mauser Ridge. In the moonlight the wood could be distinguished as a dark blur on the horizon. The 10th and the 16th would be the first Canadians to attack an enemy since the Boer War. At the assembly point there was a welter of quiet commands to confuse everyone—"Remove packs but leave on overcoats"—"Fix bayonets and remove overcoats"—"Unfix

---

* Corps soon changed this all too apt name by order to "Mouse Trap Farm."

bayonets"—"Fix bayonets." Then the men waited in the silence of suspense. The only sound was the cheery voice of Canon Scott, the 16th's padre, "A great day for Canada, boys. A great day for Canada."

The formation employed might well have been copied from some old Napoleonic campaign, but it had been stipulated in orders from 3rd Brigade Headquarters and signed by Lt. Col. Garnet Hughes, son of Sir Sam Hughes, Canada's Minister of Defense. There were eight waves advancing thirty yards apart with no attempt being made to provide flanking fire, or even to secure the flanks. Although none of the men had ever seen the ground they were to cover, there was to be no reconnaissance. The enemy lay ahead somewhere and the two battalions were being sent in shoulder to shoulder in eight waves on a narrow front only two companies wide. A bullet missing its intended target in the front rank could hardly fail to claim a victim in one of the seven succeeding waves. The artillery support for this venture supposedly consisted of three batteries (two Canadian and one British) which were firing *beyond* the enemy's first line and into the northern end of the wood. The only noticeable support was supplied by a single gun of the 75th Royal Field Artillery. It had been undergoing repairs at the Ordnance Workshop in St. Jean, and its scrappy subaltern had galloped it forward with all the ammunition available—60 rounds.

One hundred bombers* would accompany the two battalions. Seventy of these were provided by the 3rd Brigade and thirty by the 2nd. When all were reported in position Lt. Col. Hughes, the Brigade Major, gave a direction on the Pole Star. The first allied counterattack was ready to begin.

"Watches were synchronized at eleven-thirty p.m., and the advance, covered by one field battery (sic) which fired a round into the wood about every five minutes, commenced at approximately eleven forty-five p.m.," wrote the 16th's historian. "The distance from the assembly position to the south of the wood, where the enemy was entrenched, ran somewhere between eight hundred to one thousand yards. In covering the first part of this ground the attacking troops must have made considerable noise, for some platoons had to turn

---

* Bombers—this term was used to describe the battalion men trained in the use of the hand grenade.

into file to get through openings and hedges, jump ditches, and regain touch with flanking platoons on the other side; but notwithstanding these mishaps, the preliminary stage was carried out unmolested."[6]

The front rank had arrived at a beech hedge which they pushed through. There began a terrific clattering and scraping of bayonet scabbards against wire. This hedge was supported by a wire fence! Suddenly a flare hissed upwards and burst into a white glare. There was a second of stunned silence as the field and hedge full of men lay bathed in light, then the German machine guns opened up from positions forty yards in front of the wood.

"Instantly the word was given to charge, and on we rushed cheering, yelling, shouting, and swearing, straight for the foe," wrote one of the attackers. "At first the Germans fired a little too high, and our losses until we came within fifty yards of them were comparatively small. Then some of our chaps began to drop, then the whole front line seemed to melt away, only to be instantly closed up again."[7]

"Cheering and yelling all the time, we jumped over the bodies of the wounded and tore on," wrote another. "Of the Germans with the machine guns not one escaped, but those inside the wood stood up to us in the most dogged style. We were so quickly at work that those at the edge of the wood could not have got away in any case. Many threw up their hands, and we did not refuse quarter.

"Pressing on into the wood itself, the struggle became a dreadful hand to hand conflict; we fought in clumps and batches, and the living struggled over the bodies of the dead and dying. At the height of the conflict while we were steadily driving the Germans before us, the moon burst out. The clashing bayonets flashed like quicksilver, and faces were lit up as by limelight."[8]

"I vaguely saw some Germans and rushed at the nearest one," a diarist recorded. "My bayonet must have hit his equipment and glanced off, but luckily for me, another chap running beside me bayonetted him before he got me. By this time I was wildly excited and shouting and rushing into the wood up a path towards a big gun which was pointed away from us."[9]

Nearby a dejected horse tied to a tree by its reins stood on three legs holding up its wounded leg. Alongside loomed a battery of huge 4.7 guns of the 2nd London Regiment, Royal Garrison Artillery.

Major Ormond of the 10th reported, "They were piled high with dead—British, Turcos and German. In my opinion it would have been impossible to have recovered and removed these guns."[10]

The survivors pushed on past the guns and through the small coppice. Bursting out of this narrow portion of Kitcheners' Wood, the men discovered another of the hedges fifty yards in front. Lance-Corporal Hugh Wallis of the 16th was one of the first to reach this hedge. Peering through it he saw a body of men approaching led by a huge figure. Wallis challenged, but on they came. At the last moment the figures charged and Wallis and his four companions fired. The gigantic leader collapsed and the rest fled. Firing from the hip, the Highlanders bulled their way through the hedge after the enemy, leaving one behind to guard the wounded officer. Onward they ran into the darkness. Suddenly a barrage of Verey lights burst above them. Wallis was face to face with hundreds of Germans in position along a road. The enemy was in complete confusion, many standing with their arms raised in surrender while others began opening fire with rifles. Wallis and his small party retired at once. They were more fortunate than several of their comrades farther along who were captured in this way.

Back at the hedge three or four hundred men of both battalions had begun digging in. The work was agonizingly slow for the ground was so hard that enemy rifle bullets sparked and ricocheted off it hitting the men from all directions.

At this time Lt. Col. Boyle of the 10th had just received a report from a junior officer of the Scottish and had flashed his torch for a second or two on his map to confirm the position. Seconds later he was mortally wounded. Major McLaren now took command of the 10th.

Colonel Leckie of the 16th had sent out patrols in the optimistic hope of linking up with the 13th Royal Highlanders who were in reality over a mile and a half to the east. It was soon obvious that the 10th and 16th were in a precarious position. Flares shot up from both their right and their left flanks and from well behind, where the enemy still held the southwest corner of the wood. Nevertheless, it was decided to hold on in hopes that reinforcements would arrive to extend the line.

While these events were unfolding at the hedge beyond Kitcheners' Wood, a party remained in the captured trench on the south side of the wood. Major Ormond, Adjutant of the 10th, had returned to the southwest corner with an uneasy feeling that this flank was open. He found only the dead and wounded plus a few men with prisoners. A voice called from the left in passable English, "We have you surrounded. Surrender!"

Ormond set about probing this flank, but two advances were beaten back with severe casualties and the survivors hastily began strengthening their captured trench on the fringe of Kitcheners' Wood. "The trench taken was about 1-1/2 feet to 2 feet deep with a good parapet in construction consisting of dirt and sand bags, but the trench was filled with dead and wounded among which were several German officers . . . . At this time we were subjected to fire from all directions except Southeast," Ormond reported. Casualties continued to mount under heavy small arms fire, and one wounded Highlander later counted fourteen bullet holes in his kilt.

By this time Major McLaren, the new C.O. of the 10th, had been wounded and evacuated. He was killed in Ypres later that night. Major Ormond, back in the trench south of the wood, became the 10th Canadians' third commanding officer within an hour. "Despite the arrival of reinforcements (the 2nd Battalion), the tactical position had not improved," noted the 16th Battalion's historian. "The men alongside the hedge were getting under cover very slowly and both flanks of that position were still exposed. The shouting and commotion in the enemy's lines to the front of us was still going on. Judging by the loud guttural sounds from that direction the German officers were trying to rally their men for a counter attack."

As dawn approached, there was another consultation of officers. A difficult decision would have to be made now. Should the two sadly depleted battalions hang on to their costly gains or should they withdraw, surrounded on three sides as they were by a much superior force? Whichever was decided, it must be carried out before dawn revealed their sparse numbers to the enemy.

Meanwhile the desperate plea for reinforcements had reached Brigadier General Turner V.C. Some time after two Major Godson-Godson, the Adjutant of the 16th, had staggered into his headquarters at Mouse Trap Farm. His throat had been torn open by a bullet and he could not speak but he conveyed the two battalions' urgent request in a pencilled note. Turner had received word that two battalions were about to arrive at Mouse Trap Farm. He would perhaps be able to relieve the situation with them.

The men of the 2nd and 3rd battalions from Ontario had left Vlamertinghe in darkness at nine o'clock. Strangely comforting was the sillouette of a lone Canadian trooper sitting impassively on his horse at the crossroads while the crowd of refugees flowed in a babble around him. Private Peat of the 3rd Toronto Battalion wrote his impressions:

"The German shells rose and burst behind us. They made the Yser Canal a stream of molten glory. Shells fell in the city, and split the darkness of the heavens in the early night hours. Later the moon rose in the splendour of springtime. Straight behind the tower of the great cathedral it rose and shone down on a bloody earth."[11]

As the two battalions marched in column of route parallel to the German positions half a mile away, they were escorted by a thin screen of 19th Alberta Dragoons. When they passed through shallow depressions their feet stirred up wisps of the deadly gas which caused coughing and some pain. The two battalions arrived at Mouse Trap Farm—the 3rd at 1:15 and the 2nd fifteen minutes later. There the casualties began.

Brigadier General Turner received these reinforcements gratefully. The 2nd (Eastern Ontario) Battalion, under a former Quebec newspaperman, Lt. Col. David Watson, was to split and extend the flanks of the 10th and 16th. In addition, one company must be used to clear the German redoubt in the southwest corner of Kitcheners' Wood. It would have to be accomplished before daylight enabled the Germans to concentrate their artillery fire and their machine gun fire on the attackers.

Major Bennett's A Company advanced into position in a shallow fold in the ground. Patrols went out to locate the enemy. They did not return. Next, the second-in-command, Captain Leslie Gordon, went forward into the darkness. He was never seen again. Finally Bennett himself went out to reconnoitre. The minutes of precious darkness ticked away. Soon it would be too late to attack with even a hope of success. Dawn was almost upon them. Finally, Lt. Col. Watson decided to attack regardless. He had just given instructions to Lieutenant Kidd when Bennett's large form loomed out of the graying darkness. He promptly resumed control and the order was passed to fix bayonets. The 2nd Battalion was about to make its first attack.

The 3rd Toronto Battalion (minus two companies which garrisoned the G.H.Q. Line) was to move farther east. C and D Companies trekked on another 2,000 yards eastward to extend the Canadian line a further 2,000 yards to the Hannebeek, northwest of St.Julien. They would, in all probability, not make it till after dawn. If that proved to be the case, they would suffer heavily.

All through that April night thousands of men were moving almost soundlessly through darkened fields, sometimes lit up for hundreds of yards by flaming farm buildings. The heavy crash of shells drowned out the occasional clatter of equipment and the clumping of thousands of feet on the spring sod. Men in khaki, gray, and blue worked through the hours of darkness to reach their designated spot on a map or to prepare entrenchments before the first light of dawn revealed them to their enemies. Behind the new German line running the length of Mauser Ridge, battalions of *feldgrau* worked to ready their positions before daylight. In the wide-open fields to the south of them hundreds of fugitives, remnants of the 45th Algerian Division, searched for a place from which to fight or in which to die lonely deaths from the slow effects of chlorine gas. For hundreds of Canadians there was miles of marching to God-only-knows-where, finally to dig hasty trenches facing the invisible enemy.

Among the latter were three companies of the 14th Royal Montreals. B Company had been at St. Julien when the fateful Thursday had dawned. Immediately after the gas attack had been launched the 14th's remaining three companies had been marched into the General Headquarters Line.* This the men found was a rather grand title. "For the most part, it existed on maps and in imaginations only. A few shallow trenches and pits had been dug, but these provided protection for individuals rather than for organized bodies of troops," recorded the battalion historian. Lt. Col. Meighen

---

* Commonly known as the "G.H.Q. Line," the term which will be employed in this work.

placed his three companies into position with C and D facing east and A facing north with its left 'in the air,' "the imaginary line stretching quite ungarrisoned as far as the Yser Canal."[12]

Shortly after midnight the distant roar of artillery could be heard off to the east. The Germans were attacking again. This was a feint against the 28th Imperial Division by the German troops opposite them. Although the enemy never reached the British trenches, the attack was mildly successful as a division and it certainly impressed the rookie Canadians on the right of the line. "For an hour there was a veritable pandemonium of noise, rifle and machine gun, the latter being especially wicked," wrote Lt. Col. Tuxford of the 5th Western Cavalry Battalion. "For over an hour the everlasting noise rose and fell, whining as it increased its fury, to a high crescendo, then falling to a deeper note, as though played on some gigantic instrument. We had never heard anything approaching this before."

Further to the southwest, St. Julien was still under siege. Major V.W. Odlum of the 7th British Columbians, had been sent over by his C.O. to see the Town Commandant, Lt. Col. Loomis, "casualties all around him, his Headquarters filled with moaning, groaning, bleeding men," Odlum recalled. "All Loomis knew was that it happened out 'that way.' So I went back to Colonel McHarg and told him the situation as I had found it and then we started to move into that black darkness and be ready to block it up when daylight came."[13]

Thus three companies of British Columbia men came across from the support trenches at Gravenstafel Ridge to join the defenders of St. Julien. It was a polyglot mixture — one company of the 14th Royal Montreals, one of the 15th (48th Highlanders), three of the 7th, headquarters staff of the 13th and 15th plus a motley collection of *zouaves* and *tirailleurs*.

North of St. Julien near the village of Keerselaere, the 10th Battery, Canadian Field Artillery, still sat exposed and alone firing into darkness. After driving off the German infantry attack at point-blank range shortly after seven, Major King had kept two of his guns firing north and two firing west. At 8:00 he received orders to evacuate his exposed position, but it was not till 11:00 that the 10th Battery completed its withdrawal. Each time the horses were brought up they were cut down by German rifle and machine gun fire from west of the road. Ammunition wagons were thus left sitting in the open some distance behind the guns, and a party of infantry laboured mightily bringing up the desperately needed ammunition by hand. Eventually, a little after ten o'clock, teams were able to take out two of King's guns and the rest were man-handled back until more teams arrived. There were not enough horses however to bring back the ammunition wagons and two had to be left behind. By 4:00 a.m. the 10th Battery was in position west of the Yser Canal near Brielen ready to support the first French counterattack.

The commandant of St. Julien, Lt. Col. Loomis, was in a desperate fix. He had a gap on either side of him and nowhere near enough men to fill either. Judging the gap to the north between the British Columbians and the original front line to be the more critical, Loomis sent off his last reserve, two platoons of his own 13th. They moved through the darkness along the Poelcappelle Road, but ran into a large body of Germans dug in where their comrades had been overwhelmed earlier that evening. It was an unequal fight, and the two platoons withdrew to St. Julien.

By this time Colonel Loomis had received a company of the Buffs under Captain Tomlinson. Together these British regulars and the Canadian Highlanders left for the apex by a much more circuitous route. With a lot of luck they would reach the line where the 13th were presumed to be.

At the other end of this 1,500 yard gap the 13th was still hanging on doggedly. On the left flank Major McCuaig was busy with his men trying to extend the defenses down the Poelcappelle Road to St. Julien. They had been reinforced by 200 survivors of the 1st Tirailleurs with one machine gun. All the while heavy fire had been raining down upon the nearly obliterated trenches, and casualties had mounted alarmingly. McCuaig wrote, "The Germans attacked a couple of times, but our fire was too intense for them and they were driven back. In fact, the firing was incessant the whole night . . . . In the meantime, from the progress of the Germans' flares it was possible to note that they had penetrated for a considerable distances and were working round in rear of us."[14]

As dawn drew perilously closer it became more and more evident to McCuaig and the other officers that the makeshift line along the road was a poor defensive position. Therefore, work began 300 yards to the rear on a new line which at least offered a reasonable field of fire. It was decided that the line along the road would be abandoned if reinforcements did not arrive before dawn.

Thus, at the last possible moment the mixed force of Highlanders and *tirailleurs* slipped silently out of their shallow trenches and moved to the rear. Lieutenant Ross and Corporal McFarlane's party kept up a brisk fire with their machine guns and rifles to cover the withdrawal. It began without a hitch. At the same moment, in the eastern sky, pale shafts of light began to appear, lending an illusion of peacefulness to the tortured countryside of Flanders. The long night of anguish was nearly over. What would the dawn bring?

Chapter Seven

Quit Yourselves Like Men
(4:00 a.m. - Noon, 23 April, 1915)

"Be strong and quit yourselves like men."
I Samuel IV, 9

Before daybreak the first of No. 6 Squadron's planes was cruising in the cold air above the Salient. Again it was Lieutenant L.A. Strange, this time with Captain Harold Wyllie as observer. As soon as there was sufficient light they flew over the old French front line. "To our amazement we could find no signs of troops in the usual trenches, but soon discovered a new front line of trenches about four or five miles nearer Ypres," Strange wrote. "Whether these were occupied by French or Germans it was impossible to tell, but as soon as we dropped down low enough we obtained ample evidence that this new line, extending from Boesinghe to St. Julien, was held by the enemy. Wyllie hastily sketched it in his map and then we hurried back."[1]

This was the critical situation in which the Allies found themselves when dawn broke on Friday. To the north, at the hinge of the Salient, the enemy held Steenstraat and its vital bridge. The Belgians and the French 80th Territorial Regiment had re-established a rather tenuous linkup east of Lizerne, but could this stand the test of a renewed German assault?

From Steenstraat to beyond Boesinghe all that stood between the Germans and open country were a few exhausted battalions and the Yser Canal. The bridges over this barrier had been prepared for demolition by Lieutenant Hardelay and his volunteers. Now as dawn broke he had arrived back near the vital railway bridge south of Boesinghe. Hardelay climbed to the top of the railway embankment where he called out to Sergeant Mathieu who lay hidden in a small shelter hastily dug in the canal bank at the south end of the

75

bridge. It was from this shelter that the charge would be fired. Could he make it across he asked Mathieu? The latter thought it was possible, but only if Hardelay moved quickly. The lieutenant then jumped to his feet to make a dash for it, but a burst of machine gun fire from the gate-keeper's house across the canal cut him down and he fell from sight. The enemy fired all day at the unfortunate lieutenant, and it was not till nightfall on the 23rd that his body was retrieved, riddled with bullets. But Hardelay had not died in vain. At seven that morning Sergeant Mathieu detonated the charges and destroyed the railway bridge of Boesinghe.

Could the remaining crossings be held by the scattered French survivors and reserves? The only French troops still east of the canal were Mordacq's *zouaves* in the area of Zwaanhof and Mordacq Farms. On their right they had been groping eastward in hopes of connecting up with the Canadians.

There was no contact however, for a wide gap extended to Kitcheners' Wood where the survivors of the Canadian midnight attack had dug in. Fortunately, this gap was not completely open. In the middle the lone French machine gun crew stood firm, and behind it were scattered British battalions. At that moment two Canadian units were forming up to the east of the Ypres-Pilckem Road behind a slight rise known as Hill Top Ridge. These were the 1st and 4th battalions and they were preparing to advance into this wide gap.

As dawn approached, a difficult decision was being made by the commanding officers of the 10th and 16th battalions at the hedge north of Kitcheners' Wood. The 10th was by this time under its third C.O. of the night, Major Ormond, and he met with Lt. Col. Leckie of the 16th. Should the two sadly depleted battalions hang on to their dearly-won gains? Surrounded on three sides, without artillery support, and thrust into the lion's mouth, the senior officers decided to give up the suicidal positions they now held. Reluctantly the orders were passed to retire back through Kitcheners' Wood, past the four silent guns which could not be saved, over the bodies of hundreds of their comrades to the trench they had first captured in front of the wood.

Thus as dawn approached the two shattered battalions reoccupied a weak defensive line facing Kitcheners' Wood. On the left,

the 10th Canadians in the captured German trench had been reduced to five officers and 188 other ranks — all that was left of the
816 who had charged at 11:45 p.m. On the right in a series of hastily
dug rifle pits the 16th Canadian Scottish took roll call. This revealed the tragic fact that only five officers and 263 other ranks remained.

It was at this moment that A Company of the 2nd Eastern Ontario Battalion received the order to attack. They moved diagonally
across the 10th Canadians' trench out of the dead ground in which
they had waited. With Major Bennett in the lead they charged wildly over the low ridge as dawn rolled away night's sheltering curtain.
The long thin line charged down the gentle slope towards the German redoubt. The German machine guns and rifles opened up at
close range and in less than two minutes the attack was all over. The
slope was littered with lifeless or writhing figures. No one reached
the redoubt and only a dozen managed to join the men of Ormond's
decimated 10th Battalion.

The men of C Company had taken possession of Oblong Farm
to the left of the wood and they would long remember that terrible
charge made by their comrades. "One thing that I noticed more
than anything else in the front lines was the noise," recalled Private
Graham. "The screaming of wounded men was something you'd
never thought of before. You never realized that things like that
would happen."[2]

The enemy had not finished though. Immediately after, he
struck back. In overwhelming numbers the Germans attacked the
16th's depleted Colt machine gun crew. Two survivors were captured but not before the gun's firing mechanism had been
destroyed.

The weary fragments of the 10th and 16th now looked back
over the field they had crossed a few hours earlier. In places bodies
were heaped, but most lay in long even lines where they had been
mowed down. Half were in khaki and half in tartans. Even at that
distance it was clear how the different companies of the 16th had
met their fate — the yellow line on the pleats of the Gordon kilts
revealed where A Company lay in a line; B Company's Seaforth's
were identifiable by the white line; and C's Argylls by their sombre
Black Watch tartan; rows of D Company men were easily identified
by the Cameron's red lines.

Weak movements and agonized groans announced that the wounded still lay where they fell. Rescue work began at once and the enemy commenced sniping. When a stretcher-bearer was pitched forward on his face by a sniper's bullet the life-saving came to an end. The remaining wounded were destined to lie another sixteen hours till nightfall brought back their rescuers.

At 5:30 that morning a lone German plane reconnoitered above Kitcheners' Wood. In a short time deadly accurate artillery fire descended on the trench and the First Aid Post. Heavy casualties resulted. In the meantime a party of Canadian Engineers had prepared to demolish the ammunition dump beside the howitzers in the wood. The sudden unexpected roar and the rain of branches, dirt, and iron which clattered onto the trench brought everyone instantly to the alert, but the morning dragged wearily on with no further excitement.

From Kitcheners' Wood to east of Keerselaere ran a makeshift Canadian line. No part of this line was held by a complete battalion; it was merely a succession of companies representing seven battalions interspersed with blue-clad fugitives, all crouched in shallow depressions scratched into the hard earth.

For two of these companies dawn had arrived too soon. The 3rd Toronto Battalion's C and D Companies had trekked through the early morning hours but were still short of their intended position on the western bank of the Haanebeek, several hundred yards north of St. Julien. These two unsupported companies were to take a newly-dug German trench situated about four hundred yards away, across a field. They formed up in skirmishing order. "I heard no command," wrote Private Peat, "but of a sudden we heard a 'CLICK!' to the left. No one even glanced in the direction. Every man fixed his bayonet. The man on the extreme left had fixed his, the 'CLICK!' had warned his comrades eight paces away . . . In front were our officers, every one of them from junior to senior, well ahead of their men. A wave of the hand, a quarter right turn, one long blast of the whistle and we were off. We made mad rushes of fifty or sixty yards at a time, then down we would go . . . The machine gun fire was hellish. The infantry fire was blinding. A bullet would flash through the sleeve of a tunic, rip off the brim of a cap, bang against a water bottle, bury itself in the mass of a knapsack.

"I don't know what other men may have felt in the last advance. For myself the thought flashed across my mind — 'What's the use? It is certain death to stay here any longer; why not lie down, wait till the worst is over and be able to fight again — it is useless, hopeless — it is suicidal to attempt such a task.' "

But Private Peat charged with his surviving comrades. The Torontonians suffered well over one hundred casualties and nearly all of the officers were hit. The men's blood was up.

"When we reached the enemy trench and presented the bright end of the bayonet, Mr. Fritz went down on his knees and cried, *'Kamerad! Kamerad!'*

"What did we do? . . . 'Kamerad!' — Bah!'"[3]

And it was in this way that the Canadian line was stretched as far as Keerselaere.

But from Keerselaere north to the old front line there was nothing. In their flimsy trenches the men of the 13th and 15th battalions greeted dawn with apprehension. At the apex where the line had been torn open and a 'refused flank' had been established along the Poelcappelle Road, Major McCuaig and his men had begun their stealthy withdrawal to the new line 300 yards to the rear.

Arriving in the new position McCuaig was surprised to discover the despaired-of replacements — two platoons of the 13th and a company of the Buffs from the 28th Imperial Division. After a short consultation the party turned around and recrossed the three hundred yards back to the road. The return journey was completed without the enemy becoming aware of it, and a desperate spate of sandbagging ensued as a redoubt was constructed at the intersection of the road and the front line.

Thus, at dawn ten and a half Canadian and British battalions (plus seven in the so-called second line) now faced forty-two German battalions. The Germans had a preponderance in field artillery of at least five to one, plus an overwhelming advantage in heavy artillery.

These unpleasant facts were brought home to the staff officers snug at G.H.Q. when the two aviators reported there at 8:30. "We expressed our apprehension of the fact that we had failed to discover any traces of British troops confronting the Germans in their new positions," wrote Strange. "We wondered why the latter had taken the trouble to dig themselves in, when, as far as we could see, there was nothing to prevent them continuing their advance."[4] These apprehensions were communicated to the generals who had begun to realize the critical situation facing them.

To meet the German attacks which day would undoubtedly bring, it was necessary to do two things. First, scattered units in the area must be organized into fighting formations with command structures. Secondly, a pool of reserves must be established to meet the enemy's thrusts. If the battered and shrinking battalions could hang on for another day or two until fresh troops were rushed to the rescue then the Salient, and—what was more important—its garrison, could be saved.

To organize the various detached formations in the area was Alderson's job, and a number of British units were put under his command. One of these was a composite brigade created on paper at one o'clock that morning. It consisted of the 2nd Battalion of The Buffs, the 3rd Battalion The Middlesex Regiment, the 5th King's Own Regiment, and the 1st York and Lancaster Regiment. These were battalions from various brigades of the 28th Imperial Division and they came under command of the senior officer, Colonel A.D. Geddes of the Buffs. A skeleton headquarters staff of one captain, a lieutenant, and a platoon of cyclists was improvised, but there were no supporting arms. At 3:00 while the unfortunate colonel was attempting to establish some sort of order out of chaos, he had received orders to move his 'brigade' into the gap between the French and the Canadians, "driving back any enemy that may have penetrated." Thus, "Geddes' Detachment," as it became known, was given its first assignment two hours after its birth in a headquarters many miles away.

Because the Headquarters of the Canadian and 28th Divisions were west of the canal and completely out of touch, Smith-Dorrien formed his Corps Reserve under the only Divisional Commander in the Salient, Major General Snow of the 27th Imperial Division. Snow's headquarters were at Potijze Chateau immediately behind the imaginary G.H.Q. Line and south of Bellewaardebeek. Accordingly, order was imposed somewhat superficially upon chaos.

Behind the French sector similar attempts to restore order were in progress. The French Official History recorded "Towards midnight General Foch instructed General Putz that it was necessary above all, first to make certain of the retention of the occupied points, second, to organize upon them a base of departure for a counter-attack which would recapture the lost ground, and third, to deliver this counter-attack."

Meanwhile at the front senior French officers, embarrassed by the disasters so recently befallen them, were proposing the only solution they knew. Mordacq wrote, "To stop the Germans, the French High Command had reported that it had only one practical solution: counter-attack."[5] In this way the French reliance on *élan* was to be tested again. Whether or not such attacks could be successful or were even possible was scarcely considered.

This French doctrine of attacking, no matter what the circumstances, had proved to be disastrous on many occasions, but seldom had it been adhered to with less reason than on 23 April, 1915. The French generals' confident assertions that they were about to counterattack were either face-saving or self-delusion on a grand scale. The 45th Algerian Division had been shattered, its artillery had been captured to the last gun. The weak 87th Territorial Division was in worse shape, if anything. Still, generals talked boldly of counterattacks. Unfortunately for all concerned, the true extent of the French defeat was not known at Canadian or British Headquarters. As a result, several ill-advised and totally unprepared attacks were launched by these rather naive officers under the illusion that they were co-operating with powerful French counter-strokes.

It was not till 1:30 that General Putz issued the order for the French counterattack. It was a wildly optimistic document including the information that "the 28th English Division and a Canadian Brigade" would also be attacking. Did Putz believe this, or was it an attempt to encourage his decimated battalions?

The orders were equally unrealistic. Mordacq's 90th Brigade was to attack with two battalions and capture Pilckem. Meanwhile, General Roy's 87th Territorial Division was ordered to force a crossing of the Yser to cover the left flank of Mordacq's attack. This formation of elderly territorials was expected to advance against the powerful German 45th Reserve Division, cross the canal, and "occupy the 2nd line of trenches to the north of the 45th Division."

It was 3:45 a.m. when Alderson received his copy of these impossible orders. Two minutes later he sent the following message to

Brigadier General Mercer of the 1st Brigade:

"At 5 o'clock two French battalions are to make a counter-attack against Pilckem with their right resting on Pilckem-Ypres Road. You will co-operate with this attack at the same time with your left on this road. Acknowledge." Mercer was not destined to read this till 45 minutes before zero hour.

At 4:10 Alderson sent a similar message to Geddes' Detachment requesting that they too join in, adding hopefuly, "If possible you should connect with this attack and co-operate." Fifteen minutes before zero hour, Colonel Geddes received this, his second set of orders. A copy of this order arrived at Mercer's headquarters nearly twenty minutes after the attack was to have begun.

But zero hour passed and no one advanced. Lt. Col. A.P. Birchall of the 4th Central Ontario Battalion was in charge of the small attacking force, 1st Brigade Headquarters being on the west bank of the canal. Birchall's 4th and Lt. Col. F.W. Hill's 1st Western Ontario Battalion had been at Vlamertinghe the evening before, four miles away. At 12:30 that morning they had been released from Corps Reserve by Smith-Dorrien and had marched off towards Brielen and the canal. At 1st Brigade Headquarters, an *estaminet* on the west bank, Major Beatty, the Chaplain, had read them a passage from scripture and collected numerous last messages from the men before they went into action. Then it was over the Yser by the Brielen bridge, already prepared for detonation by Canadian engineers, and along a cart track to an abandoned farm. The 4th lined up on a frontage one company wide (150) yards, with the 1st Battalion in the rear. Thus seven waves lay ready to advance by 4:30.

Artillery support for the entire attack was very meagre. Two batteries of British 4.5-inch howitzers and the 10th Canadian Battery were to support from a distance. Now two half batteries (the 2nd and 3rd Canadian)* had also been brought up at the last moment. "We had just nicely got the horses settled in the horse lines when the bugle blew 'Stand To' and we were told we were going into action at once," recalled John Armstrong, a former member of the Dominion

---

* Nearly all of the Canadian Field Artillery batteries were composite units until 4 May for they had been caught in the midst of a relief when the attack came on 22 April.

Police in Victoria, B.C. "So we hitched up—by that time it was nearly daylight—and we started down the road. By the time we left Ypres and got to Hellfire Corner, Fritz had spotted us and opened up on us. It was the one and only time we went into action at the gallop. For about three miles down the road we went as fast as we could. Fritz followed us all the way up with 5.9 shells. We got in behind the canal bank and we were ordered to prepare for action." Sixteen guns were to attempt to silence a mile of entrenched riflemen and machine gunners.

Meanwhile on the far side of the canal the 4th and 1st battalions behind Hill Top Ridge waited to advance with their French allies. Five o'clock came and went, but there was no sign of Mordacq's *zouaves*. Unknown to Birchall, the end of the French line was several hundred yards farther ahead, and the Canadians were considerably to the rear.

Officers who moved up to the crest of Hill Top Ridge could see a broad panorama. On the crest of Mauser Ridge, 1,500 yards in front, swarms of Germans could be seen working on trenches and placing barbed wire entanglements. Ahead, on the east side of the Ypres-Pilckem Road, lay a long field dotted with stacks of cut sod and manure piles. At the far end grew a row of willows. The ground sloped gently from there to the top of Mauser Ridge a mere thirty feet above the surrounding plains. As it grew lighter, a traditional Flemish farm—house, barns, and sheds surrounding a manure-filled courtyard—could be seen on top of the ridge. This would be known to history as "Turco Farm."

Across the canal the two half batteries were now "Ready for Action." "We were told that just about 200 yards farther up we'd go through a gap in the bank then along the canal to go into action. And of course when we left there it was at the dead run again," Gunner John Armstrong remembered.

"Down through this gap we went, right along the canal bank. We pulled up under some trees, and though the Germans had a direct view, the trees prevented them from finding out just where we were. We got orders to 'Action Front.' We unloaded the gun limbers and they took them away. There were shells popping all around us and machine gun bullets too."

It was now 5:25 and Colonel Birchall, looking tall in his British Warm, decided to delay no longer. He assumed that Mordacq's *zouaves* were attacking behind several hedges which blocked his vision to the left. The waves moved off towards the crest of Hill Top Ridge. All was quiet as the advancing lines swept past Foch Farm where unmilked cows lowed in the yard, and the farmer's untouched supper of the evening before sat on the table. As they topped the rise and emerged from the hedge there, they were met by a tornado of fire. Brigadier Mercer near the reserve line could still see the whole advance "being carried out in the most perfect order as if on parade." Into the field of manure piles the men advanced in short rushes.

"Ahead of me I see men running," wrote George Bell of the 1st. "Suddenly their legs double up and they sink to the ground. Here's a body with the head shot off. Here's a poor devil with both legs gone, but still alive. A body of a man means nothing except something to avoid stumbling over. It's just another obstacle. There goes little Elliot, one of the boys from the print shop where I worked in Detroit, only ten yards from me. Poor devil. There's nothing I can do for him. What's one man more or less in this slaughter?"

The Canadians were surprised to find in front and to the right British soldiers in shallow rifle pits. They were men of Geddes' 3rd Middlesex Regiment. "What's the matter with them? Their faces are ghastly gray," noted Bell. "They're coughing, tears are running down their faces, and some are rolling on the ground in agony. But those who are able to stand are holding grimly on, and they give us a faint cheer as we pass through their weakened ranks. What soldiers they are, holding on to the last man." Few Canadians realized that the Middlesex Regiment had, a century before, earned its nickname — "The Diehards." They did not propose to lose it now.

The men of both Canadian battalions were soon mixed together, and the front had widened as they approached the enemy's advance positions. These were now empty, the Germans having withdrawn to their main line on top of Mauser Ridge. The order was passed to halt in a shallow ditch marked by the row of pollard willows. One survivor wrote, "We heard the bullets whistling around us, and the calls for 'stretcher bearers wanted' to left and right . . . Their machine gun and shell fire was terrible, but you would not hear a complaint; instead perhaps you would hear,

'Throw us over a cigarette, Bill,' or 'Have you got a match?' or some joke."[6]

Now Colonel Birchall called for reinforcements. He threw his reserve company from the 1st Battalion in with the two companies of the 3rd Battalion The Middlesex Regiment, "the Diehards," who had been advancing on the right, and they pushed forward another hundred yards. The Canadian composite battery was now hitting Turco Farm with deadly accuracy and the Germans pulled out chased by the Tommies and the Canucks. But when the victors attempted to occupy the old Flemish farm themselves they found there was no way to call off the fire of their own artillery. They withdrew to the bottom of the slope in sheer frustration.

Now at eight o'clock the isolated survivors looked back over "The Field of Manure Piles," as it came to be known. There they saw hundreds of sprawled figures; some were in khaki and some in the bright blue, white, and red of the 45th Algerian Division which had passed through the field the previous day going the opposite way. Most now lay still, but there was still the occasional man clutching at his throat or eyes and making weak convulsive movements on the ground. Looking up the slope in front of them the survivors saw trenches already protected by barbed wire and swarming with *feldgrau*. A sergeant summed it all up. "My God, if they had any sense at all, or any guts at all, they'd come over here and they wouldn't have to fire a shot. They could just take us all prisoners."[7]

Certainly, considering the short time the Germans had held Mauser Ridge, their position was formidable. Several strongpoints dominated the crest of the ridge, but slightly farther back out of sight lay the German main line — well-sited, scientifically constructed, with loop-holes, gabions, and parados, and well armed with numerous machine guns. "Ah! The Germans since last night had not wasted their time," Mordacq marvelled. "They accomplished there, it must be admitted, a truly superhuman task."

On the opposite side of the Ypres-Pilckem Road Mordacq was struggling with his own problems. First he had been ordered to attack although he had no artillery of his own to support the assault. Secondly, he was desperately anxious to link up with the Canadians. Thus as dawn brightened the eastern sky his outlook from Mordacq Farm must have been bleak. Unknown to him his *zouaves* were much farther to the north and closer to Mauser Ridge than were the

1st and 4th Canadian Battalions who were preparing to attack. Therefore the Canucks would have to advance a considerable distance to draw even with his command. For this reason, his patrols ran into enemies rather than Allies, and the Canadians' advance which began half an hour late, was not known to him.

As for Mordacq's own advance, the French Official History enigmatically states, "On the forenoon of 23rd April the Groupement d'Elverdinghe carried out two counter-attacks which miscarried." Even Mordacq, who was in charge of the attack, devotes only eight lines to it, and this is mainly a mild criticism of the rate of fire put down by an unnamed Canadian battery supporting his troops.

Evidently the French attack never took place in any meaningful manner, certainly it did not begin at 5:00 as ordered. It seems that elements of the 7th and 2nd Half-Battalion of Zouaves made a gradual and brief advance under heavy fire similar to that which mowed down so many members of the 1st and 4th Ontario battalions.

All that morning the Canadian survivors and their comrades of "the Diehards" lay in the hot sun hardly daring to move. Finally the moment arrived that every man had been dreading — gas! " 'Piss on your handkerchiefs and tie them over your faces,' yells our lieutenant. That's a break for us. Our lieutenant had been an analytical chemist in civil life, and when he got a sniff of that gas he must have known what it was," recalled George Bell. "Those who have no handkerchiefs tear strips from their puttees. At any rate it works as the gas sets up some sort of chemical combination with the urine and it crystalizes on the outside. There are some who do not take this precaution. They roll about gasping for breath." Fortunately most would survive, for although the enemy plastered the area with gas shells, they were the lachrimatory T Shells. When the bombardment was over the vapours soon dissipated.

Thus noon of Friday, 23 April, found the situation the same as at dawn except for the narrow Canadian-British advance to the foot of Mauser Ridge. These troops were now totally isolated — at close range, overwhelmingly outnumbered, almost without artillery support, and with two unprotected flanks. It was impossible to advance; it was equally impossible to withdraw across that long field dotted with manure piles and hundreds of fallen comrades. For men of the 1st Western Ontario Battalion and the 4th Central Ontario Battalion it would be a long afternoon.

From Duke Albrecht of Württemberg's point of view, Friday morning had been intoxicating—without doubt the highlight of his military career to that point. During the night, as the reports had poured in announcing success on every hand, he had begun to realize the potential that 'Disinfection' had opened up. Now he had decided to broaden substantially the objectives for the second day. Rather than rest along the Yser Canal, XXIII Reserve Corps under von Kathen was ordered to press on across the canal and take Poperinghe itself—over six miles behind Ypres! The secondary operation, to be undertaken by von Hugel's XXVI Reserve Corps, was to drive south and take the Canadian and 28th Imperial divisions in the rear.

As the morning progressed some of this euphoria began to wear off. After the long night spent beating off Belgian and French attacks around the bridgehead at Steenstraat, the 45th Reserve Division was exhausted. The German official history recorded, "The German troops did indeed beat off the attacks, but after that were not in a fit condition to continue the advance as ordered." The 51st Reserve Division too had been startled by the ferocity of the Canadian attack on Kitcheners' Wood during the night. That attack had hit the German line very close to the junction of the 51st and 52nd Reserve Divisions and if the Canadians had known that, even more disruption could have resulted. For their part, the 52nd Reserve Division had expected to find nothing to bar their way to Ypres that morning. Thus they had been thrown somewhat off balance by the relentless advance of the two Ontario battalions. As a result, both of Duke Albrecht's planned advances had been delayed.

To carry out his ambitious scheme the Duke needed reserves. These were few indeed—one brigade from his already hard-pressed 45th Reserve Division at Steenstraat and two regiments of Marines. All other available troops were hundreds of miles away heading for Galicia.

Meanwhile von Falkenhayn was basking in the warm glow of Kaiser Wilhelm's approval. In an audience with the monarch he was warmly congratulated and embraced three times. Colonel Tappen was promised a bottle of pink champagne by the Kaiser. Fortunately for all three, Wilhelm had not been informed that von Falkenhayn had just finished sending all his reserves in the opposite direction.

While the Kaiser and von Falkenhayn sipped their pink champagne the world's common folk were hearing about Disinfection for the first time. Canadian newspapers of 23 April declared, "Poison Gas Shells Forced British Back"; a French official report stated that "Bombs of Chloride" had been used against them and described the Germans throwing the bombs "by a hand-sling as used by boys for throwing stones"; British accounts told of the four lost *Canadian* guns and their subsequent recapture.

In Germany however, a different tone was adopted. The official communique read as follows:

"Yesterday evening, along our front from Steenstraat to the east of Langemarck we attacked the enemy position north and northeast of Ypres and advanced on a front of about five and a half miles to the heights north of Pilckem and east of these heights.

"Simultaneously our troops, supported by artillery forced a passage across the Yser Canal near Steenstraat and Het Sas, where they gained a footing on the western bank. The places of Langemarck, Steenstraat, Het Sas and Pilckem were taken, and we captured at least 1,600 French and English prisoners and 30 guns, including four heavy English guns."[8] Of chlorine gas there was no mention.

Chapter Eight

The Uncertain Trumpet
(Noon, 23 April - 5:30 a.m., 24 April, 1915)

*"If the trumpet shall give an uncertain sound,
who shall prepare himself to the battle?"*
I Corinthians XIV, 8

At the headquarters of *Groupe Provisoire du Nord* at Cassel Sir John French, The British Commander in Chief, had just arrived to have an urgent conference with General Ferdinand Foch. Sir John had driven over to warn the commander of all French troops in the area* that he was about to pull back the British and Canadian troops in the Salient. This decision had been made at his own headquarters at St.Omer after careful consideration. Sir John felt that the situation was so precarious that only immediate and decisive action on the part of the French to retrieve the situation in their sector would enable him to hold on. It was this grim ultimatum that the British Field Marshal had arrived to deliver in person to Foch.

Ferdinand Foch was the personification of the French will to win. He had for several years been lauded as the pre-eminent military theorist of France. Pronouncements such as, "The will to conquer sweeps all before it," and "A battle won is a battle we will not acknowledge to be lost," had had a great impact on French strategy and tactics. Early in the war he had been given the opportunity to carry these precepts into action. Under heavy attack on the

---

* Foch's Groupe Provisoire du Nord included Tenth Army (Arras-Vimy Sector), Groupement d'Elverdinghe (Ypres Salient, between the Canadian and Belgian forces), and Groupement de Nieuport (between the Belgians and the coast). The latter two groups were usually referred to *en masse* as the Detachement d'Armée de Belgique, and were commanded by General Henri Gabriel Putz.

Marne, legend has it that Foch reported, "My centre gives way, my right is retreating, situation excellent, I am attacking."

After four days of repeatedly attacking, Foch's command had been reduced to mere fragments. When a subordinate had protested, Foch had grandly retorted, 'You say that you cannot hold on and cannot retreat, so the only thing left is to attack to-morrow morning." When morning came the Germans had gone. Although their withdrawal had nothing to do with Foch's performance, it seemed to vindicate his reliance on the offensive. From then on 'Attack' was the only French strategy.

As Foch became more senior he grew more mystical and began to speak in parables, displaying a cavalier disregard for logistics and facts. A biographer wrote, "Foch was a natural disorganizer — indeed, he seemed to many not to understand the needs and principle of either organization or training."[1]

This morning Sir John found Foch in an excitable euphoria — in a fever pitch of energy and supremely optimistic. Crises always had that effect on the French commander. Feeling anything but optimistic himself, Sir John was ushered into the conference room.

History cannot tell us what transpired behind those doors but when the British Field Marshal re-emerged at noon he had made a complete about-face on the ultimatum he had brought with him. On the strength of Foch's enthusiastic optimism and several vague promises — obviously impossible to fulfill — Sir John had committed his forces to making the *major* counterattacks. What was more, these assaults were not to be well prepared offensives in the near future. They were to be hasty, ill-prepared attacks carried out immediately. Thus his tiny reserve was to be squandered in an attack *that afternoon* in the *French sector,* whereas an hour earlier he had been convinced that these reserves were insufficient to enable him to even hold his own sector.

As Sir John drove back to his own headquarters he apparently had second thoughts — a common occurrence with him — for immediately on arrival he ordered up, not only the troops in the immediate area, but the whole of the Second Army reserve. These consisted of the 50th (Northumbrian) Division, two brigades of the 4th Division, and the Lahore Division of the Indian Corps. Sir John's intention was to mount a much heavier counter attack when he had sufficient strength to do so. Nevertheless he gave orders to General

Plumer at V Corps to proceed with the attack that afternoon. The sector occupied by Mordacq's *zouaves* was to be taken over by Brigadier-General Wanless O'Gowan's 13th Brigade sent across the Salient by the 5th Imperial Division.

Foch, for his part, left shortly after his meeting with Sir John to visit General Putz. Putz, the fifty-six year old veteran of the Tonkin, Madagascar, and China campaigns, unlike Sir John, remained unimpressed. "Putz was of stronger fibre than Sir John French, and owing responsibility only to the King of the Belgians, was less suscep-tible to political pressure. He had seen the front imperilled by the collapse and flight of two French divisions and felt little inclined to sacrifice the lives of the few remaining Belgian troops in hasty counter-attacks before French reinforcements arrived. Consequent-ly Foch could get no specific assurances."[2]

Nevertheless on his return from this obviously unsuccessful meeting with Putz, General Foch called on Sir John and advised him that Putz was being "massively strengthened." This, Foch knew to be absolutely untrue.

Others closer to the front were under fewer illusions than their leaders. When Canadian Divisional Headquarters forwarded a message from French headquarters advising that the Germans had run out of ammunition, Brigadier-General Turner V.C. at Wieltje simply wrote across it, "An example of the value of information received from the rear."

As a result of Sir John French's meeting with General Foch, two sets of orders were sent out almost simultaneously. The first came from General Quiquandon of the 45th Algerian Division. It was hastily drafted and included at least three errors — one of which was to prove deadly. It began as follows:

I.   The Germans appear for the moment to have exhausted their am-munition.
II.   The time for the general counter attack has arrived.
III.   Consequently the Colonel Commanding 90th Brigade (Mordacq) with all the troops at his disposal will attack on the front Boesinghe-Pilckem on the East of the Canal their right resting on the Ypres-Pilckem road in close touch with the British.
IV.   On our right the English warned of our attack will advance on Langemarck.

This was a vital error: the British were in fact to attack towards Pilckem, and Quiquandon was hereby ordering Mordacq to attack over the same ground as Alderson's troops. In error, this order further stipulated a *three* minute bombardment instead of five as intended. This would leave the German defenders two minutes to recover before the attack commenced. Lastly the time of issuing was noted incorrectly at 1:40 p.m. rather than 1:20. The hour of attack was fixed by Quiquandon at 3:00 p.m.

The second set of orders was issued at 1:30 by General Alderson of the Canadian Division. They announced that the 13th Brigade now under his command would attack along the west side of the Ypres-Pilckem Road where Mordacq's *zouaves* were situated. On the other side of the road, over the ground crossed by the 1st and 4th Ontario battalions that morning, Geddes' Detachment would advance. The surviving Canadians and Middlesex men were to follow up once their positions had been passed by the attackers. Zero hour was listed as 3:30, half an hour later than Quiquandon's orders stated.

When copies of these orders reached their destinations many brows were furrowed in bewilderment. At 2:30 the 1st Canadian Brigade contacted Divisional Headquarters asking if the French would be asked to cancel their attack because of the larger British attack. The reply Mercer received was puzzling.

"No, let French commence their attack and if possible you might cooperate as far as possible and then let the 13th Brigade go through you."

It was into this confusing flurry of paper that the 13th Brigade was marching. Wanless-O'Gowan's brigade was made up of four battalions of the old regular Army and one Territorial battalion, Queen Victoria's Rifles (9th County of London Regiment). The regular battalions had been in France from the start and had seen action at Mons and LeCateau. They were proud remnants of the "Old Contemptibles," as they had been dubbed. These battalions were the 2nd King's Own Scottish Borderers — dour Lowlanders — the 1st Queen's Own (Royal West Kent Regiment), and the famous King's Own Yorkshire Light Infantry — "the Koylies" (from their initials). The other battalion, The Duke of Wellington's (West Riding Regiment) remained in reserve with the 5th Imperial Divison.

"A lot of Imperial battalions are going up along the road," wrote a man of the 16th Canadian Scottish Transport Section very early in the morning. "They are in great spirits, singing, and some of them almost on the trot. The thought came to us that they were going to be thrown in, as our battalion was, to stem the tide."[3]

Everyone they met was eager to inform the Tommies of the horrors of the enemy's poison gas. But this they could see for themselves as they passed numerous casualty clearing stations. There the victims of chlorine gas lay in rows were they had been placed in the fresh air to pass their final hours of agony. From the north too came a steady stream of wounded Canadians still being brought in from the dawn attack.

"Ambulances were everywhere, and the village of Brielen, through which we passed, was choked with wounded and gassed men," wrote Anthony Hossack of the "Vics." "We were very mystified about this gas, and had no protection whatever against it."[4]

With the Borderers leading, the 13th Brigade made its way across the Brielen Bridge at mid-afternoon when observers described them as "cheery, but physically very tired."[5] This was hardly any wonder, for the brigade had eaten early last evening and had been on the march ever since. Immediately prior to that they had lost sixty-two officers and 1300 men on Hill 60. "We are tired and weary men who would like to rest," Captain Fleming of the "Vics" told his Company. "However, there are men more weary than we who need our help. We may not have to do much; we may have to do a great deal. Whatever happens, fight like hell. I shall at any rate."[6] This pretty well summed up the attitude of the 13th Brigade.

Orders were sent out postponing the attack till 4:25 p.m. as it had become obvious that the 13th Brigade would not be in position till then, since it had to push its way through roads congested with French troops and transport. Thus it came as a surprise to everyone when, a few minutes before three, the "massed" Allied artillery opened up. The feeble bombardment continued for three minutes then all was silence. Most of the batteries had not been warned of the change in the time of the attack. Several had just arrived — loaned by the I Cavalry Corps — but all were scattered, came under different commanders, and were connected by separate telephone nets. What was worse — the Allied artillery had now expended their ammunition; there would be no preliminary barrage when the assault did go in.

While these preparations were going on, survivors of the dawn attack were still hanging on one thousand yards to the front. "We lie under protection of the ridge for the rest of the day," George Bell wrote. "Lord, but I'm hungry and thirsty. What wouldn't I give for a drink of cold water. Even bully beef and hard tack would taste good. If only the artillery would stop long enough so a man could rest." All the while scores of wounded lay under the April sun amongst the manure piles.

Farther to the west and south the 13th Brigade was assembling in almost complete silence. On the east bank of the canal were the Queen's Own Royal West Kents flanked by the King's Own Scottish Borderers whose right rested on the Ypres-Pilckem Road. Their advance would take place in the sector supposedly occupied by Mordacq's 90th Brigade. Once the attack got under way, the plan was for the 'Koylies' and the Queen Victoria Rifles to move across the canal and form up behind them. The Yorkshiremen were to be in support while the 'Vics' were a local reserve.

Across the road on the east side two battalions of Geddes' Detachment were lined up—the 2nd East Yorkshire Regiment and the 1st York and Lancaster Regiment. Behind them in reserve lay the 5th King's Own (Royal Lancaster Regiment) from Lancashire. They were in almost the same position that the 1st and 4th Canadians had occupied early in the morning, and they would advance over the same Field of Manure Piles.

Also to be thrown into this travesty of an attack were two newly arrived battalions from the 27th Imperial Division—the 2nd Battalion, Duke of Cornwall's Light Infantry, and two companies of the 9th (Highland) Battalion, The Royal Scots.

At 4:25 the advance began. Each battalion of the 13th Brigade had been allotted 500 yards of front and had been formed up in six lines. The shelling began immediately from the German side with only feeble response from the British and Canadian batteries whose communications were still not linked up. As the waves advanced and reached the range of the machine guns and Mauser rifles on the ominously named ridge, whole waves went down in swaths. Companies disappeared in seconds. "They were just simply bowled over like ninepins," noted one observer.[7]

On the 13th Brigade's front the terrible confusion was compounded as a result of Quiquandon's orders. From the left, on the bank of the Yser Canal, appeared a formation of French troops. It was a battalion of the 7th Zouaves and they were advancing *across* the line of attack of the West Kents and the Borderers. While this strange manoeuvre was carried on, the two British battalions continued their advance, being pushed more and more to the right. Platoons were then pulled out of the crowded line and the attack halted — all the while under vicious fire. The French intruders soon withdrew and the calamitous advance resumed. The King's Own Yorkshire Light Infantry moved up to take over the now open left flank between the West Kents and the canal.

By this time smoke and dust from the German shells had provided a rather nebulous cover for the advancing Tommies. Their own artillery fire had increased and had begun to inflict casualties on the defenders of Mauser Ridge. The advance no longer consisted of waves but of small groups and individuals working their way forward despite the terrible fire. Little information came back, for the losses amongst officers had been fearful.

The three battalions chased in the German outposts but were forced to halt around 5:45 at the foot of the ridge. Over 3,000 men had fallen without having come to grips with the enemy. There was now not one officer or one man surviving who had fought at Mons with these units eight months ago.

In the centre, Geddes' Detachment suffered similarly. Led by Colonel Geddes himself, the men had pressed on regardless of the destruction amongst them. The reserve battalion, the King's Own, had early in the attack been moved into the front line to fill a gap which occurred between the East Yorks and the D.C.L.I. Eventually, Geddes' men reached the line of willows held by the 1st and 4th Canadians and the two companies of the Middlesex Regiment. There the survivors from the dawn attack jumped to their feet cheering and joined the advance.

Eighty yards from the enemy's position Colonel Birchall of the 4th gave the order, "Charge!" Immediately they surged forward — men from Ontario and four counties of England. "We advanced as far as a little old farm — I don't remember its name — on top of Pilckem Ridge, which we took at the point of the bayonet, surprising Fritz somewhat, because I don't imagine he thought we were able to do it," recalled Captain Williamson of C Company, 1st Western Ontario Battalion. "The centre of that old farm and the stink-pot in the middle of the courtyard was a regular shambles. I saw more wounded in a radius of about fifty yards than I think I ever saw before or hope to see again."[8]

Here the men saw an example of German heroism. An enemy observer was discovered in the ruins telephoning information back to the guns. He stuck to his post and continued telephoning until he was killed by one of the D.C.L.I. Hand-to-hand fighting raged in and around the farm buildings, and a party of the East Yorks passed beyond and almost reached the German's main position, before being cut down.

The movement forward was shattered. Some units made it a little farther than others, but outside of the little knot of East Yorks, no one got closer than 100 yards to the German front line. Most lay 200 yards away pinned down by vicious rifle and machine gun fire. Here they remained till nightfall enabled them to pull back in small groups.

Casualties were appalling: The "Yorks and Lancs" had lost 425 men including their C.O., Lt.Col. Burt; the East Yorkshires were reduced to 7 officers and 280 men, having lost 383 all ranks; only 20 "Diehards" were left out of the two Middlesex companies, and their C.O., Lt. Col. Stephenson, was dead.

Despite the terrific cost, Turco Farm could not be held, and by night the Cornishmen had been moved southwest to end up between the Borderers and the York and Lancaster Regiment.

On the extreme right of this futile advance was the 9th Royal Scots. They were only at half strength, two companies having been sent to St. Julien and then returned too late to take part in the attack. The half-battalion advanced almost to the main enemy line, but they too were cut down, suffering severely from enfilade fire from the right flank, and those who lived through this experience withdrew with difficulty back down the valley.

And so the attack on Mauser Ridge ended. Only for a few minutes at Turco Farm had the enemy been met face to face. Nowhere had the German front line been reached. There were no gains of any sort to be seen. The lowest British loss per battalion was 200 although several were over 400. If anything could be claimed for the advance it was from the point of view of morale. General Alderson had that in mind when he wrote to the decimated 13th Brigade, "Words cannot express what the Canadians owe the 13th for their splendid attack and the way they restored confidence."

Colonel Mordacq later wrote, "The losses, without doubt, were heavy, but the results were important; this time, not only were the Germans stopped but it was we who had taken the initiative of the attack. From the morale point of view, this was enormous and it is that which I pointed out in the reports to superior authorities."[9] In truth, Mordacq could report little else that day. His troops had made an almost negligible advance in the morning, and the 7th Zouaves' sortie across the front of the 13th Brigade was the sole French involvement in the afternoon attack ordered by General Quiquandon.

The British Official History gave a much less charitable verdict on the attack on Mauser Ridge: "No ground was gained that could not have been secured, probably without casualties, by a simple advance after dark."

As dusk settled on the Salient the situation appeared to have changed little in the last twenty-four hours. On the left, the Belgians had held firm. At six o'clock that night General Codet's often-postponed attack on Steenstraat began. It was soon beaten off by the German 45th Reserve Division which later that night launched its own attack against Lizerne. By two in the morning, after very severe fighting, Lizerne was in Germans hands.

Farther south, opposite Boesinghe, General Schopflin's 46th Reserve Division drove the remnants of the 45th Algerian Division back to the banks of the Yser Canal. This was a costly operation for both sides, and the fighting went on throughout the night. It meant that the only French troops on the east side of the canal were those from Zwaanhof Farm to the Ypres-Pilckem Road.

East of that road was a very broken and uneven line of British and Canadian battalions several hundred yards south of the German positions atop Mauser Ridge. From his vantage point on the west bank Gunner John Armstrong of the 3rd Battery, Canadian Field Artillery could see the 13th Brigade's battlefield. "There was one horse out there between us and the Germans. For three days after the attack he went around with just the lower part of a man's body in the saddle. From the waist up there was nothing. A good-sized shell had hit him. One thing that brightened our day up though was seeing some Germans come out under escort of four Frenchmen who were only about half as tall as the Germans."

In front of Mauser Ridge the vestiges of the old 13th Brigade had been drawn back somewhat and ordered to dig in. This ground was totally unsuitable, being muddy and water-logged as well as being completely dominated by the Germans. It was to be a harsh night for those weary veterans. The temperature descended below freezing and the soldiers in their wet and sweaty uniforms shivered uncontrollably. But worse than that was the fact that the majority had not eaten for twenty-four hours. The brigade reported, "The position along the front line was rather a medley as a number of *zouaves* had taken shelter in our trenches and the line on our right ran far back and was not garrisoned."

This statement was not totally correct for in a very uneven line lay the survivors of Geddes' Detachment and the 1st and 4th Canadians. The latter had lost all its stretcherbearers and their duties were being performed by the remaining Battalion Bombers. By 9:00 p.m. the two shattered Ontario units were moving to the rear, their places taken by British battalions. The 23 April had cost the 1st 404 casualties and the 4th, 454, including Lt.Col. Birchall who had been killed while conducting the relief of his battalion. There were only four officers left, but the survivors had not lost their spirit. "It was a glorious day for the Canadians because these men had practically no training. But was I ever proud of them," G.W. Twigg of the 4th stated years later. "If they'd have been trained for ten years they couldn't have acted better. To think of those kids that had been pulled from all over the country and the way they behaved! In a murderous fire like that. I never felt so proud of a bunch of boys in my life."[10]

Friday night was bright and moonlit until 2:30 the next morning. This effect was heightened by the flames still shooting skyward from Ypres in the southwest. Through the doomed town refugees still flocked in such numbers as to cram the desperately needed roads. From the front line however the scene was one of frightening silence as the flames outlined with their eerie flickering light the black ruin of the Cloth Hall and the Cathedral.

In front of Kitcheners' Wood the 2nd, 10th, and 16th Battalions had put in a quiet afternoon and evening. On their right the badly depleted C and D Companies of the 3rd Toronto Battalion endured. Water bottles empty, iron rations finished, and wounds unattended, they had clung through the hot day to their hard-won trench. During the afternoon Colonel Rennie had been advised that the Algerian troops with his battalion would have to be returned to French control. This meant that the thin line would have to be stretched even thinner. By night the wounded were finally taken out, the seriously wounded to an aid post in the stables at Mouse Trap Farm. There the straw-covered courtyard was soon overflowing with badly wounded men awaiting horse-drawn ambulances which could operate only after dark. During the long daylight hours Captain Haywood, the Torontonians' medical officer, had worked unceasingly in his improvised operating theatre — bullets spattering on the walls around him and above the wounded.

In front of St.Julien it had been quiet. From their sketchy line of trenches and rifle pits only inches deep the Canadians could see swarms of German reinforcements arriving both by lorry and on foot. Shortly after four Lt.Col. Hart McHarg of the 7th British Columbians set out to reconnoitre his front accompanied by his second-in-command, Major Odlum, and Lieutenant Mathieson. McHarg was mortally wounded, and as a result, Odlum became the 7th's new C.O.

Farther north along the Poelcappelle Road the 13th Royal Highlanders' refused flank had come under severe pressure. At nine that morning Major McCuaig and his garrison had been forced to give up their redoubt situated where the old trench line crossed the road. Four enemy attacks were beaten back by withering rifle fire and the rest of the line held. Yet the situation remained critical as patrols revealed the left flank was still open.

By mid morning General Alderson back at Canadian Divisional Headquarters had accepted the evidence that in spite of promises made by Foch and other generals the French were not going to re-establish their line. Therefore at 11:03 Alderson issued orders for the 13th Royal Highlanders to withdraw from the line, extend southward, and thus smooth out the apex. This manoeuver, however, would only be possible at night.

Thus at eight that evening the perilous operation began. Moving in file from the right, the Highlanders and Buffs slipped along their battered trenches to take up new positions (already prepared for them) 1,200 yards to the rear. The Germans followed them as closely as the small, tenacious rearguard would allow, and the operation was made even more difficult by the hundreds of wounded who had to be evacuated. Gassed *tirailleurs* and wounded Buffs and Royal Highlanders were laboriously carried out on the few stretchers, supplemented with blankets, fascines, planks — anything that would bear the weight of a man.

All these wounded continued down the trenches occupied by the 15th (48th Highlanders) Battalion before moving southwest through St. Julien, Wieltje, St. Jean, Ypres, and eventually to safety. The 15th had spent a reasonably normal day under intermittent shell and rifle fire, suffering only a handful of casualties. Of course they now held the northern side of the newer, blunter apex and they could expect to bear the brunt of future attacks. For the moment however they assisted the Buffs who had no entrenching tools, and next to them the 13th, as they strengthened the new line of defense during the night.

Next in line was the 8th "Little Black Devils." Kettles full of water stood in every section of trench and the men had been instructed to wet a strip of blanket, a handkerchief, or a piece of cloth and tie it over the nose and mouth if a gas cloud approached. Seeing the Germans working a few yards in front of their trenches, Lt.Col. Lipsett decided to test the artillery arrangements by a trial S.O.S. With a gratifying roar, the 18 pounders of the 2nd Canadian Field Artillery Brigade went into action. The response was immediate and effective. Now the 8th too could meet the hours of darkness with some sense of security.

At the right end of the Canadian line was "Tuxford's Dandies," the 5th Western Cavalry. Here as elsewhere every man was suffering somewhat from gas fumes, and sore throats and eyes were prevalent. However only 3 men had been killed and eight wounded, so it had been comparatively quiet along the Stroombeek. At midnight the 5th reported succinctly, "Perfectly quiet. Perfectly prepared."

On the other side of no man's land Friday had been a frustrating day. First, Duke Albrecht's ambitious plans to smash through the Franco-Belgian line at Steenstraat and break out towards Poperinghe, miles to the rear of Ypres, had been foiled by his troops' exhaustion, his shortage of reserves, and the unexpectedly savage resistance. Secondly, the fierce Canadian and British counterattacks, although failures in themselves, had prevented his XXVI Reserve Corps from advancing and cutting off the British Divisions in the Salient. Hence it appeared that there would have to be a one-day postponement. But that afternoon the German High Command intervened by informing Albrecht that "Poperinghe did not primarily enter the question at all as an objective for the operation," and reminding him "that it was strictly a matter of cutting off the Ypres Salient."

Whether or not the Germans' caution was justified is still a moot point. Every battalion in the British divisional and corps reserves had been thrown in, plus two brigades from Second Army reserve. These had all suffered severe casualties and there were no more British reserves immediately available. The French were in a slightly less serious predicament, but were unwilling, despite Foch's assertions, to take offensive action. However, many German generals had begun to lose confidence in their chief weapon — and this was not chlorine gas. The War Diary of the XXVI Reserve Division bluntly recorded: "Unfortunately the infantry had become enfeebled by trench warfare and had lost its daring and its indifference to heavy losses and the disintegrating influence of increased enemy fire effect. The leaders and the brave-hearted fell, and the bulk of the men, mostly inexperienced reinforcements, became helpless and only too inclined to leave the work to the artillery and trench mortars."[11]

Nevertheless, the usual boastful communique was prepared to appear in Saturday's newspapers. It told of continuing successes but again made no mention of chlorine gas and concluded with the following prophetic lie: "The English are using German uniforms in order to gain cheap successes, and are carefully employing bullets emitting asphyxiating gases and dumdum bullets, and by other means are carrying on a brutal war."

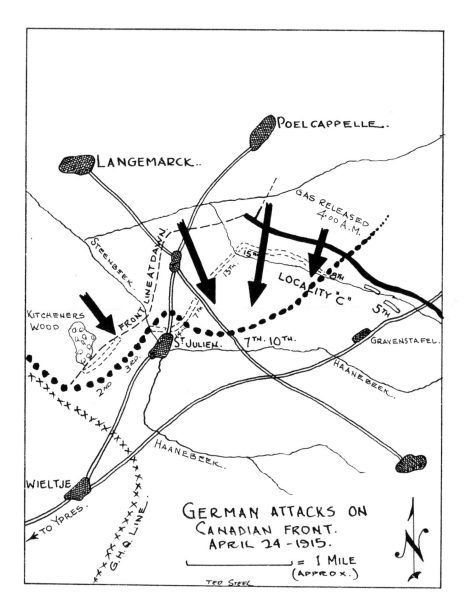

POEL CAPPELLE.

LANGEMARCK.

GAS RELEASED 4.00 A.M.

STEENBEEK.

FRONT LINE AT DAWN.

15TH

13TH

8TH

LOCALITY "C"

5TH

KITCHENERS WOOD

7TH

3RD

ST. JULIEN.

7TH. 10TH.

GRAVENSTAFEL.

HAANEBEEK.

2ND

HAANEBEEK.

WIELTJE

TO YPRES.

G.H.Q. LINE

GERMAN ATTACKS ON
CANADIAN FRONT.
APRIL 24 - 1915.

= 1 MILE
(APPROX.)

TED STEEL

N

102

Chapter Nine

Faithful Unto Death
(4:00 a.m. - 1:40 p.m., 24 April, 1915)

*"And for ten days you will have tribulation. Be
faithful unto death and I will give you
the crown of life."*
Revelation II, 10

As dawn broke on Saturday morning the weather promised
to be lovely. The sun's rays brightened the eastern sky in a ra-
diant arc unbroken by cloud, while a mild breeze sprang up from
the north-northwest. The terrible battlefields of Flanders enjoyed a
few moments of tranquility. At 3:30 the peaceful interlude was over,
and shells crashed down upon the allied trenches. Another day had
begun.

At three the front line units had gone on stand-to and at four
were just preparing to stand-down when sharp-eyed sentries along
the northern face of the apex noticed the burst of three red flares
from the captive balloon. At once there was activity across the line;
above the German parapet several figures wearing mine-rescue
helmets appeared with hoses in their hands. "I saw the Germans hop
over their trenches and put these cans in front of their trenches. I
wondered what they were doing, see, just one here and one a little
further along," recalled Lester Stevens of the 8th 'Little Black
Devils.'

Stevens and his mates opened fire but they did not have long to
wonder. "Smoke from that boiled up and the wind blew it towards
us. I thought it was smoke and they were going to come up behind
it, see . . . And then when it came along towards us it turned green,
a greeny yellow colour."[1]

At the same moment, further to the east, George Tuxford,
C.O. of the 5th Western Cavalry Battalion, was awakened from a

restless sleep by his Adjutant, Captain Hilliam. From his battalion's position on the extreme right of the Canadian line, Tuxford was amazed to see rolling towards him from the northwest a cloud of greenish fog.

"It rolled along like a heavy Scotch mist, swallowing up the landscape as it came.

" 'What do you make of that? What do you think it is?' Hilliam questioned.

" 'I wonder if it has anything to do with the gas we have heard about,' I replied.

"I went to the telephone and called up Lipsett, for his Head-quarters was now enveloped by the vapour. He replied himself, at once, his voice choking, and gasping for breath. 'It's gas—very bad—can't talk,' was all that I could make out."

Tuxford and his men had no experience with gas although they had been told that a wet handkerchief over the nose and mouth pro-vided some protection, but that the best thing was to stand up on the trench to get above the heavy gas which would hug the ground.

"But this gas was a solid wall, and to step on the parapet for air was to step into a solid sheet of rifle and machine gun bullets. The gas drove directly at the 8th Battalion, extending around to the 5th, and soon we were getting our share, blinding the men and choking them. They died or lived as they stood," wrote the former homesteader from Moose Jaw.

For ten minutes the trenches on the northern side of the apex were pounded by artillery and mortar fire, at the same time being smothered in the deadly greenish fumes. Then the artillery moved on.

"The gas wave passed through and at once the German infantry followed its course, to be met with a withering fire. The trenches stood and no man budged from his post . . . The Ross rifle jammed . . . Men cursed the rifle and threw it away to grab a fallen one and try again. I have seen strong men weep in anguish at the failure, with a useless rifle in their hands and the enemy advancing in full sight. We instructed the men to lay the handles of their en-trenching tools alongside them on the trench, so when the jam oc-curred, by sharply hitting the bolt, it might be released. If this failed, as a last resort the man placed the butt of the rifle on the ground and stamped hard on the bolt with his heel."

Farther towards the northwest the 8th 'Little Black Devils' had endured an even worse experience with the gas. Colonel Lipsett, the likeable Irishman from Winnipeg, quickly got on the telephone to Brigade Artillery and repeated his S.O.S. of the night before. The response was immediate and accurate, and the German trenches began receiving their share of shrapnel which arrived, screaming over the 8th's trenches, at the rate of a ton every two minutes. But regardless of this storm of steel the Germans attacked in heavy waves, and were mowed down. On the right of the battalion where the gas was less dense the advancing lines of grey were routed by accurate rifle and machine gun fire, but on the left the situation became more serious. The gassed Manitobans, undaunted, somehow managed to drag themselves onto the parapet above the swirling fumes and shoot down the fast-approaching enemy—all the while gasping for breath through their improvised respirators. Dizzy, with running eyes and aching lungs, still they fired into the hordes. Then their rifles began to jam. Boot heels and entrenching tools cleared some temporarily. One man was killed when his own rifle blew back. Those wounded and unable to stand lay dying in the filthy trench but continued to load rifles for their comrades standing on the parapet above.

It became obvious that the critical point lay on the left flank. Here there was a one hundred yard gap between the 8th and 15th Battalions. C Company of the 8th were slightly to the rear in support and now they were instructed by Colonel Lipsett to secure the left. Tom Drummond was one of those waiting behind the front line for that moment. "Came the order to advance and the thrill which comes with the idea of meeting the enemy face to face; then all hell seemed to let loose—high explosive, shrapnel, coal boxes, whizz bangs, machine gun fire," he wrote later. "Men went down like ninepins, and looking around, I found myself and one other man to be the only ones still standing of our platoon. As if by common consent, we both dived into shell holes and then the nature of the greenish cloud became apparent. Gas! I wet my scarf and wound it about my face, but this did not seem to have much effect, although there is no doubt that it helped."

Drummond continued his progress to the left sector moving from shell hole to shell hole. He joined two comrades in one such hole. "Both of them were choking and spitting. It seemed impossible to get air into the lungs; or, having got it there, to get it out again. Strings of sticky saliva drooled from their mouths." He was at the edge of the critical spot.

"Quick peeks over the edge of our shell hole discovered a line of men on our left leaving the line, casting away equipment, rifles and clothing as they ran. Some managed to get halfway to where they were going only to fall writhing on the ground, clutching at their throats, tearing open their shirts in a last struggle for air, and after a while ceasing to struggle and lying still while a greenish foam formed over their mouths and lips." These were the shattered remnants of the 15th Battalion's A Company.

What happened in those few minutes in those trenches of A Company of the 15th will never be known, for no officer survived to submit a report and the company was virtually wiped out. Like the 8th Battalion, the 15th sent an S.O.S. to its supporting batteries of the 3rd Artillery Brigade. Their reply was tragic:

> "4:01 a.m. — We have to admit that it is impossible for us to respond to your S.O.S. and along the entire original front, as the trenches are out of range of our present positions."

Like a tennis player dashing madly from one corner of his court to the other, trying to return the volleys of a more skillful opponent, the allied artillery had been inevitably caught out of position. All of the 3rd Brigade's batteries were now in distant corners. The 10th and half of the 11th Batteries were west of the canal in support of the French. The remainder were in the St. Jean-Wieltje area behind Geddes' Detachment. The 3rd Canadian Infantry Brigade would have to go it alone.

The doomed companies in the front line never read the response to the S.O.S. The men of the 15th endured the ten minutes of shelling and chlorine gas without knowing that their foe was advancing unmolested. The makeshift respirators failed where the gas was thickest. Shouted orders died on frothing lips amid hacking coughs. Watering eyes failed to see hand signals otherwise only dimly discernable from a few yards. The savage shrieking of German shells and their ear-splitting concussions obliterated all other sounds. Archie McGregor's A Company disintegrated, fighting it out to the choking finish, silent in this maelstrom of death.

To their left, three platoons of C Company under Major

McLaren endured an almost equal share of hell. However, the edge of the gas cloud lay in line with McLaren's Number 12 Platoon so survivors were able to pull to the left and rear into more or less clear air. Here Lieutenant Smith of 12 Platoon had lined a communication trench at right angles to his position with a few riflemen. These Highlanders were therefore able to fire into the flank of the enemy who had already crossed the trench formerly held by A and C Companies.

Lieutenant McKessoch's two Colt machine guns came into action at this point, one fired by the gigantic daredevil, Rolly Carmichael, the tallest man in the 15th. The two guns plus the feeble rifle fire from Lieutenant Smith's communication trench halted the German advance. Then out of the gas cloud staggering and swaying came a broken line of kilted figures, Captain McLaren stumbling at their head. From A Company's former position the Germans opened up a heavy fire. In the fog of gas the survivors would vanish momentarily to reappear, fewer each time. Only a handful of stricken men reached Smith's trench and these were completely helpless.

Others took refuge in the reserve trenches. Here most of them died a slower death from asphyxiation. Lieutenant Geoff Taylor, the well known footballer and former stroke with the Argonauts, was found by a stretcher-bearer. "Let me alone, just let me alone," he croaked. Stretched on his back gasping for air, he died. Those able to stand there by the Stroombeek fought it out to the last, finally being overwhelmed in an unequal hand-to-hand struggle.

In the meantime on the left where the original line ended and which now abutted upon the line prepared last night, Lieutenant Fessenden's platoon was withstanding a heavy attack. This efficient young officer had spent the hours of darkness building several new traverses and sandbagging them as strongly as possible, expecting to be enfiladed by the enemy during the coming day. Now his work was paying off as the Germans made their way down the abandoned trench in hopes of taking the battalion in flank. Despite everything, the apex held firm.

In the interim on the northwestern face of the apex — the line retired to last night and now extending to St. Julien — the Germans had launched another attack. The assault came at five, after an hour and a half of accurate artillery fire. This was directed from observation posts in the village of Poelcappelle, and was unhampered by counter-battery fire. The attack was directed at St. Julien itself. In a thin uneven line in front of this shattered village lay two companies of the 7th British Columbians, one of the 15th, and two of the 14th Royal Montreal Regiment.

Already, gassed and wounded men from the northeastern side of the apex had appeared behind the defenders. With them came the most lurid rumours—the front was broken; the 3rd Brigade had been wiped out; Fritz was right behind; a cloud of gas was coming. Meanwhile in front, without any pretense at cover, waves of Germans were forming to advance up the slopes towards the flimsy Canadian trenches. Although they presented an incredible target for the allied artillery, not a shell could reach them. In the distance their reinforcements could be seen moving up in marching order in endless numbers.

"Across the open space the attack came, not in dense masses as we had been led to expect," wrote Herbert Rae, "but line on line, like waves in an advancing flood. No wild charge of cheering warriors, and without the glorious rush of battle, they came on methodically and silently, as men with a duty to be performed in which they took small delight. It was a magnificent example of their discipline.

"Every man had his greatcoat rolled up; we saw their water-bottles and their haversacks hanging as if on parade. Across the fields they stumbled forward, running clumsily with their fat legs and ridiculous boots. And behind each line we saw their officers urging them on. From the trench our rifles cracked and machine-guns spat; before the hail of bullets the Germans fell. Soon the field was spotted with fallen figures, some lying still, others trying to crawl away. But still they came on. Now we could see their features and count the buttons on their tunics as they lumbered forward . . . Now the wave lapped against the edge of our trench. Suddenly a fat German, with bulging eyes, recognizing death staring at him across the mud-bank, turned to fly. A bullet caught him on the buckle of his waistbelt, causing his equipment to fly apart as it passed onwards on its way. A huge red-headed warrior, his mouth open and breathing hard from running, got it square between the eyebrows; the force of the rush carried him onward to fall against the parapet, where he lay, the back blown out of his head and with a look of mild surprise upon his face. One or two rushed the parapet, but they were not fighters, and fell like sheep on the points of our bayonets."[2]

The stolidly advancing Germans had also been severely punished on the left flank by infilade fire from two advanced companies of the 3rd Toronto Battalion across the Hannebeek. This attack had been beaten back, but every man from Kitcheners' Wood to the Apex knew that this was only the beginning.

When the foregoing events began there was an immediate scramble for reinforcements. The first unit called upon was the 10th Canadians in their trench before Kitcheners' Wood. At four they had seen the gas cloud 4000 yards to their right and they knew what to expect when their phone rang half an hour later. They were to move out of their captured trench and go to 'Locality C' which lay northeast of St. Julien on the crest of Gravenstafel Ridge. Evacuating their trench was a very tricky proposition. First the skeletal 16th had to be advised to stretch its line even farther to the left and take over the 10th's position, then in broad daylight the men of the 10th had to work their way through the shambles to the rear. Some idea of the conditions can be gleaned from the fact that two officers and twenty men could not get out till five o'clock because their trench was blocked with wounded and dead for ninety yards.

Those who made it formed up and marched to 2nd Brigade Headquarters at Fortuin Farm. "General Currie himself came out and gave the men a cheery word," recalled Major Ormond, the new C.O. "He pointed out the so-called Locality C which is the crest of Gravenstafel Ridge."[3]

Ormond reconnoitered the site and got in touch by telephone with Colonel Lipsett of the 'Little Black Devils' who warned him not to let the Germans take Locality C whatever the cost. The vestiges of the once powerful 10th were then ordered forward. "The men responded with a spirit and tact which was all that could be desired." Upon arriving they were joined by A Company of the 7th British Columbians under Captain Warden.

Ormond went forward to scout, and fell in a hole full of water. After scrambling out amid rifle fire and shrapnel, he was hit on the shoulder and knocked down again but was merely bruised. He was then almost overcome with gas, and only a share of Lieutenant Crichly's wet handkerchief saved him. Surviving all of these ordeals, Ormond returned to the top of Gravenstafel Ridge where he found his 10th Battalion dug in, 146 strong—less than company strength.

By this time every available man from Currie's 2nd Brigade had been brought into action. Colonel Lipsett of the 8th realized that the critical spot was his left flank where the junction with the 15th had been swept away. Therefore he called up the two remaining platoons of C Company from Boetleer Farm.

Lieutenant O'Grady was killed, and Colour Sergeant Hall, a former clerk and one-time Cameronian, took charge. Hall got his men into position under a terrible fire then went back and brought in two wounded men. Hearing the groans of a third, he and two volunteers went over the top to rescue. Both his comrades were wounded and Hall brought them back. On his second attempt he refused to be accompanied. Somehow he reached the badly wounded man but as he struggled to put the soldier on his back the Colour Sergeant was hit in the head by an enemy bullet.

By 5:15 the only unit of the 2nd Brigade still in reserve was Tuxford's C Company. It too was rushed to the left to protect the 8th Battalion's flank. They suffered severely on their way, Captain Bertram and two officers being shot and many of the men falling in the storm of iron and lead. But the survivors shored up the left flank of the 2nd Brigade and stayed there in the crucial hours to come.

Meanwhile, back in front of Kitcheners' Wood the 16th Canadian Scottish were ordered to withdraw after the 10th, leaving the sector to the 2nd (Eastern Ontario) Battalion. It was the usual scramble and crawl under heavy fire to the fragile shelter of a hedge. There they found in orderly rows their packs discarded the night before as they had launched their attack. Groups of men wandered about searching for their own kit.

There was only one figure not wearing the kilt. "I saw a disconsolate Algerian wandering around. I hailed him in French. He grinned all over, bowed and returned my greeting. I passed the time of day, asked him if he would care to join my section, and he replied with great eagerness that he would. Afterwards he explained that he was the only one left of his battalion, or more probably the only one who did not retreat, and that he was the son of a sheik."[4]

"Mr. Moroc," as he was dubbed, was soon issued the kilt, and he stayed with the 16th, becoming every inch a Highlander. He was very popular and his vivid pantomime descriptions of his adventures amused everyone.

The small bank of Highlanders that had once been a battalion were ordered into a gap in the G.H.Q. Line. This they were instructed to hold till the last man. As further remnants of the 16th came in they were marched off as reinforcements to St. Julien and Locality C. As a result, several 16th Battalion men figure in the casualties of almost every small desperate action that took place that Saturday.

The Germans now had the apex at their mercy. Their penetration of 700 yards through the 15th Battalion's right had enabled large numbers to fan out and take either side in the rear. Vast arrays of grey-clad reinforcements were forming up on both faces of the apex, while through the gap poured a flood of masked Germans in the wake of the gas cloud. Their elation can be judged from an entry in the history of the Regiment Reussner. "Like a fiery steed that can be reined in only with difficulty, the battalions of Regiment Reussner stood fast under their commanders and waited the advance of the 233rd R.I.R. with which the Regiment had to link up on the right . . . At 7:10 a.m. Regiment Reussner could be restrained no longer and dashed forward. At 7:20 a.m. it had already gone forward 600 meters."

The four hours after the initial breakthrough at 4:20 were spent in wiping out pockets of resistance and attempting to smash through into the open country behind Locality C. At six the last stubborn vestiges of the 15th's right and centre were overwhelmed on the banks of the Stroombeek, a few yards behind their abandoned trenches. Then, full of confidence, the men of Sturmbrigade Schmeiden, who had so recently quaffed the Kaiser's beer, advanced on Locality C.

Atop the minor eminence of Gravenstafel Ridge, stretched ever so thinly, were the men of A Company of the 7th British Columbians plus the 146 survivors of Alberta's 10th Canadians. Added to this tiny garrison were small clusters of fugitives who had escaped extermination or capture when the front line fell. Almost 500 yards to the right and totally isolated lay D Company of 'Tuxford's Dandies,' the 5th Western Cavalry Battalion.

"We looked over there," recalled Private Critchley of the 10th, "and all we could see was masses of the Germans coming up in mass formation. Their officers were still on horseback then."[5]

Major Ormond remembered, "They came on in close order with their rifles at the high port and some of them had put on the kilts of the 15th Battalion that they'd come through.* And they were a queer looking mob. We stood up on our parapet and gave three ruddy cheers and shook our fists at them. We gave them everything we had, and they figured it wasn't worth while and they just turned around and went back."[6]

At the same time Major Ormond reported a small party approaching up the gap on his left. This was a particularly sensitive area for it lay between Locality C and the line north of St. Julien still held by assorted Canadian companies. No one was able to tell who these newcomers were although the officer closest to that sector thought they were Turcos. Ormond's field glasses were full of water after his tumble into the shell hole, and the after-effect of the gas prevented him from distinguishing colours at any distance. They came on steadily carrying a white flag and several stretchers. Two of Ormond's men went forward cautiously to identify these interlopers. As they drew closer the two were suddenly set upon by a small party of Germans who popped from a fold in the ground. The strangers then disappeared into an abandoned house with their stretchers and white flag, and a moment later several machine guns opened up on Ormond's men from that point. Despite this, the second German attack was beaten off although the house remained a thorn in the Canadians' side.

After each attack the shallow trench on top of Gravenstafel Ridge was subjected to a fierce artillery shoot. The trench lay in the open and every shell seemed to find its mark. The thinly-manned position continued to lose five or six men at a time, and German aeroplanes soared overhead to correct any slight errors in range.

---

* Although several similar observations have been recorded, the *British Official History* points out that this has never been proven and suggests that the Germans were in fact wearing their knee-length great-coats.

At 8:30, the Germans, having for the moment given up their attempt to break into the open country behind Locality C, launched a massive assault to eliminate the apex entirely. From Kitcheners' Wood to the severed end of the original front line, masses of *feldgrau* advanced in relentless waves. They were preceded by artillery fire which was described by Major Cory as "absolutely hellish in its accuracy." The surviving defenders were literally being blown out of their trenches.

From his position in the extreme end of the apex Major Osborne of the 15th witnessed a most professional but heartrending demonstration of the German artillery's prowess. Starting at the southerly end of the 13th Royal Highlanders' line they dropped shell after shell of high explosives into these shallow ditches, each time shortening the range to demolish them yard by yard thus forcing the kilted Canadians to evacuate or die futilely. Close behind the shells came German infantry in hundreds led by one man bearing an artillery marker seventy-five feet behind the curtain of shells. As fast as this flag-bearer was picked off another took his place.

It was the same all along the western side of the apex. "People were being blown up all around us, bodies flying in the air," explained H.G. Brewer of the 14th Royal Montreals. "So eventually they just blew us out of that position and we had the order to retire, and retirement was up a long slope right out in the open, no cover at all. The bullets were — well, it was just like being out in a rainstorm. I don't know how we ever got up, the few of us that did. But by that time we were disorganized and there were 13th and 14th and Engineers and Signallers and everybody all mixed up."[7] The slope that everybody was heading for was the end of Gravenstafel Ridge, the gap to the left of Major Ormond's 10th Canadians.

The order to retire spread to the north but it was too late for most. Major Rykert McCuaig's company, now reduced to 40 men and three officers, many of whom were wounded, made for a hedge in their rear. Rifle fire from three sides burst upon them and only twelve made it to the hedge. McCuaig, accompanied by young Lieutenant Pitblado, was shot through both legs and lay helpless on the bullet-swept field. "Pitblado, in spite of my protests, refused to leave me and bandaged up the wounds in my leg under a very heavy fire. He was then wounded a second time in the leg, which finished his chances of getting away. I was subsequently wounded four times while lying on the ground. We both remained there until picked up by the Germans an hour or two later. Their firing line passed us about ten minutes after we were wounded."

Similar scenes were taking place all over the apex — small groups of men fighting to the last or being exterminated by bursts of shrapnel or high explosive. The individuals that survived these last-stands were mostly picked off by German machine guns and rifles or were trapped and captured. Those few who eventually escaped were generally so exhausted and battered that they were incoherent. Said one who made it, "I've never seen such marvellous men in all my life. They adjusted themselves to anything. It would be difficult to pick out any man for bravery, because they were all brave. I expected to see panic. There was no thought of panic. There was a job coming along, and they just knuckled down to it, and really they were marvellous."[8]

At the very tip of the apex two isolated companies realized that it would be impossible for them to retire. B Company of the Buffs and the 15th Battalion's D Company fought attackers coming up the trenches from the west, south, and east, while on their respective fronts they faced swarms of Germans advancing from the northwest and northeast. Southeast, in their rear, German machine guns in an abandoned farm ranged along their position. Nevertheless the Buffs and the Highlanders fought on till their ammunition was exhausted. By this time Major Ewart Osborne, the senior officer in the line, had been wounded twice and captured. He watched from a distance as the German artillery began to work down the trench held by his helpless men. The first shell killed two. Then at 9:10 the senior surviving officer, a young lieutenant, ordered the men to surrender. Osborne breathed a sigh of relief. "Had another shell landed along the trench it would in all probability have killed 30 or 40 men."

Sullenly the fragments of a battalion raised their hands. Captain McKessoch's 31 men were now 3, Lieutenants Fessenden and Smith had more men but not one round of ammunition although the remaining Colt machine gun had twenty-five rounds left. Also in this final stand were the last of the gallant Buffs — Lieutenant Ryder and 13 men.

The apex was no more. The Germans after five hours of costly fighting against a numerically inferior enemy without artillery had, even with the use of the chlorine gas cloud, only broken off the end of the line. They had not broken through the frail defenses into the open country behind. The original line remained intact to the end of the 8th Battalion's position. Here there was a gap resembling a brick torn from a wall. But the mortar and the neighbouring bricks held firm. Men of the 5th Western Cavalry and the 8th Battalion manned a line running southwest to Locality C. There on Gravenstafel Ridge Warden's British Columbians and the decimated 10th, mixed with shreds from the old front line companies, clung doggedly. The line was intact.

Communications between the front line and 3rd Brigade Headquarters had broken down completely, and Brigadier Turner V.C. was not aware of the destruction of his companies at the apex. Consequently, several sets of impossible orders were issued, one sending Lt. Col. Loomis from St. Julien to head a counterattack leading fifteen odds and sods from his headquarters.

He did not get far. From the top of Gravenstafel Ridge he could see the pitiful remains of his own 13th Royal Highlanders and the companies from the Buffs, the 14th, and the 15th fighting off swarms of the enemy approaching frontally. At the same time he could see masses of the enemy, crossing the broken line and moving into position in their rear. Loomis turned, and without stopping, ran almost two miles back to Mouse Trap Farm to try and describe the terrible situation to Turner.

Thus at 7:50 the tragedy was for the first time clearly understood at 3rd Brigade Headquarters and a message was sent to Division:

"Our line is broken C.6c Keerselaere to right. Organizing at St. Julien and occupying G.H.Q. line. No troops in rear. Support needed. Please give situation on our left."

As no reply was received, this plaintive message was repeated at 8:20 with the added plea, "Is there any prospect of help?" This was the message which was finally received by General Alderson at Divisional Headquarters at 8:47.

Up till this moment unduly high hopes had prevailed at the various headquarters—Divisional, Corps, and Army. True, as early as seven, Alderson had established that there was some sort of minor breakthrough by the enemy, but recent confident messages had reassured him. Now the situation was belatedly made clear. A short time later, the high hopes based on the French counterattack at Lizerne were dashed when news arrived of its failure. Realization dawned that despite General Foch's dramatic pledges, there was little hope that the French would recapture their original line, thus repairing the terrible situation which had arisen.

Alderson cast about for reinforcements. These were very few and very distant. The closest were three widely separated British battalions—The Royal Irish Regiment (1st Battalion) at 27th Divisional Headquarters, the 12th County of London Regiment (The Rangers), and the 1st Battalion, The Suffolk Regiment. The latter two were in 28th Divisional Reserve at Verlorenhoek and Frezenberg. West of the canal Alderson could call upon the decimated 4th Central Ontario Battalion and the equally shattered 13th Brigade. There were however some fresh troops—four raw battalions direct from England—the 150th (York and Durham) Brigade. This new formation was at present manning the west side of the Yser Canal near Brielen Bridge. This brigade was part of the 50th Northumbrian Division which was being rushed to the Ypres sector. Other British formations, primarily cavalry, were *en route,* but much too far away to be of assistance.

Already at 7:30 Alderson had ordered two battalions of the 150th (York and Durham) Brigade to move to the G.H.Q. Line astride the Ypres-Poelcappelle Road. Now at 8:45 he sent the remaining two battalions up to the same position. From there the first two were ordered forward at 11:35 to counterattack.

Meanwhile for Brigadier General Turner one of the most pressing problems was artillery support. There were no guns within range of the German artillery wreaking so much havoc northeast of St. Julien. The 9th Battery was now firing by request on the front between Kitcheners' Wood and Keerselaere, but its four 18-pounders were of little consequence against an array of fire-power so vast.

In the meantime northeast of St. Julien, events had far out-stepped the plans being devised at rear headquarters. At right angles to Gravenstafel Ridge, astride the road from Keerselaere, were the men of three companies of the 7th British Columbians. They were in their original positions aligned with the garrison of St. Julien and the trench recently held by the 13th and the Buffs. Now they had become the hinge of the line where it bent back along Gravenstafel Ridge.

This hinge was immediagely assaulted by the victorious Ger-mans. The two platoons on the north side of the road were virtually annihilated. "It was every man for himself," recalled L.C. Scott. "Shoot what you can see. Every man stood his ground . . . Sergeant Peerless was behind waving his rifle and saying, 'Give the sons of bitches hell, boys,' " Ammunition was desperately short and Major Odlum called for volunteers to take it up. He reported, "Having volunteered for the duty, and in attempting to take up ammunition for his own platoon, which was with Captain R.V. Harvey on the North East of the Cross Roads, my brother, No. 16608, Corporal J.W. Odlum, was blown to pieces by a shell."

L.C. Scott summed it up: "We got trapped. We were out behind the German lines. We stayed too long."[9] He was captured by the Germans, one of a small handful who survived.

At this point the Germans should have ripped through the Canadians' makeshift line. But for Lieutenant Edward Bellew, the Machine Gun Officer of the 7th, they probably would have. Bellew was one of those rarities — a man born on the high seas. He had held a commission in the Royal Irish Regiment before emigrating to Canada where he became a civil engineer with the Public Works Department of Vancouver. Today he stepped into the breach by bringing two of his machine guns into action on the high ground at the crossroads.

Enemy fire was almost overwhelming and the crews promptly became casualties. Bellew seized one gun and the other was taken over by Sergeant Peerless. Their fire was so accurate and rapid that the onrushing Germans were halted for the moment only one hun-dred yards from the two Colt guns. The enemy encircled the two almost immediately and Peerless was shot dead. Bellew was wounded but rose again and resumed firing until his ammunition ran out. Then seizing a rifle he smashed his Colt and single-handedly met the final rush of the enemy with the bayonet. Lieutenant Bellew was captured and it was not until his release in 1919 that his winning of the Victoria Cross was announced.

All this while the pressure had been mounting against Locality C perched atop Gravenstafel Ridge. The Germans launched a third attack against the decimated defenders. "When they went back the third time we thought we'd won the war," recalled Major Ormond, C.O. of the 10th Canadians. "We'd stopped them, but within a few minutes, the Boche started to play the piano on us. He really started to go after us with the four-ones and the five-nines and machine guns, and we were being lifted right out of the ground. We had no machine guns. Our four guns had never reached us, so we had nothing to come back at him with except Ross rifles, and instead of getting off twelve or fifteen rounds a minute we could only get off two or three. They were jamming and men would have to lay down and take their heel to force the bolt open."[10]

At eleven o'clock at Enfilade Cross Roads, just behind Gravenstafel Ridge, a conference was held under fire. Lt. Col. J.A. Currie of the 15th, and Major Odlum, now C.O. of the 7th, met with the officer in charge of the firing line, Lt. Col. Burland of the 14th. Theirs was a difficult decision. Both flanks of their frail line along the ridge were now being enfiladed, and the line itself, being on the crest, lay in full view of the enemy artillery and riflemen. Should they hang on to the last man or withdraw to a more defensible position? They decided to withdraw 300 yards to the bottom of the ridge.

As Major Ormond put it, "We decided that we'd better pull back and let him come up onto the skyline and then we'd get our own back."[11]

The order to retire was given around noon. The companies in the middle of the line were able to take advantage of dead ground behind the crest. These men retired in sections bringing their wounded with them and all reached the bottom of Gravenstafel Ridge.

On the left however, Major Odlum's three companies of the 7th British Columbians had no dead ground, and the enemy had chosen that moment to attack. Private Perley Smith recalled, "The wounded and the dead were lying everywhere, and there was everything in the German Army coming towards us over the fields for miles."

At least one Colt machine gun was out of action at this point and its crew was calmly trying to carry out 'immediate action.' "It had a hundred and fifty parts inside," recalled Private A.D. Corker. "We had sheets but the minute you spread your sheet out a shell would explode nearby and cover it with dirt. The shelling was so bad it made me deaf.

"They came over in masses. You couldn't miss if you could fire a gun. That's what made me so sore. If our guns had been working, or just if we had good rifles—some fellows picked up Lee-Enfields and threw the Ross away. There were some fellows crying in the trenches because they couldn't fire their damned rifles."

When the order was passed to withdraw, the men retired in small groups, some by heading to their left where B Company of the 15th still stood under Major Cory. Most, however, tried to cross the open ground in their rear. The majority never made it.

With others Private Corker stayed behind too long trying to fire his Colt machine gun. When he was wounded he knew it was too late. "It was one of those things you never thought of when you went overseas. I thought, well, you might get wounded or you might get killed, but I never thought about being taken prisoner. I don't think we would have been taken prisoner if we had the Lee-Enfield. We could have held them—we could have held them till we got a bit of help."

And thus the withdrawal ended. The 7th Battalion had been almost wiped out. Major Odlum reported, "In the new position on the St. Julien-Fortuin Road I succeeded in collecting 100 men of the 7th Battalion and a few stragglers of other Battalions." Of B Company, 15th Battalion, only a few individuals had escaped, and most of them were wounded. Fortunately the 14th and 10th had made it back with most of their wounded. But still up on the ridge was its original garrison—A Company of the 7th under Major Warden. He later reported, "About 12 noon, I only had one officer left, Lieutenant Scherschmidt. . . . All my N.C.O's except the Company Sergeant Major were either killed or wounded and I only had about 50 men left. (I took in a full company of 234 men with some 50 Turcos, and about 12 men and 2 officers of the 16th Battalion.)"

At 12:30 another meeting was held. This time Major Ormond of the 10th was present and he urged that the others join his battalion (now consisting of about one hundred men) and "go back and clean up this ridge." But to the others his idea did not seem too feasible, nor did their present position which was subject to shelling and heavy machine-gun fire from the northwest. No one wanted to retire as far as the G.H.Q. Line, so that too was vetoed. Then word was received that the 8th, the 'Little Black Devils,' had been ordered to retire, and this swung the balance. A decision was reached to withdraw to some old unused trenches 1,000 yards to the rear and southeast of St. Julien.

So the pitiful few survivors from fourteen companies of five different battalions sullenly retired once more. This was no panic or rout; it was a disciplined and determined body of men who retired in successive rushes through the fields erupting with shells. Each party ran back several yards then flopped to the ground and provided covering fire for their comrades whose turn it was next. Many fell in those one thousand yards, but the wounded were brought back, and the thin line of infantrymen withdrew for the last time. "I never saw anything more wonderful for what you'd call semi-trained troops. They went out on the brow of a hill and they ran at about six pace intervals and most of the time you couldn't see them for bursting shells. The Germans were really throwing the big stuff into them. And these fellows took their position up and then they started to fire. I tell you I was proud to be a Canadian! It was really a wonderful thing!"[12]

In the meantime the village of St. Julien and its small garrison had been taking a fearful pounding since dawn. When ammunition began to run short in mid-morning the Ammunition Column of the 9th Battery had just arrived at Mouse Trap Farm. Brigadier General Turner came out and told the men the situation.

"He stressed that he wouldn't ask anyone to do it, but, if anyone cared to volunteer—? Everyone, of course volunteered," Jim Grey recalled, "but he would only allow the first two crews to attempt it. He had an orderly take the names and numbers of the two crews, and away they went—on the dead run.

"Arriving at St. Julien safely, a very irate officer popped out of a doorway and ordered them to 'Get those goddamned horses out of here!' Unhooking and dumping the contents of the 'pill boxes' in the middle of the road, the boys told the officer where to go then headed back down the road."

The garrison of St. Julien officially consisted of B Company of the 15th (48th Highlanders) and B and D of the 14th Royal Montreals in a line slightly forward of St. Julien with the highland company adjacent to the 7th British Columbian position so recently overrun. In actual fact there were also odds and ends of details from all over—Engineers, Turcos, 16th Canadian Scottish, and 3rd Toronto Battalion—to name but four.

The men had been so badly depleted and the shelling had forced them to move around so often that every position included men from several units. When the right of the little garrison was exposed by the destruction of the 7th, they were augmented by its fugitives, notably seventy men under Major Byng-Hall.

The relentless German pressure mounted minute by minute. Although the terrible odds were partially hidden from the little garrison by folds in the ground, the masses of enemy had been watched by others for some time. Several battalions had crossed the 'Little Black Devils' front sometime earlier and had been sniped at very long range by the Manitobans. While Locality C was still in Canadian hands dozens of battalions could be seen forming up unmolested for the drive towards St. Julien. At the same time on the left flank the forward companies of the 2nd and 3rd battalions east of Kitcheners' Wood had watched a massive build-up take place. At noon the avalanche descended on St. Julien.

The last message from the doomed village had been sent out at 11:30 by Captain Brotherhood of the 14th:

"Enemy have shelled us out and are advancing from our left and front. Will hold every traverse if we have to retire along line to our right. Captain Williamson killed."

Part of D Company the Royal Montreals managed to withdraw on the left into shattered houses, but for the rest it was a bitter hand-to-hand fight to the finish. The enemy outnumbered the Canadians well over ten to one and the artillery fire had lengthened those odds by inflicting huge casualties all morning. There could be only one ending.

"Our rifles were jammed and the only machine gun that remained had been clogged with mud," related Private W.C. Thurgood of the 7th. "Then the enemy broke into the trench further along and started bombing their way toward us. One of our officers, Major Byng-Hall it was I think, ordered us to surrender and we threw up our hands. It was a portion of the 232nd* Regiment of Bavarians that took us prisoners. Though we held our hands aloft and were now unarmed, the cold-blooded crew started to wipe us out. Three of our men were bayonetted before an officer arrived and saved the rest of us. Even then our rough captors struck us with their rifle butts and kicked some of our men who were unfortunate enough to be laid out with wounds."[13]

Now as prisoners of war the handful of survivors not murdered by the Germans straggled up the Poelcappelle Road. They included Major Byng-Hall and about 70 men of the 7th, Major Cory and 39 highlanders of the 15th, four from the 16th Canadian Scottish, two from the 3rd Torontos, and two from the 13th Royal Highlanders. The battered shell of St. Julien lay undefended behind them as they began their weary trek to the Fatherland.

Five miles behind St. Julien, at Divisional headquarters, General Alderson was being bombarded with warnings of the Germans' midday advance and its consequences. Every division in the Salient sent its messages and advice, but unfortunately these were of little use to the harrassed Alderson. Just before one that afternoon, Colonel Romer, Alderson's chief staff officer, spoke to Brigadier General Turner VC on the telephone. The result was a written order from Division finally cancelling instructions to counterattack and ordering Turner to use the battalions of the 150th (York and Durham) Brigade "to strengthen your line and hold on."

There was a misunderstanding implicit in this. Turner's 3rd Brigade no longer held what could be termed a line. Certainly as a defensive line the positions in which his surviving troops found themselves were wholly inadequate. For Turner's part, he interpreted the message to mean the G.H.Q. Line which had so often been stressed in previous messages. Despite another telephone conversation with Colonel Romer, the misunderstanding continued. Thus Turner immediately sent the following message to all battalions now under 3rd Brigade's jurisdiction:

---

* Thurgood was here mistaken, for the 232nd Regiment was not serving in the Salient at this time. However the XXVI Reserve Corps was made up of all the regiments from the 233rd to the 240th. (Appendix I)

"To 5th Durhams, 4th Yorks, 2nd, 3rd, 14th, 15th, 16th Canadian Battalions.

"You will hold G.H.Q. Line from St. Jean-Poelcappelle Road south.

"From 3rd Canadian Infantry Brigade 1:40 p.m."

The result of this order would be the creation of a gap almost three miles wide between the G.H.Q. Line and the old front line still held by the 8th and 5th Battalions. As the remnants of the 3rd Brigade began their withdrawal, neither they nor their Brigadier knew that the orders previously given to the 2nd Brigade to retire had been cancelled. "Tuxford's Dandies," and "The Little Black Devils" were being left on their own.

Chapter Ten

For Want of a Shepherd
(1:40 p.m. - 7:00 p.m., 24 April, 1915)

*"For the teraphim utter nonsense
and the diviners see lies:
the dreamers tell false dreams
and give empty consolation.
Therefore the people wander like sheep
They are afflicted for want of a shepherd."*
Zechariah X, 2

On the Canadian right, Brigadier General Arthur Currie's 2nd Brigade still held its original positions. It was in fact only half a brigade at this stage for both the 7th British Columbians (less D Company) and the 10th Battalion had been put under command of the 3rd Brigade. As a result, the 5th and 8th Battalions now held the only original section of the line between Steenstraat and Berlin Wood. Unfortunately, these two battalions had been forced to use all of their own reserves to shore up the end of the line where the breakthrough had occurred and to hold Locality C's eastern extremity.

All morning the men of the two battalions had hung on confident in their own ability, but in the dark as to what was happening on their left. There had been several orders to withdraw, but each had been cancelled. Then at about one o'clock came an order which, unrealistic as it proved to be, was to have far reaching consequences. Briefly it informed the beleaguered 2nd Brigade that their neighbours, Brigadier General Turner's 3rd Brigade, were to counterattack in the neighbourhood of Locality C. "Also two battalions York and Durham Brigade will be employed to restore situation on the left of the 2nd Infantry Brigade." This was certainly welcome news and meant that no withdrawal was necessary despite

125

the critical situation of the moment. The message was passed forward at 1:15.

The former homesteader, Colonel George Tuxford of the 5th Western Cavalry Battalion wrote, "Upon telephoning the order to Major Tenaille in the right front line, I can still hear ringing in my ears the cheer that sounded in the telephone from these unbeaten men. Likewise, telephoning to the left, Major Edgar's bluff voice immediately responded, 'We'll stay till the cows come home.' " The 'Little Black Devils' for their part were no less emphatic.

One small withdrawal however had become imperative. On the extreme left flank of the 8th a platoon had been pushed into the 100 yard gap between that battalion and the 15th early in the morning. This little party had been almost wiped out and Colonel Lipsett ordered their withdrawal at one o'clock to avoid being cut off. They began to move out, one man at a time, running the gauntlet of fire.

"It was hard to leave the wounded where they lay," Tom Drummond stressed. "One man in particular with his foot hanging by the sinews, with the bone protruding, begged to be taken along. I and another man dressed the foot as well as we were able, but he continued screaming as first one and then another left him. This may seem hard-hearted on our part, but the effect of the gas was such that every effort increased the difficulty of breathing and, moreover, there was a wire entanglement to cross which would have made it almost impossible to take him even had a stretcher been handy."

Drummond was the last man to cross the open ground, but his arrival coincided with that of a 'coal box,' a large German shell which put out vast quantities of black smoke. He was blown almost twenty feet away but woke up some time later unscratched. "I crawled into the H.Q. trench and found myself alongside the R.S.M. who appeared to be badly gassed. He was sitting with his back against the trench wall gasping for breath. I gave him a sip of water which seemed to ease him somewhat, but nothing could be done for him, and indeed, he died a few minutes later."

The Canadians' opponent at this point was Sturmbrigade Schmieden which had been assigned to capture Hill 32 (the German name for a point between Locality C and Boetleer Farm). They did not reach this their first objective till 2:40, and made no attempt to advance on their second objective, a line from Hill 37 to Gravenstafel. German regimental histories emphasize the heavy casualties, especially from artillery fire. This must be taken as a high compliment to the sixteen gun crews of 2nd Canadian Field Artillery Brigade.

Although their assault was directed against the unoccupied Hill 32, the Germans had to pass between Boetleer Farm, held tenaciously by D Company 5th Western Cavalry Battalion, and Locality C still occupied by Captain Warden's dwindling company of British Columbians. German reinforcements were brought up from the 5th Matrosen Regiment. These men were part of a naval brigade, and their flat waterproof hats caused them to be mistaken for Britishers for a moment.

The Germans too were worried about gaps in their line although there seems to be little reason for this caution. Many halts were made while battalions waited for neighbouring units to draw even. The rifle and machine gun fire which they encountered appears to have convinced front line officers that they were up against a numerous enemy when in actual fact the Germans outnumbered the Canadians ten to one.

From the Canadian point of view reinforcements seemed to be the only salvation. The men of the 2nd Brigade could extend no farther to the left—they were stretched too thinly as it was, and all reserves had been thrown in. Brigadier General Currie realized that he had to fill the gap between his line and Localitiy C if a disaster was to be averted.

As early as 8:15 Brigade Headquarters had received a message from Division informing them that two battalions of the 150th (York and Durham) Brigade were in the G.H.Q. Line and could be called up if needed. Thus Currie had sent a staff officer, Lieutenant M.K. Greene, to get in touch with the two battalions. At eleven o'clock with the Germans on the skyline east of Keerselaere, Greene returned, having met no one. Thereupon, he was sent back with orders to remain until one of the battalions made its appearance.

At noon an English battalion arrived* and Greene reported to its commanding officer. But the battalion had been given orders to support *both* Canadian brigades, and its colonel would not budge until he received orders detailing how this was to be done.

It was shortly after noon that Brigadier Currie received this astounding report. By that time Currie knew of the gap on his left between the old line and Locality C. He also knew that Turner's 3rd Brigade was being blasted out of its positions and that the gap might widen. Now just to the rear had appeared ample reserves to plug this hole, but they would not come forward. Shortly after this Currie received the message previously alluded to telling him of a counterattack being launched by the neighbouring 3rd Brigade. Currie therefore decided to go back to the G.H.Q. Line himself to secure the troops he needed to close the breach between the two brigades. As he later wrote, "It being thought that they might move for me when unlikely to move for officers of lesser rank."[1]

Currie's path lay towards Wieltje and near there he met 3rd Brigade's scant reserves milling about. From them he learned of the critical situation at St. Julien and Locality C. By the time he arrived at the G.H.Q. Line Currie had changed his mind; he had decided that the first priority was a counterattack in the 3rd Brigade's area rather than plugging the line in his own.

"In General Headquarters Line I met the battalion (5th Durhams), but it would not move. There it was joined by its Brigadier." Brigadier General Bush agreed with Currie that a counterattack was necessary but wanted to wait for his other battalion, the 4th Battalion, Alexandra, Princess of Wales' Own (Yorkshire Regiment) better known as the "Green Howards." This battalion was moving up by way of Potijze. Bush set out to hurry them on, but he missed them.

"In due time (2 o'clock) the battalion arrived and their records will disclose that they were urged by a Canadian Brigadier to advance towards St. Julien," Currie wrote. "I was the Brigadier who urged them. They would not move without instructions from Bush and I went along the road Bush had taken in the hope that I might

---

* There is confusion regarding the battalion Greene met. Duguid states that it was the 5th Battalion Durham Light Infantry, which was later met by Currie himself. However a signal message from the 4th Battalion Alexandra Princess of Wales' Own (Yorkshire Regiment) suggests that it was the latter battalion which Greene met.

find him. Before going I had a conversation with Lt. H.F. Mac-Donald of the 3rd Brigade Staff who told me that the 3rd Brigade had been ordered to retire to the General Headquarters Line."[2]

This news must have come as a real jolt to Currie. He had left his brigade to find the troops promised to plug the gap between his own and the 3rd Brigade. Now he had located them, they refused to move and the neighboring 3rd Brigade, instead of attacking, was pulling back to a position three miles behind his own. His men, it appeared, were being left to total destruction while he, their commanding officer, was three miles to the rear and out of touch with his Command Post.

If Currie was worried before, he must have felt desperate now. He pursued Bush and tracked him down at Lane Farm southeast of Wieltje where he begged him to commence the agreed-upon counter attack. But Bush was helpless in the matter for his troops were now under command of Turner's 3rd Brigade. As such they were to remain in the G.H.Q. Line because the counterattack had been cancelled. Currie was stymied. Then he discovered that a Divisional Headquarters of some sort lay five hundred yards to the southeast. Assuming it would be in close communication with his own division he made for there. It turned out to be the headquarters of the 27th Imperial Division and Major General Snow was present. Snow had been given command of all reserves in the area early that morning by order of General Plumer. It was now three o'clock and Currie had been absent from his own brigade for two hours. He presented his case to Snow. The latter however was under the false impression that there had been a breakthrough on Currie's right at Berlin Wood and that Currie's own Command Post at Fortuin* was now in German hands. Indeed he had already dispatched troops to retake Fortuin. It is therefore no surprise to find that Currie was unable to obtain assistance in securing his left flank. He did however forward from Snow's headquarters to the headquarters of the Canadian Division a brief account of the situation and his own actions. He then turned his weary footsteps back towards Lane Farm. On the way he met a group of stragglers, formed them up under an NCO, and sent them up to Fortuin. They were pitifully few.

---

* There was no town named Fortuin. It was the name of a locality on the map, Fortuinhoek (Fortuin Corner), really a crossroads among scattered farms.

At Lane Farm he found that Brigadier Bush had left, but was surprised to find his own Brigade Artillery's signals section in occupation. They were establishing a station in anticipation of 2nd Artillery Brigade Headquarters moving back. This was a shock to Currie for his own Command Post was situated in the same dugout as the Artillery Brigade H.Q. which was being evacuated.

Assuming therefore that his own staff was also pulling back, he went forward to meet them at his rear headquarters in Wieltje. There Currie found no one but the Adjutant of the 5th Western Cavalry Battalion. Captain Hilliam had been sent back to try and find out what was happening. Where was Currie's headquarters staff? Where were his two battalions? What had happened?

In the meantime in the front line tension had been steadily building. At first everyone had waited hopefuly for the promised counterattack. The Germans however had begun to penetrate the gap between the line and Locality C. Attempts had been made early that morning to hold the most vital sections, and Tuxford's 5th Western Cavalry Battalion had without hesitation sent D Company under Major Pragnell to line a hedge and a section of a grain field at the eastern end of Locality C. Five hundred yards farther to the west was Captain Warden's Company of the 7th Battalion, the only portion of the British Columbians still under 2nd Brigade's command.

Unfortunately these moves did not prevent swarms of Germans from infiltrating through between Locality C and the front line trenches. Isolated groups of Canadians, mostly stragglers from the old front line, hunted them down. From his battalion command post Colonel Tuxford watched two such struggles. In the first a strong party of Germans with a machine gun fortified a farm 700 yards to his left rear. While Tuxford was desperately trying to locate a field gun to reduce the place he saw a party of Canadians of various units advance towards the farm house. They did not seem to be aware of the Germans occupying it, and Tuxford watched helplessly as they approached in the open. An officer detached himself from the party and advanced alone. He was shot down and his small command flopped to the ground to engage the enemy — unsuccessfully, as it turned out.

Currie's absence from his headquarters seemed to have caused some alarm, as had the apparent delay in 3rd Brigade's promised counterattack. At 1:45 Lt. Col. Betty, Currie's Brigade Major, sent the following message to 3rd Brigade.

"How soon may infantry counterattack be expected to reach left flank of Section II about Locality C to relieve pressure on that flank? Upon your answer depends the decision of O.C. 8th Battalion as to whether to hand on to trenches or not. General Currie missing. Do you know his whereabouts? Last seen going to G.H.Q. 2nd Line."

Almost immediately the illusions were shattered when Turner's reply came back:

"Have instructed troops to hold G.H.Q. Line. Orders for counterattack cancelled."

Should the two battalions fall back in echelon by companies as planned? If so, who should give such orders? Any withdrawal would have a drastic effect on the British troops to the right and they too would be forced to withdraw. With no Brigadier present to make the decision who should take the responsibility?

Before the brigade had even reached France the latter problem had been solved. The four colonels had agreed that the one professional soldier amongst them should take command in case of emergency. This was Lieutenant Colonel Lipsett of the 8th. Of him, George Tuxford (who was actually senior) wrote: "Lipsett was an Irishman. One of those men you call God's gentlemen. Brave to the point of recklessness, generous, and of a most kindly and courteous disposition, he was loved by all. To use a hackneyed expression he 'was devoted to duty.' "

Lipsett, formerly of the Royal Irish Regiment, had been on loan to the Canadian Militia, responsible for training in Western Canada. On the outbreak of war he was given command of the "Little Black Devils" and thus found himself the lone professional in a group of talented amateurs.

Lieutenant Colonel Lipsett at once rang up Tuxford informing him of the new situation and of Currie's disappearance and asked for Tuxford's opinion regarding a withdrawal. "I replied that I did not understand why we should have to retire. In spite of our casualties my men were full of fight. Lipsett then . . . said, 'I am temporarily in command of the Brigade, and if you think it advisable, suppose we stick?' It was mutually agreed there and then, and we stuck."

In the meantime Lt. Col. Creelman of the 2nd Canadian Field Artillery Brigade had estimated that all his remaining ammunition could be fired by six guns. He therefore ordered the withdrawal of the 7th and 8th Batteries and half the 6th. This cross-country move began at 2:45.

All that day ammunition allotments had been ignored, and the various ammunition columns had been seizing shells wherever and whenever they could. In those trying times only one battery is known to have kept a record of its consumption—Major A.G.L. McNaughton's 7th. Over five days his four guns averaged 248.6 rounds per gun per day.

That grim Saturday the 7th had fired over 1,800 rounds, and the shell cases now lay in great heaps around the gun positions. So did the German dead in front of the 'Little Black Devils' ' trenches for McNaughton had been shelling them "over open sights down to eight or nine hundred yards with shrapnel." After every major assault he had held fire, "waiting for them to line up so we could get the greatest number of people in the line of fire."[3]

McNaughton and his gunners were still exhilarated by the noise and the excitement. They had laboured on despite a severe shelling from the enemy that morning. "A German shell burst in my face," McNaughton recalled. "It blew me about ten or twelve feet back, and part of it went through my shoulder."[4] He stayed on for another twelve hours with two orderlies to hold his maps and keep his telephones in order, for miraculously, the lines were still intact to the 8th 'Little Black Devils.' But now two and a half batteries had been ordered to retire and the guns were galloped to the rear.

By this time Sturmbrigade Schmieden had captured the unoccupied Hill 32 between Locality C and Boetleer Farm. They were jubilant. "Lieutenant Colonel Reussner was obviously delighted. With riding-switch and monocle, and puffing a cigar, he was everywhere in evidence, even under the heaviest fire." The panoramic view from this spot provided two surprises as Regiment Reussner's historian recorded. "All enemy moves were clearly observed. Thus it was reported . . . at 2:45 p.m. that the enemy's artillery were going back; and at 2:52 p.m. that two more waves of infantry were advancing in a north easterly direction."

At the same time from their dugout at Fortuin 2nd Brigade staff officers had spotted two lines of skirmishers advancing from the southwest. Field glasses were quickly focused to reveal khaki uniforms. They must be Canadian or British, but who were they, and how had they come to arrive there at this critical moment?

At nine o'clock that morning General Plumer had deputed control of all troops in V Corps Reserve to Major General T.D'O. Snow, Officer Commanding the 27th Imperial Division. (This was the General whom Currie met later in the day during his search for reinforcements.) Snow had also been given power to employ these reserves at his own discretion. Unfortunately, these orders do not seem to have been circulated to other formations, notably the Canadian Division.

In mid-morning Snow had received word that the Germans were advancing through St. Julien. This, of course, was not the case. He had also been erroneously informed that there had been a breakthrough near Berlin Wood causing a gap between the 5th Western Cavalry and the 27th Division. As a result he had ordered up from his own Divisional Reserve the 1st Battalion The Royal Irish Regiment. This depleted unit only 370 strong, moved off at noon from Potijze Chateau with orders to secure and defend Fortuin which Snow imagined to be overrun by the Germans. General Snow next located two battalions from Major-General Bulfin's 28th Imperial Division. Without asking Bulfin's permission, he ordered these two battalions forward from Verlorenhoek to close the presumed gap. These were the 1st Battalion, The Suffolk Regiment and the 12th County of London Battalion (The Rangers).

Next, at 2:15 Snow issued the following order to the harassed Brigadier Turner V.C. at Mouse Trap Farm:

"The enemy's advance from Fortuin must be stopped at all costs. You must move every man you have got to drive him back. I have directed two battalions under O.C. Suffolks from Frezenberg against Fortuin. I am also sending you up the Royal Irish Regiment from here . . . You will get in touch with these troops and take command in that part of the field and drive the enemy northeastwards. I am issuing these orders as I am on the spot and communication appears to be dislocated and time is of the highest importance. Act with vigour."

It was not till almost two hours later that Turner received the above message. There must have been a colorful scene around Mouse Trap Farm when the Brigadier read Snow's peremptory orders. Here he had instructions from an unknown divisional commander whose front was three miles away to drive the enemy to the northeast from Fortuin which was part of Currie's 2nd Brigade area. This must have been exasperating, piled as it was upon his own troubles. It was little wonder that Turner ignored Snow's commands. After all, he was in constant touch with his own Divisional Headquarters, and they had made no mention of any Major General Snow. He must, however, have begun to feel uneasy about his right for he did set out on foot to Fortuin to discover for himself the situation there.

General Snow's intervention did fortunately have one beneficial result. The Suffolks and the 12th London (The Rangers) had advanced beyond Fortuin in compliance with their orders to drive out the Germans who were supposedly in the area. These were the khaki-clad troops spotted by the beleaguered 2nd Brigade as its artillery pulled out. Reinforcements at last!

The Brigade Major, Lt. Col. Betty, hurried out to meet them. On discovering the futility of his current orders, Lt. Col. Wallace of the Suffolks agreed to move the two battalions up to close the gap on the 'Little Black Devils' ' left. Thus at four o'clock the advance recommenced with Betty guiding the right flank and Major C.J. Mersereau the left.

By this time the enemy had Gravenstafel Ridge almost entirely in his grasp. Major Warden's company of the 7th had been reduced from 234 plus 64 Turcos and Scottish to 35 men and one other officer, Lieutenant Scherschmidt. Warden himself had been badly wounded at two o'clock but had just been evacuated, passing a small party of reinforcements going up to Locality C. They were 27 Sappers from 2nd Field Company, Canadian Engineers. They and their officer, Lieutenant H.F.H. Hertzberg, were going up to fight as infantry. Together the British Columbians and the Sappers held the short stretch of trench at Locality C till early next morning when the combined force, then numbering only 40, were ordered out by the Brigade Major. Under Lieutenant Scherschmidt they slipped back through the German lines in a heavy mist which made their escape possible.

But by four o'clock the rest of Gravenstafel Ridge was in German hands. So were the farm buildings to the left and the town of St. Julien. From these vantage points the enemy poured an accurate fire into the two advancing English battalions. The Tommies had also entered an area shelled by their own batteries. There was no way to stop this fire for it came from distant British field guns firing without observation and according to orders from their Divisions. Thus the Suffolks on the right and the Rangers on the left were forced to dig in along the Haanebeek facing Locality C 700 yards away. The casualties totalled 203, including the Rangers' commanding officer. The 1,300 yard gap between Locality C and the 'Little Black Devils' was still open.

At noon the call for reinforcements of the G.H.Q. Line had sent the 'Koylies' and the Queen Victoria Rifles up from their reserve position west of the Yser Canal. Heavy shelling caused numerous casualties, and entire platoons were erased by German 'heavies.' There were other heartrending sights. Wrote Anthony Hossack of the Queen Vics, "We pass a field battery; it is not firing, as it has nothing to fire, and its commander sits weeping on the trail of one of his guns."[5]

The two battalions closed a gap in the G.H.Q. Line on the eastern side just north of Wieltje. "There we found ourselves amongst a crowd of Canadians of all regiments jumbled up anyhow, and apparently fighting a desperate rearguard action. They nearly all appeared to be wounded and were firing as hard as they could."[6]

The Yorkshiremen and the Cockneys were ordered to "dig in" at the side of a road but the ditches were full of liquid mud. " 'Tis balers we need," the men retorted. They were amazed to see a woman completing her washing and hanging it out to dry beside a cottage a few yards away. But the Germans had the road ranged in and soon 5.9's began to crash along the road.

"Their last shell has pitched on our two M.G. teams, sheltering in the ditch on the other side of the road," wrote Hossack. "They disappear, and all we can hear are groans so terrible they will haunt me for ever. Kennison, their officer, stares dazed, looking at a mass of blood and earth. Another crash and the woman and her cottage and water jars vanish and her pitiful washing hangs in a mocking way from her sagging clothes line. A bunch of telephone wires fall about us. To my bemused brain this is a catastrophe in itself, and I curse a Canadian Sapper beside me for not attempting to mend them. He eyes me vacantly, for he is dead. More and more of these huge shells, two of them right in our midst. Shrieks of agony and groans all about me. I am splashed with blood. Surely I am hit, for my head feels as though a battering-ram has struck it. But no, I appear not to be, though all about me are bits of men and ghastly mixtures of Khaki and blood."[7]

Further south several Canadian batteries had been gathered around Potijze. Lieutenant Stan Lovelace of the 9th Battery (which had been there all day) wrote in his diary: "A 5.9 blitz came in the afternoon so we did a 'horse artillery' move to the rear of the wood at Potijze. We signalled for the horses, now depleted by at least a third—both my dear Paddy, a Toronto Police horse, and Speckles had been killed. The drivers came up at the gallop—elbows waving as they forgot the proper methods of riding and rode like cowboys and Indians. God bless them, they were just showing the rest of us they were in this too."

The battery limbered up under showers of debris from the 5.9's which were quickly zeroing in. Away went the first gun and limber across the field, down a ditch, then crashing up onto the cobbled road, gunners hanging on for dear life. The signallers had found a pram which they loaded with telephones and equipment. This too had rushed towards the gate.

"This move was coming off with gusto," the diary records. "A shell cut down a thin tree about six inches in diameter between the wagons. Now the horses got into this too and didn't even pause but went over the tree like jumpers. But one gun and limber wheels hit that tree. The gunners couldn't hold on but flew into the air like trapeze artists."

While these events were transpiring in the G.H.Q. Line, men of the 2nd and 3rd Battalions were enduring their most difficult hours to the west of the wasted village of St. Julien.

In front of Kitcheners' Wood lay three companies of the 2nd (Eastern Ontario) Battalion. 'A' Company, it will be remembered, had been completely destroyed in its dawn attack on the German redoubt the morning before. Now the three remaining companies held the trench formerly occupied by the 10th and 16th Battalions' survivors as well as their own stretch of so-called trench — really nothing more than inches-deep scratches in the hard soil.

The situation was such that Brigadier General Turner V.C. had ordered the 2nd, which was temporarily under 3rd Brigade control, to withdraw at one o'clock. Lt. Col. Watson, the former editor of the *Quebec Chronicle* and now C.O. of the 2nd, sent back Captain Willis O'Conner, his Adjutant, to plead for a deferral till nightfall. This Turner agreed to. However this situation was short-lived as Turner shortly after sent out his 1:40 order to withdraw to the G.H.Q. Line.

Watson went up to the front line with his second-in-command, Lt. Col. Rogers, to supervise the retirement. It would not be easy — three companies held pieces of trench stretching over three-quarters of a mile. In addition, three groups of farm buildings had been seized and held as advance posts — Oblong Farm on the left in front of C Company, Hooper's House to the east of Kitcheners' Wood, and Doxsee's House even farther in front and on the right flank.

The word was passed verbally along the line. Captain Chrysler's C Company on the left was to commence the withdrawal followed by Culling's B Company on the right. When these flanks were clear D Company under Major Bolster was to withdraw. This plan was simple enough, but the problem was getting the word through to those affected because the 2nd Battalion's line was not a continuous one. The problem of passing the word to the three advanced posts was even greater. These posts did not receive the withdrawal order till well after 3:30.

The situation at each of those posts during that final afternoon was probably similar to that described by Private A.W. Bennett of the 10th Battalion's machine gun section. He and his crew had been sent up to support the 2nd Battalion garrison in one of these farms, probably Hooper's House. "Gradually we were being surrounded. We had been holding the house up to this time for about 35 hours — yet, it seemed like a week. It looked hopeless for us to keep the gun in the loft any longer. The fire from their machine gun, coming through the shell-hole, was cutting down our barricade in front of our gun. Soon we wouldn't have any cover left at all." Bennett and his partner, Private Foss, fired a long burst into a hedge full of Germans then dismantled their gun and crept back to a hole in the floor. After crawling across the muddy courtyard they reached the house. "Back into the house again, and what a place! Just a handful of men left — no water to drink and nothing to eat — and 'Hell Let Loose' outside. All the same, Foss and I were glad to get out of that loft with our gun. If we got trapped up there with a jammed machine gun it would have been 'all up' with us as I couldn't imagine them taking us prisoners with so many of their dead lying out there by the hedges.

" 'Here they come again!' the men called out. I immediately opened fire cutting through the sacks hanging in front. I had a clear view of them over the window sill. They were coming through the hedges, from one end of the field to the other — starting to advance in short rushes. I traversed my gun right along the hedge and I saw some of them fall, killed and wounded, with the wounded crawling back to the hedge. Others had stopped and with their entrenching tools were lying on the ground, trying to make shallow holes to lie in. For the moment we had stopped their attack."

It was in such conditions, under almost constant attack that the 2nd Battalion was to withdraw. On the left flank, C Company crawled along their shallow trench to the right, then each man had to make a break across the open fields to some farm buildings in the rear. These fields were swept with machine gun fire and shrapnel as the enemy attempted to prevent the withdrawal. The men in Oblong Farm remained at their posts. Behind them a trench choked with wounded and dead showed where many had tried to carry out the withdrawal order. The situation there was hopeless, but the tiny band of men from eastern Ontario fought to the last man.

On the right the story was almost identical except that Doxsee's House was successfully evacuated by Captain Richardson and his men. The withdrawal then commenced. "It was a most terrifying experience to see your chums going out, one after another, out the end of this little trench that we had, out into the open where machine gun fire was just squirting in like through a hose," A.B. Beddoe recalled in later years. "One after another they would go like jack rabbits, and they were piling up there. And we were moving towards this ultimate destiny, you might say, and feeling, well, my turn is next."[8]

A torrent of fire hit the men and scores lay where they fell. Only about a dozen B Company men and Captain George Richardson reached the road to Wieltje. When he had collected this remnant of a company Richardson organized them, exhausted as they were, and moved off. Presently they came across an English battalion moving up. They were mostly youngsters with London accents. It was the 12th County of London (The Rangers) moving towards Locality C with the Suffolks. The little group of Canadians watched the newcomers move by in extended order. Then Richardson turned to his remnants, "We're going forward."

Not another word was spoken, but the little band shook itself into open order and joined the advance on Locality C. They suffered further casualties here, but it was not till after dark that B Company rejoined the 2nd Eastern Ontario Battalion.

In the centre, the men of D Company were ordered to remove the bolts from rifles that could not be carried out. This proved impossible for a large number of bolt rings had been broken off by men who, in desperation, had tried to kick them open. As the men withdrew under heavy fire, Major Bolster, their Company Commander, remained behind as their rear guard. He was never seen again.

For the men in Hooper's House the end was not far away. One group had been ordered to retire. "Out through the back door we ran," wrote Private Bennett. "I was carrying the gun, Foss the tripod, and the others the ammunition boxes. The Germans saw us leave and we ran right into their fire which seemed to be coming from all angles. Bullets were flying and hitting the ground around us as we ran. They turned a machine gun on us. I dropped after running about 25 yards. I was soon up again and running when a bullet hit the gun, which I was carrying under my left arm, ripping a piece off the handle, and tearing a hole through the sleeve of my tunic. I tripped and fell. I looked back and saw Foss lying on the ground not far from the house. Two of our men dropped — killed outright. There were two ahead of me crawling along the ground, while over to the left I could see two or three crawling and running, trying to get through. I took another look back and saw the Germans were coming out from behind the hedges, advancing in rushes towards the house."

Bennett was one of the fortunate ones. He made it back to the front line with only one other member of his crew. "I looked back over the field and it was hard to realize how I had got through to the trench—about 75 yards in the open—under fire all the way across! It was too late now. The others would never make it. I could see one of our men standing in the doorway at the back of the house. Out in the field I could see four of our men dead. The Germans had now captured the place and what had been the fate of our men who had been unable to get out?"

One of the last to leave the front line was Lt. Col. Watson who with Lt. Col. Rogers, the second-in-command, had waited by the dressing station to see the last of his men begin the perilous journey to the rear. Shaking hands, the two separated and commenced their own ways back. In the meantime Private Wilson fell, shot through the leg. It was still half a mile to comparative safety, but Watson swung the wounded soldier onto his back and carried him to shelter.

That night Watson took stock of his battered battalion. Of twenty-two officers only seven remained. The other ranks had suffered equally. There was nothing for it but to combine all the survivors into two companies under the two remaining Captains, Richardson and Chrysler.

On the right of the 2nd were the two companies of the 3rd Toronto Battalion to the left front of St. Julien. Their situation had not become serious till shortly after noon when St. Julien's defenders on the other side of the Haanebeek had been overrun. Then Major Kirkpatrick of D Company reported his fears that the flank of the neighbouring company (C) would be turned. He was subsequently ordered to hold on and await a counterattack which, of course, never came.

Despite the courageous efforts of Lance Corporal Gravely who carried the message under fire, the order to withdraw to the G.H.Q. Line did not reach these two companies until after the 2nd Battalion had begun their difficult retirement. At that same moment (approximately 3:00) the Germans launched their fourth major assault towards St. Julien. Coming from the north, they were an awesome sight. "All you could see in the woods was a succession of spiked helmets," noted Eric Seaman. "There were hordes of them came at us there."[9]

Hundreds of *feldgrau* overran the Torontonians' shallow

trenches while hundreds more swarmed into the outskirts of the deserted village of St. Julien. By 3:30 it was all over. The survivors were ordered to surrender. "After they caught us and took all worthwhile souvenirs from us we went back through their reserve lines," said Seaman. "There was trench after trench after trench chuck full of Germans. If they had known they were so close to a break-through, and they'd kept on going, they might have done something."[10]

The men who returned from C and D Companies were few. Of C, which was on the right, only forty-three straggled back, almost all of them wounded, and two of these were totally blind.

So it was that at 3:30 on the third day of fighting the Germans had at last entered St. Julien, now a blasted shell littered with scores of Canadian dead. Cautiously the grey figures worked their way through the rubble-strewn streets. They halted at the ruined church, but there was no need for that, for there were no living Canadians left to defend St. Julien.

While the Germans were entering St. Julien, another set of General Snow's orders was being delivered 3,000 yards away behind the G.H.Q. Line. Here a staff officer from the 27th Imperial Division was presenting Lt. Col. M.H.L. Bell of the 4th Green Howards yet another copy of instructions "to make Fortuin good and stop the Germans who were in St. Julien and probably advancing."

Bell accepted these orders from an unknown divisional commander even though he came under the command of the Canadian Division and had earlier refused Currie's urgings to advance. His own superior, Brigadier General Bush, could not be contacted, but Colonel Bell set off with his battalion plus the 4th Battalion The East Yorkshire Regiment. No senior officers were informed of their move.

Thus it was that they advanced to the Haanebeek where they wheeled left and approached the area between Kitcheners' Wood and St. Julien. A captain from one of the rear companies spotted a section of the 6th Battery C.F.A. below Fortuin and sent a runner with the written query, "Can you tell me where the enemy is?" It was in this manner that two battalions of green troops of the 150th (York and Durham) Brigade went into action for the first time.

They were not alone. Slightly ahead and to the right were the men of the 1st Royal Irish Regiment. Earlier that afternoon, following General Snow's orders to recapture Fortuin, they had come up from Potijze Chateau. Finding Fortuin occupied by a motley collection of Canadians, they had advanced north-northwest towards St. Julien. The possibility of occupying the village was rejected when the Irishmen came under a terrific concentration of fire several hundred yards short of the outskirts. However, they had discovered several old trenches on a rise five hundred yards from the village, and these they occupied. It was shortly after four when the beleaguered battalion spotted the long ranks of Yorkshiremen moving up on their left.

At this same moment the *coup de grâce* was administered by the exultant German commanders. It came in the shape of another massive assault — their fifth of the day. Swarming from Kitcheners' Wood the grey hordes came. Immediately troops in the northeastern sector of the G.H.Q. Line opened up with rifle and machine gun fire. The 'Queen Vics' rushed forward to occupy a set of farm buildings. The Germans, more methodically, advanced towards it at right angles. On they came in dense masses, but the weary Vics burdened with four bandoliers each ran through the shrapnel and machine gun bullets. Which would reach the farm first?

"Shall I ever get there?" Anthony Hossack wondered. "My limbs ache with fatigue and my legs are like lead. But the inspiring figure of Seymour urges us on, yet even he cannot prevent the thinning of our line or the gaps being torn in it by the German field gunners, whom we can now plainly see.

"At last we reach the farm, and we follow Culme-Seymour round to its further side. The roar of enemy machine guns rises to a crazy shrieking, but we are past caring about them, and with a sob of relief we fall into the farm's encircling trench. Not too soon either, for that grey mass is only a few hundred yards off, and 'Rapid fire! Let 'em have it, boys!' and don't we just. At last a target, and one that we cannot miss. The Germans fall in scores and their batteries limber up and away."[11]

The din was terrific along the eastern flank of the G.H.Q. Line and it continued for over half an hour as the enemy surged back to the attack. "We allow them to come a bit nearer, which they do. We fire till our rifles are almost too hot to hold, and the few survivors of our mad quarter of an hour stagger back. The attack has failed, and we have held on."[12]

Farther to the east, however, the Germans advanced almost unscathed. Across the Wieltje-St. Julien Road they came, unhurried and in perfect order. Suddenly before them they sighted for the first time the long rows of advancing khaki. It was Lt. Col. Bell's two battalions of Yorkshiremen. A fierce burst of rifle fire erupted and the battle had begun.

A few hundred yards behind the Yorkshire Battalions the 5th and a section of the 6th Battery, C.F.A. were in position facing northeast towards the Stroombeek which they were shelling with the last of their ammunition. The observation officer of the 6th hearing the rattle of musketry to the northwest swung his binoculars over to discover the Germans, rank upon rank of them, crossing the fields unmolested in the sunlight. Lt. Col. Creelman ordered two sections of his guns to engage this enormous new target. It took only a few moments to swing the 18 pounders around.

At 5:15 the eight guns opened up over open sights firing twenty rounds a minute. At this rate the ammunition would be expended in no time at all. Each battery commander directed his own fire and prayed for more ammunition. Seated astride the roof-ridge of Brigade H.Q., Major Harvey McLeod called out orders. "Range 1600" — then, "Drop 100." As the enemy drew nearer he called once more, "Drop 200." In this tense atmosphere there were sudden shouts of exultation. "Four ammunition wagons, sir," reported a subaltern saluting. Into the farmyard careened his sweating teams with their welcome loads.

"Drop 100," came the order. The Germans were now 900 yards away, just a few yards from the Yorkshiremen. It was at this point that the enemy broke. The grey waves disintegrated as the Germans began to flee at first in small groups and finally by hundreds. The rifle fire from the East Yorkshires, the Green Howards, and the Royal Irish crackled into them as dusk settled behind the retreating masses. All the while the Canadian gunners blazed away at the target they could hardly miss. At 6:30 they ceased fire when it was reported, "our troops advancing from St. Julien to Kitcheners'

Wood."* In actual fact the troops moving from St. Julien to Kit-cheners' Wood were Germans evacuating the village in face of what appeared to them to be a massive allied attack. It was now assumed by both sides that St. Julien was occupied by a force of Canadians, but the only Canucks who would occupy St. Julien that night were the dead that still littered the streets.

Darkness descended and the firing died away. This day of calamitous disorders and unfortunate muddles should have ended at this point. It did not. It will be recalled that Brigadier Turner V.C., alarmed by Snow's obsession with Fortuin, had set out on foot to visit the place. He had set out only moments before the final German assault was launched, and his route lay directly across the path of their advance. Thus at the height of this ferocious battle Turner could have been found alone striding towards Fortuin completely unaware of the danger or of the catastrophic consequences of his capture by the Germans. Nevertheless he made it unscathed, and discovered the 1st Royal Irish Regiment shortly after they had joined the Yorkshiremen and the Canadian gunners in smashing the Ger-man attack. Turner ordered the battalion to withdraw at dusk to the G.H.Q. Line. Then he returned to Mouse Trap Farm. The Irish, as they withdrew, passed these two orders on to the Yorkshire battalions which in turn pulled back. The gap was again open.

---

* It is not known who sent this report.

Chapter Eleven

We Have Piped Unto You and Ye Have Not Danced
(24 April, 1915)

"But to what shall I compare this generation?
It is like children sitting in the market
places and calling to their playmates,
'We piped unto you and ye did not dance.' "
Matthew XI, 16 & 17

The Allied Command organization had broken down entirely. If events at the front seemed confusing and orders contradictory, they were no less so in the rear. For instance, General Alderson at Canadian Divisional Headquarters did not discover that his 3rd Brigade had fallen back to the G.H.Q. Line till after four o'clock that afternoon. That was at the same time that the final German attack was debouching from Kitcheners' Wood.

Prior to this information at last reaching him he had planned to relieve the 3rd Canadian Brigade that night with the British 10th Brigade. This formation, detached from the 4th Imperial Division, was then to counterattack and restore the situation. Alderson was therefore amazed when an inkling of the true circumstances reached him. Just how small an inkling it was can be gathered from the order he sent to Brigadier Turner at 4:35. After listing the troops supposedly available, he concluded: "I have no exact knowledge of your situation at the present moment, but hope that you are still blocking St. Julien and in close touch with the 2nd Canadian Infantry Brigade." Of course, neither of these hopes had been in effect all that afternoon. At the moment that Alderson was sending this message both his brigadiers were on foot far from their headquarters—Currie heading for Wieltje and Turner to Fortuin.

145

At Corps Headquarters, "Daddy" Plumer was equally in the dark. At 9:00 that morning he had given command of all the reserves to Major General Snow of the 27th Imperial Division because he of all the divisional commanders was closest to the critical point. In turn, Plumer appears to have received most of his information from Snow who it seems was poorly informed despite his proximity to the front line.

Above Plumer in the chain of command was Sir Horace Smith-Dorrien. He was not on good terms with the Commander-in-Chief and it appears that where possible he was by-passed by Sir John French, although shortly after 9:30 a.m. he did receive the following observation from "Wully" Robertson, Sir John's Chief of Staff: "Evidently not much reliance can be placed on the two French divisions on your left . . . the Chief (Sir John French) thinks that vigorous action East of the Canal will be the best means of checking the enemy's advance." Smith-Dorrien was not at all convinced that "vigorous action" was the solution to the problem. Constant attacks appeared to be only wearing down his troops, making them less able to hold the Salient. His "defeatist" attitude was known at headquarters, and Sir John sent him specific orders shortly after four: "Every effort must be made at once to restore and hold the line about St. Julien or situation of 28th Division will be jeopardized." Sir John's views were expanded upon later in a letter from his C.G.S., Wully Robertson: "He does not wish you to give up any ground if it can be helped . . . The Germans must be a bit tired by now and they are numerically inferior to us as far as we can judge. In fact, there seems no doubt about it."

Sir John, for his part, still adhered to the agreement made with Foch the previous day. Foch had assured him that the French were about to "take a vigorous offence against the front of Steenstraat, Pilckem, Langemarck, and east of these places." As evidence of this Foch added that a fresh division, the 153rd, was arriving and that a second had been called up for the next day. What he did not mention was that the 153rd was only ten days old and consisted entirely of untried units. It is truly amazing that either Foch or Sir John could believe that four French divisions (two of them almost shattered as Wully Robertson had recognized) backed by only a handful of batteries, could drive an equal number of victorious German divisions supported by an overwhelming preponderance of artillery, not only out of their prepared positions, but back three miles to the original line. Nevertheless, illogical as it may seem, this supposition was the sole reason for hanging so tenaciously to the original line and for launching the constant succession of British attacks.

Thus it was that Sir John ordered at the end of this day of carnage yet another attack. Actually, it was the re-staging of the attack planned for early that morning. The order was passed down the chain of command till it reached Alderson shortly after 6:30. He realized that the 3rd Canadian Brigade could not be relieved as planned.

New operation orders were formulated and sent out by Alderson at 8:00. In brief, the attack was to be commanded by Brigadier General Hull whose 10th Brigade was to provide the bulk of the attacking force. The assault was to go in at 3:30 the next morning in hopes of nullifying the Germans' superiority in artillery. The area to be attacked was the German line running from the front of Kitcheners' Wood to St. Julien. Hull was given, besides his own 10th Brigade, the following battalions to support his attack: The 4th Central Ontario Battalion, the 1st Suffolks, the Rangers, the 1st Royal Irish, the "Queen Vics" and the 2nd K.O.Y.L.I., plus the four battalions of the newly arrived 149th (Northumberland) Brigade.

Hull was new to the area and desperately needed a conference to communicate his plans to these widely scattered battalions representing six different brigades. Thus Hull sent out orders for all fifteen battalion commanders to meet at his headquarters at nine that night. Unfortunately, the message was rather ambiguous regarding the actual site of his headquarters.

Brigadier General Turner too was still in difficulties. At 8:45 he forwarded a situation report outlining his position in the G.H.Q. Line. He also estimated that 200 Canadian troops still occupied St. Julien although they were surrounded. In this he was mistaken; no living Canadians remained in St. Julien. Of a link-up with the 2nd Brigade he made no mention. It appears that Turner believed General Snow was now responsible for this.

In the meantime Snow had realized that there had been no link-up between the two Canadian brigades although several battalions he had ordered to "recapture" Fortuin had passed through the locality and disappeared into the gap. He notified Plumer at V

Corps. The result was a scathing message sent to Alderson. This message accused Alderson's subordinate, Turner, of "giving up all the ground for which such a struggle has been made today and leaving the 2nd Brigade in the air." Plumer then ordered "instant action" to re-establish a line near St. Julien, and added ominously, "If necessary you are to appoint an officer to take command."

Alderson received this bolt from the blue incredulously. He then sent Lt. Col. Gordon-Hall forward with powers to take whatever action the latter deemed necessary, and ordered the Divisional Cyclist Company to occupy Fortuin. Thus at midnight, Captain Robinson and his cyclists pedalled away from the Chateau des Trois Tours into the inky blackness, across the canal towards the supposed gap at Fortuin. His men were inspired and felt a great nobleness of purpose, for their orders concluded with the grim injunction "to hold position at all cost." When the weary cyclists stopped momentarily at Wieltje to report to the O.C. of the 150th Brigade they were abruptly let down.

Brigadier Bush did not want them and he sent Captain Robinson to the 3rd Canadian Brigade instead. Turner himelf was not there, but eventually someone ordered the exhausted pedalers to turn about and ride back to St. Jean where at 4:30 they collapsed into a series of reserve trenches.

The reason for Brigadier General Turner's absence was that he had received from General Snow another inflammatory and inaccurate message. The attitude and instructions expressed in the message were to Turner so "inexplicable, inappropriate and incomprehensible"[1] that he jumped on a motorcycle behind a dispatch rider and tore off to visit his own Divisional Commander, General Alderson. Unfortunately, this early morning interview did nothing to clear the air. Each became convinced that the other did not understand what was going on. Both at last were totally correct.

Amongst the Generals there was at least one more plaintive voice crying unsuccessfully to be heard. General E.S. Bulfin, commanding the 28th Imperial Division had seen two of his battalions vanish into thin air as it were. He signalled Canadian Headquarters:

"Please direct my two battalions, 1st Suffolks and 12th Londons now at Fortuin to return to 84th Infantry Brigade Headquarters at earliest possible moment as their presence is urgently required here. These battalions were sent to Fortuin at 3 p.m. today by General

Snow's orders as he was out of touch with me and heard that Germans were occupying Fortuin."

No one at Canadian Headquarters had heard of the two battalions. Furthermore, Snow had been responsible for them only as long as they were reserves. As such he had sent them; there his responsibility ended. Only two headquarters knew where the Suffolks and Rangers had gone — 2nd Canadian Brigade which was given no control over them, and their own 84th Brigade. However their own brigadier had too much on his plate in his own sector to bother contacting them and no one asked him of their whereabouts. Thus General Bulfin fumed and sent more messages.

At 8:40 he tried General Snow, although at this stage he seems to have given up hope:

"Whilst I am responsible for holding a line of defence I must protest against troops allotted to its defense being moved without my knowledge."

Fortunately for everyone except General Bulfin, the Suffolks and the Rangers stayed where they were in front of Locality C.

It was on this day, Saturday, 24 April, that the first small step was taken towards providing gas masks for allied troops. Lt. Col. Wingate of No. 10 Field Ambulance, at Vlamertinghe, appropriated a gauze mask taken from a German prisoner. It was delivered to headquarters at St. Omer for an examination which revealed that the gauze was saturated with glycerine and impregnated with alkali. There appears to be no record of what happened to those found on the deserter captured nine days earlier on 15 April. It is known that the 28th Imperial Division had on that date offered V Corps a sample of the first deserter's mask for analysis "if desired." There is no way of telling if Corps followed up this offer.

The French too had finally taken action to combat the gas cloud, for the next day, Sunday, General Weygand, back at Cassel, instructed the Tenth Army as follows:

"An attack with asphyxiating gas is always to be apprehended.

"For protection the Germans place over the mouth and nostrils a little bag of rubberised cloth filled with cotton waste, impregnated with a solution of hyposulphite of soda and a fixed alkaline hydrate (sodium or potassium). The same precautions are to be taken by us."

On the French and Belgian sector Saturday had been a difficult day. The village of Lizerne, six hundred yards west of Steenstraat and the canal, had been the scene of bitter fighting. It began shortly after midnight when the Germans' 46th Reserve Division had attempted to seize the village in preparation for a drive two miles southwest to Vlamertinghe. The defenders, men of the 80th Territorial Brigade, had been surprised by the sudden fierce bombardment and the swarms of infantry which struck the place from three sides in the blackness of night. The Territorials were steadily driven back by these overwhelming numbers although it took several hours of confused bayonet fighting to clear the battered ruins. When silence finally returned to Lizerne the Germans had become its new inhabitants.

General Foch had issued orders shortly before midnight outlining two attacks which Putz's *Détachement d'Armée de Belgique* was to undertake. The first to be conducted by General Quiquandon had a simple if enormous objective, "to throw back upon the right bank all elements of the enemy forces which had crossed it (the Yser Canal) and to gain footing on that bank." This difficult mission had now been complicated even further by the loss of Lizerne. To carry out this task Quiquandon had been given the 87th Territorial Division (General Codet), almost destroyed in the first gas attack, plus the untried 418th Infantry Regiment of the newly-formed 153rd Division.

The 418th was made up of *bleuets*, raw recruits of the class of 1915. Their commanding officer was an old friend of Mordacq's, Lt. Col. Barraud who had served at St. Cyr (the French equivalent of the British Sandhurst), with Mordacq. Barraud had "moved heaven and earth" to be returned directly to a fighting battalion after being severely wounded at the beginning of the war. Now he would lead the 418th into its baptism of fire.

To co-operate with the 418th, the Belgians supplied the 3rd Battalion, 2nd Regiment of Carabiniers. These troops were among the best in the Belgian Army and were easily distinguished by their quaint headdress, resembling a rather rakish silk top-hat. The

Carabiniers also wore dark green greatcoats unlike most Belgian troops.

These two battalions were to retake Lizerne and move on eastward through Steenstraat to the canal. South of that, General Codet's 87th Territorial Division were ordered to take Het Sas. The assault was to be supported by all the available Belgian artillery plus two French batteries.

Colonel Mordacq, reinforced by two battalions of Chasseurs, was to resume his drive to Pilckem with all the forces he could muster. The attack was to begin at 5:30 a.m. but the colonel did not receive his orders till 3:00 a.m. Thus he postponed the attack till 1:30 that afternoon.

At 8:30 General Codet's attack began with the 418th Infantry Regiment and the Belgian 2nd Regiment of Carabiniers advancing steadily though under heavy fire. The fire was such that Lizerne could not be reached. At eleven Codet called a halt to the attack when he decided to wait for "serious artillery preparation."

At 9:40, while the Germans were advancing on Locality C, Putz sent a report to General Foch. It was not quite what the latter had been hoping for. First, Putz explained that no action was possible in Mordacq's sector till the Chasseurs arrived. Next he reported that Smith-Dorrien had informed him that the British were too weak to attack along the whole front although they would take "vigorous action" on the left of Pilckem that afternoon. At that very moment however the handful of survivors of the Apex were being marched off to prisoner-of-war camps.

Putz then reported that the Belgians had fallen back from Lizerne. Of course, this was not entirely true — there were elements of his own 87th Division which had also been driven out of the hamlet. He ventured the opinion that, "The Territorials of the 87th are still shaken by the charge of the day before — one cannot expect much of them . . ."

Foch replied to this gloomy report with fiery rhetoric. Nothing more clearly shows Foch's ability to brush aside distasteful truths with stirring phrases and impossible orders:

Action must be taken:
1. By vigorous offensive east of the Canal in co-operation with the English who have been put in motion to this end by Field-Marshal French.

2. It is necessary to attempt at all costs to throw back from the Canal the German elements which have crossed at Lizerne and further south—push up your reserves to do this. It can all be engaged by nightfall . . . (Here Foch promised another Division plus a British reserve.)
3. Give orders to that effect and without delay.

Foch.

Shortly thereafter Foch wrote his own superior, 'Papa' Joffre. It was a rather soothing letter which began, "On the west bank of the Canal things are going well with us. We are in a fair way to begin and to take Steenstraat and Het Sas." The failure of his own troops to make any advance is laid at the feet of the British "who are being very strongly attacked near St. Julien." The letter ends with an account of the formidable reinforcements being brought up by Field-Marshal Sir John French who was about to "resume the offensive to drive the Germans back to Langemarck." He assured Joffre, "I have just seen him. He is in good form."

Colonel Mordacq's attack was scheduled to begin at 1:30 p.m. There was an attempt to provide artillery coverage for the *zouaves'* assault by calling in all sixteen 18-pounders from the 1st Canadian Field Artillery Brigade and eight large howitzers of the 118th R.F.A. However there were few French batteries available for the attack.

During the morning the *zouaves* had been greatly heartened for their ordeal by a rather bizarre ceremony. Colonel Chizelles of the 2nd Half-Battalion received word that morning that a veteran N.C.O. had been awarded the *Médaille Militaire*. Taking his Adjutant, de Montcabrier, and a bugler he headed for the front lines to present the award before the attack. The *zouaves* were amazed to see the trio arrive in broad daylight under heavy fire, but even more so when they were ordered to 'fall-in' amid the ruins of their flimsy trench. Chizelles then ordered the bugler to sound a fanfare and he presented the *Médaille Militaire* to the astonished N.C.O. The Germans were equally astonished and for a few moments quit firing. At the conclusion of the ceremony they redoubled their rate of fire however.

Some time later Mordacq had occasion to speak with Chizelles and warn him not to risk his life in this way—it belonged to his country. Chizelles replied, "Evidently it has been exaggerated a lit-

PUBLIC ARCHIVES CANADA PA1370

Above left: Arthur Currie, former teacher and real estate agent, commanded the 2nd Canadian Infantry Brigade during the Second Battle of Ypres. By 1917 he had become Lieutenant-General Sir Arthur Currie and in command of the Canadian Corps in France.

Above right: Brig. Gen. Geo. S. Tufford, original commander, 5th Battalion (Western Cavalry 1914-1916). Commander 3rd Infantry Brigade, March 1916-1919.

Below: Captain W.H. Hooper of the 2nd Canadian Battalion with trench periscope. During the 2nd Battle of Ypres Captain Hooper drove the enemy out of a fortified position named Alberta Farm. For his efforts, the position thereafter became known as "Hooper's House".

PUBLIC ARCHIVES CANADA PA107238

Above left: Pte. Tom Drummond, 8th Battalion (Winnipeg's 90th Rifles, but known as The Little Black Devils) C.E.F. Tom survived the war and returned to his adopted home of Moosomin, Saskatchewan, where in the 1950's he wrote his war-time memoirs. Tom passed away in 1976.

Above right: "Sergeant Bill", 5th Canadian Battalion, Senior Mascot Canadian Forces. Enlisted 23rd August, 1914, Arrived in France February 15, 1915. Wounded April 24th, 1915 at 2nd Battle of Ypres.

Below left: Mobilization — August 1914. The St. Catharines contingent of what would become the 10th Battery, C.F.A.

Below right: Gunner Linden Somerville survived the 2nd Battle of Ypres, only to be crippled by a falling horse in late 1915. He was released in 1916, and at the time of this publication, Linden was still enjoying life in Niagara Falls, Ontario.

10 BATTERY ORDERLY ROOM, ST. CATHARINES, ONTARIO.

Above: Indian troops on the march near Vlamertinghe. Below left: Indian troops preparing chapattis. Below right: Sikhs getting a chance to catch up on their laundry. Note camouflaged netting on the road in the background.

Above left: General Ferdinand Foch,
commanding the "Groupe Provisoire du Nord".
Above right: Field Marshal Sir John French,
Commander-in-Chief of the British Expeditionary
Force.
Below left: Lieut-General Sir Herbert Plumer,
officer commanding the British V Corps, being
decorated by H.M. King George V.
Below right: General Sir Horace Smith-Dorrien,
commanding the British 2nd Army.

The Second Battle of Ypres, by Richard Jack.

The painting *The German Poison Belt* by John De O'Bryan, depicts the retreat of the French colonial troops in the face of the gas cloud on April 22, 1915.

This 1916 photograph shows a gas cloud being projected on a Somme battlefield. A similar method was used by the Germans at Ypres in April 1915. Unfortunately no photos of the gas released in April 1915 are available due to the complete surprise use of this weapon.

Left: Typical trench conditions in the Ypres Salient. Men of the 11th Hussars and French soldiers in the trenches at Zillebeke.
Above: This type of hurriedly improvised gas alarm was to be one of the most important trench fixtures during the war. Its noise would be one of the most feared.

General view of ground over which Germans advanced after releasing gas, April 22, 1915.

Road near Fortuin and 2nd Canadian Infantry Brigade H.Q.

Above: Approximate position of the 8th Canadian Infantry Battalion (The Little Black Devils)
H.Q. on 22 April, 1915.
Below: By 1919, the date of this picture, there was little left of Kitchener's Wood, the object
of the attack by the 10th and 16th Canadian Battalions during the night of 22/23 April, 1915.
This picture was taken from the jumping off positions of the two Canadian battalions.

tle. With men like I have who each day show so much courage, such self-sacrifice, it is only right that I take a small share of the risks." That he risked an entire section of men by falling them in in a front line trench for such a presentation was not mentioned.

At 1:30 when these *zouaves* went to the attack they were met by a torrent of fire which their handful of supporting artillery could not quell. The advance continued against withering fire but finally bogged down well short of the line. Major Guého, who was in his position behind the centre of the battalion, ran forward as his men took cover. He crossed 200 yards of open ground before arriving at the front line. Guého hit the ground and gave several orders, then grabbing a rifle he jumped to his feet calling, "Let's go, *zouaves*, forward! We must seize them by the throat!"[2] He and the men who followed him were immediately shot down, but others got up and under a terrible fire recovered the body of their major a scant ten yards from the Germans.

Another brave soul who made it that close was stopped by the enemy's barbed wire. The Germans called upon him to surrender, but he fired off his whole magazine at them, and not waiting to be riddled with bullets, sprinted back safely to cover.

Despite these and many other heroic gestures, the *zouaves* did not reach the enemy front line. Five hours after it began, the attack towards Pilckem ended without results. What success there was came later at dusk when patrols discovered that the bloody shambles of Turco Farm was no longer occupied by the Germans. This old Flemish home, the scene of such bitter fighting by the 4th Central Ontario Battalion, the Middlesex, and the Duke of Cornwall's now became the junction point between French and British front lines without another shot being fired.

Resumption of the attack on Lizerne had been scheduled for 2:00 p.m. A Belgian who witnessed the advance wrote, "The French 418th, composed of young soldiers of the class of 1915 who were seeing fire for the first time, went into action. I saw it advance in perfect order under the bombardment towards the first line of trenches. It was thrilling. They had the misfortune, however, to lose their colonel, killed at the outset leading the attack."[3] Mordacq's old friend, Barraud, had died at the head of his battalion in its first attack.

German fire was severe. Machine guns and shrapnel tore gaps in the advancing blue ranks but there was no faltering. The outposts were driven in and by dusk Lizerne was surrounded on three sides by the Allies. Nevertheless this was very far short of Foch's grand plan.

Across no man's land the *feldgrau* also greeted nightfall with relief. For those units which had led the attacks that day there were heavy casualties to accept. Possibly it was these losses which had fostered such unnecessary brutality by the German infantry that day. Whatever the reason, the Germans had been seen on several oc- casions shooting wounded Canadians in cold blood. Major Ormond of the 10th Canadians reported, "The enemy shot our wounded unmercifully and with some sort of projectile that set fire to their clothing. These have the velocity of bullets, some exploding in the air, this I observed myself."

Possibly this is the reason for the surprisingly low number of Canadian gas casualties. Although captured German documents claimed 5,000 killed by gas—this was more than all the Canadians involved in the cloud gas attack—only 122 were admitted to hospital. Eleven of these unfortunates died.[4]

German brutality was not limited to murdering helpless wounded and unarmed prisoners. An incident at 2:30 that after- noon on the Belgian front was even more difficult to comprehend. An isolated party of the German 211th Infantry Regiment had been pinned down in no man's land during the attack of April 22. They were without food and water for two days, and their officers had all been killed. That afternoon, in agonies of thirst, they put up a white flag. The Belgians did not fire and soon a small forest of hankies ap- peared waving on the ends of rifles and bayonets above the trench.

"We are not assassins," declared Kempeneer, the Belgian com- mander. "I shouted to those who wish to surrender to come one at a time, without weapons, but then we witness a most distressing scene, the most poignant of the battle. One by one, as each German leaves the trench to surrender, one of their machine guns knocks him down . . . Several fall never to rise again, others die near our line."[5]

On another part of the battlefield a German officer, Rudolph Binding, wrote in his diary: "The effects of the successful gas attack were horrible. I am not pleased with the idea of poisoning men. Of course, the entire world will rage about it first and then imitate us. All the dead lie on their backs, with clenched fists; the whole field is yellow. They say that Ypres must fall now. One can see it burning — not without a pang for the beautiful city. Langemarck is a heap of rubbish . . . All that remains of the church is the doorway with the date '1620.' "[6]

Records do not show the mood at Duke Albrecht's headquarters. There was probably some mild euphoria on the part of many of the staff officers, for after all, German arms had been victorious almost everywhere. Yet this truth went hand in hand with the fact that nowhere had the advance succeeded beyond the first objective. The Fourth Army had failed to attain any of its secondary objectives for the day.

When Saturday had dawned Ypres had appeared to be within grasp. Along the Yser Canal the XXIII Reserve Corps was to have driven through the disorganized French defenders of Steenstraat and Het Sas. Once into the open country von Kathen was to have swung south and cut off the Allied retreat by seizing Vlamertinghe.

Even more dramatic had been the plans for the XXVI Reserve Corps facing the Apex and St. Julien. Here von Hugel had been heavily reinforced by the last of Duke Albrecht's reserves. His own two divisions had been supplemented by three more brigades — the 2nd Reserve Ersatz Brigade, Sturmbrigade Schmieden, and the 38th Landwehr Brigade. To pave the way to victory here Pionierregiment 35 had laboured all the previous day to dig in the remaining gas cylinders along the 51st Divisions's trenches. The Canadian line should have been swept away in moments. Then the XXVII Reserve Corps farther east would have assaulted the British as their flank began to cave in. It should have been 22 April all over again.

It had all seemed quite feasible on paper. Now after a day of the most vicious fighting there was only a moderate dent in the line. The XXIII Reserve Corps was no farther west of the Yser Canal and was not even remotely near Vlamertinghe where they were to have cut off retreat from the Salient. Von Hugel's XXVI Corps, utilizing all the available reserves, had progressed less than half the distance planned, had failed to roll up the line of the 2nd Canadian Brigade, and had been forced back out of St. Julien after expending huge numbers of men to capture it. Of course, these meagre results meant that XXVII Corps, poised to attack, had made no move against the British at all.

As a result, modified plans were being prepared for tomorrow, Sunday, 25 April. It was decided that no more attempts would be made against the French west of the canal. The whole effort was to be made in the area around St. Julien. The first objective was the capture of the shattered village believed by the Germans to be still in Canadian hands. Then the assault was to press forward and secure the ridges north of Wieltje and Frezenberg—an advance of over 2500 yards in some places. Thus the 51st Reserve Division, actively supported by the 52nd, commenced assembling all their available forces for an early morning attack stretching from Kitcheners' Wood to Berlin Wood. Duke Albrecht and his generals realized that time was running out. Tomorrow's battle would have to decide the issue.

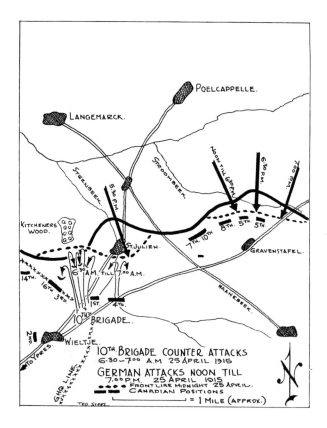

Chapter Twelve

Fuel for the Fire
(Sunday, 25 April, 1915)

*"And the people shall be as the fuel
of the fire."*

Isaiah IX, 19

Some time after midnight Lt. Col. Gordon-Hall arrived at the ravaged village of Wieltje. It will be recalled that Alderson had been instructed in a blistering message from Plumer to send a staff officer forward with plenary powers "to deal with the situation on the spot." Lt. Col. Gordon-Hall was Alderson's emissary. He was a British officer who had been on attachment to the Canadian Militia when the war broke out. He now found that Brigadier General Turner V.C. had just left, riding pillion on a motorcycle to confer with Alderson in person. However, Turner's Brigade Major, Lt. Col. Garnet Hughes, was present as were Brigadiers Mercer and Currie of the 1st and 2nd Canadian Brigades and Bush of the 150th (York and Durham) Brigade.

Gordon-Hall soon discovered the true situation and issued orders to remedy it. Currie's 2nd Brigade was to extend southwestward from the original front line to the northern branch of the Haanebeek. This was to be accomplished by bringing up the 7th British Columbians and 10th Canadians. Mercer's two 1st Brigade battalions (1st and 4th) were ordered to carry the line westward to the Zonnebeek-Langemarck Road. From there southwest to the Haanebeek's southern branch the York and Durham Brigade was to fill the breach. Finally, Turner's 3rd Brigade was ordered to extend northward from the G.H.Q. Line and join up with the York and Durhams on the Haanebeek. This would effectively seal the gap in the line. This settled, the necessary orders were sent out at 2:10 a.m.

Meanwhile, Colonels Lipsett and Tuxford had been busy

157

badgering neighbouring British units for reinforcements. The results were gratifying, and various companies on entrenching duties were given to the 2nd Brigade to shore up their battered line. Thus men of the 2nd Northumberland Fusiliers, the 2nd Cheshire Regiment, the 8th Middlesex and the 1st Monmouthshire Regiment found themselves occupying an assortment of positions scattered along Gravenstafel Ridge. Unfortunately, each Company Commander operated independently and there was no cohesion or unity of command.

In the meantime the battered Canadians clung to their trenches subsisting on their emergency rations and rations taken from the dead. Water and ammunition were almost exhausted and the men tired beyond belief. The two colonels, however, were human dynamos that night as they searched everywhere for supplies or relief. "Upon returning from one of these fruitless quests to Lipsett's Headquarters in the cellar of a farm house, every available foot of space in which was now occupied by wounded men," Tuxford wrote, "we were informed that there were two British Divisions on the road close to Zonnebeek who were only awaiting guides to come forward. It did not appear probable, but in the disordered state of things, there was a possibility and it seemed like a ray of hope."

Major Pragnell of the 5th volunteered to go back through the German-infested countryside as a guide. Tuxford vetoed this as Pragnell was already wounded in three places. There was only one person, he explained, who was available and knew the country; that person was Tuxford himself.

Thus George Tuxford set out alone to make his way through the scattered enemy posts on his left rear. He reached Bombarded Crossroads in the darkness and pouring rain to find the nearby farm filled with wounded and gassed men. There were no sentries posted so the former homesteader found a slightly wounded N.C.O. and put him in charge. "I left them to produce some attempt at organization, and proceeded up the Zonnebeek Road. The whole countryside was being systematically searched with artillery fire. There was no sign of any troops, and having assured myself of that fact I made my way, by sheer luck, back again to Lipsett's Headquarters."

Much farther behind the lines troops were being drawn to Ypres like tacks to a magnet. From all sides they came although the French pole of the magnet drew but a handful. Only one regiment out of the three divisions promised by Foch had begun to arrive as yet.

That night British reinforcements were marching hard for the Salient. The Lahore Division from India was drawing closer, their destination being Ouderdom, four miles northwest of Ypres. Much closer — only 1000 yards north of Ypres — a long column was halted at the side of the road, where the troops had been ordered to rest before entering the Salient. These were the men of Brigadier General Hull's 10th Brigade who were to counterattack the enemy at 3:30 in the morning. "We sat for the most part in great-coats and silence, watching the shelling of Ypres. Suddenly a huge fire broke out in the centre of the town," wrote 2nd Lieutenant Bruce Bairnsfather of the Royal Warwickshire Regiment. Bairnsfather was soon to become the most famous cartoonist of his time as the creator of "Old Bill."

"The sky was a whirling and twisting mass of red and yellow flames, and enormous volumes of black smoke. A truly grand and awful spectacle. The tall ruins of the Cloth Hall and Cathedral were alternately silhouetted or brightly illuminated in the yellow glare of flames. And now it had started to rain. Down it came, hard and fast."[1]

The 10th Brigade consisted chiefly of splendidly trained career soldiers from such renowned units as the Royal Warwickshire Regiment, the Seaforth Highlanders, The Royal Irish Fusiliers, and the Royal Dublin Fusiliers. The fifth was a Territorial battalion, the 7th Argyll and Sutherland Highlanders. There was one exceptional thing about the 10th Brigade — it was at full strength.

At this moment Brigadier Hull was anxiously waiting for his battalion commanders to arrive at his temporary headquarters. Hull had been given a total of fifteen battalions for the attack. Unfortunately, the three officers added to his Brigade Staff were not enough to ensure liaison with his far-flung command. Because the rendezvous for the meeting had been ambiguously stated in the orders he had issued, Hull found himself alone with the C.O.'s of his own five battalions. Eventually one other arrived along with the senior Canadian artillery officer and the Brigadier of the 149th

(Northumberland) Brigade. Hull had had no chance to reconnoitre the area himself and he was reluctant to commit his brigade to the cross-country route located by the 19th Alberta Dragoons. Thus he ordered the 10th Brigade to march for Wieltje along the main road north of Ypres. He left for that place himself at one after having sent out an order postponing the attack one hour till 4:30.

"As we went on we could see a faint, red glow ahead," wrote Bairnsfather. "This turned out to be Wieltje. All that was left of it, a smouldering ruin. Here and there the bodies of dead men lay about the road. At intervals I could discern stiffened shapes of corpses in the ditches which bordered the road."[2]

By this time Hull had discovered that there were only two openings in the wire guarding the G.H.Q. Line. Through these his own five battalions must defile before again forming up for the assault. Thus the attack was postponed yet another hour till 5:30. Hull had still not heard from six of his fifteen battalions so he decided to go ahead with only his 10th Brigade supported on the right flank by the 149th Northumberland Brigade.

What had happend to the remaining six battalions? One of these was the shattered 4th Central Ontario Battalion. It was at this moment *en route* with the 1st Battalion to fill the gap between the 2nd Brigade and the Zonnebeek-Langemarck Road. This was in accordance with the orders issued by Alderson's emissary, Colonel Gordon-Hall. When Brigadier Mercer, now at Wieltje, received word that one of his battalions was to support Hull he was nonplussed. Mercer was at the same time also ordered to wait and let the 10th and 149th Brigades pass through the wire first as they were already two hours behind schedule. Mercer accepted these more recent orders to support Hull's attack and did not continue on to the Zonnebeek-Langemarck Road.

Further to the east Lt. Col. Wallace had not as yet heard that his command (the 1st Suffolk Regiment and the Rangers) had been placed under Hull's command. It would not be till 3:45 that this message was received. Hence his two battalions held on to their positions.

Brigadier Hull's three other assigned battalions, the 1st Battalion Royal Irish Regiment, the Queen Victoria's Rifles, and the K.O.Y.L.I. were occupying sections of the G.H.Q. Line unaware that they had been transferred. Thus Hull's command had been reduced to ten battalions.

As the veterans of the 10th Brigade moved along the narrow paths through the wire they encountered the hideous remains of three days' fighting. They stumbled over the reeking cadavers of both farm animals and men. Old trenches and drainage ditches rapidly filled with slimy water as the rain beat down upon them. Everywhere lay discarded equipment, shattered wagons, and empty shell casings. At 2:30 they had heard the distant rumbling of a bombardment. This ceased by 3:15, but sharp at 3:30 (their originally scheduled attack time) another, closer barrage opened up. The batteries had not been advised of the two hour-long delays. The more distant bombardment had been provided as a preliminary to the attack by batteries of the 27th and 28th Imperial divisions firing into Kitcheners' Wood. Unfortunately, one brigade, the 146th, had been ordered to fire on St. Julien. This mistake announced to the amazed Germans that no allied troops held the embattled village.

The next barrage at 3:30 had been put down by the Canadian Divisional Artillery and two British howitzer batteries, first on the near side of Kitcheners' Wood then on the far side to catch German reinforcements coming in. The men of the 10th Brigade knew none of these details; they could only trudge and slither on glumly listening to their precious supporting ammunition being fired off into the inky gloom.

At 4:40 the British batteries repeated the bombardment in accordance with the first orders postponing the attack for one hour. Kitcheners' Wood took another short pounding although not a shell fell on St. Julien this time. The 146th Artillery Brigade had not been notified that 200 Canadians were holding St. Julien. This lack of shelling was welcomed by one group however—a patrol of shadowy gray figures about to enter the silent village from the west. They were men of the German 51st Reserve Division.

In the meantime reinforcements had begun to trickle and, in some cases, blunder into the gap between the 2nd and 3rd Brigades. Lt. Col. J. Turnbull and the 8th Durham Light Infantry had been detached from their brigade (151st (D.L.I.) Brigade) by General Snow with orders to join the 85th Imperial Brigade. However when they arrived Brigadier Chapman instead ordered Turnbull to close the gap north of the Rangers facing Locality C. On his arrival there, the bewildered Turnbull was next requested to move even farther north to relieve the badly gassed remnants of the 'Little Black Devils.' This he immediately agreed to do. As a result, the remains of three companies of Canadians were relieved before 4:30, but D Company on the right remained when daylight appeared.

The Canadian companies had endured a difficult night. Although their own battalion war diary makes little mention of the exploits of these gassed and exhausted survivors, the History of the 5th Matrosen Regiment states: "That evening the 1st and 3rd Battalions were sent against a piece of trench which remained from the 22nd April in rear of the new German front and which was heavily manned by the enemy. So as not to endanger the 77th Reserve Infantry Regiment (facing the original front line) which was in contact with the enemy, the attack would be enveloping and delivered with cold steel. In altogether unknown terrain, and on a pitch dark rainy night, the heavy task could not be accomplished; only elements of the 1st Battalion succeeded in rolling up a short length of trench, which it had however, to give up on account of strong opposition and after sustaining heavy casualties." Thus two well-rested, full-strength German battalions had been routed by a handful of gassed and battered 'Little Black Devils' and 5th Western Cavalry, augmented by a smattering of men from other Canadian and British units, notably the 2nd Northumberland Fusiliers.

Despite their own appalling condition, these men greeted their relief with mixed feelings. "They were all kids," Lester Stevens marvelled. He accosted one of the young boys from County Durham who told him, "We've just come out from England." Stevens was incredulous. "Haven't you been in any trenches before?"

"Never been in any trenches before," replied the youngster who added, "We don't know nothing!"

"Goodnight!" exclaimed Stevens, "I'm sorry for you." He complained to his chums, "It's a damn shame for them to come in here and take over from us. We should stay here and carry on."[3]

During Brigadier General Currie's odyssey on the 24th he had discovered in the G.H.Q. Line the remains of his two detached battalions, the 7th British Columbians and the 10th Canadians. Both had been brought back from Fortuin at nine to be fed after fifty continuous hours of fighting, entrenching, and marching. Currie therefore led the 150 survivors of each battalion, weary but no longer hungry, back up the road from the crowded G.H.Q. Line, through deserted Fortuin, along another mile of silent road to Bombarded Crossroads. From here they moved northwest to occupy a position west of the Suffolks, facing their old position atop Locality C. It was 4:00 a.m. before they arrived, and in the mist confusion reigned.

As dawn broke through the mist and drizzle, farther to the east, the Orderly Room Sergeant of the 5th Battalion, Sergeant F.B. Bagshaw was startled by an apparent apparition. "We saw a man on the height of land walking along the ridge from the 8th Battalion, and presently this fellow jumped down into a sap and came along the line into our battalion. And he said, 'Tuxford, who the hell was that shooting at me?' And this was Currie."[4]

Tuxford explained that there was a German machine gun post in the farm building to his left rear, but Currie seemed sceptical. So Tuxford took him to a brick wall and suggested that the Brigadier take a peek, QUICKLY. Currie did so and immediately machine gun bullets pattered against the other side of the wall. "Then those are the beggars who shot at me this morning," remarked the gigantic brigadier. "While we had been sitting in the cellar at breakfast," recalled Tuxford, "the General had been fumbling at his riding breeches, finally pulling out a spent bullet that had found a resting place there."

As dawn streaked the eastern sky, Brigadier Hull's 10th Brigade approached Kitcheners' Wood striding briskly along in column of fours. Suddenly the semi-darkness crackled into life as German rifle and machine gun fire spat out at short range. The spot where the Warwickshires were to have formed up on the left was in enemy hands. Nevertheless, the four regular battalions deployed into extended order as if they were on manoeuvres at Aldershot. The Royal Warwickshires were on the left facing Kitcheners' Wood, and next to them, in their kilts of MacKenzie tartan, was the 2nd Battalion, The Seaforth Highlanders. The two Irish regiments were to take St. Julien and the area between. On the right was the Royal Irish

Fusiliers, and between them and the Seaforths, the 2nd Royal Dublin Fusiliers. The 7th Argylls were to support the attack on Kitcheners' Wood.

The rain abated as daylight spread revealing the crack British battalions smoothly extending into open order. The German fire became even more difficult to endure as their artillery joined in. Because it was already 5:30, each battalion began its advance as soon as it deployed.

The major surprise was the enormous volume of fire which burst from St. Julien. General Alderson had arranged for a preliminary bombardment of the village, but at the last moment this had been cancelled due to the belief that 200 Canadians were still holding out there. The Germans had also believed it to be occupied until the British artillery brigade had unfortunately put a barrage on it at 3:30. If the British attack had taken place when originally planned the Irish regiments would have entered St. Julien unopposed, for it was not until 4:30 that the first German patrol had entered the ravaged village. Now the houses bristled with German guns, and the fire was devastating.

"Bullets were flying through the air in all directions," Bruce Bairnsfather wrote. "Ahead in the semi-darkness, I could just see the forms of men running out into the fields on either side in extended order, and beyond them a continuous heavy crackling of rifle-fire showed me the main direction of the attack. A few men had gone down already, and no wonder—the air was thick with bullets."[5]

Each moment lessened the precious cover of darkness. From the upper stories of farm buildings and from the houses in St. Julien the fire poured down. Nevertheless the first mile was soon covered. At Mouse Trap Farm staff officers with field glasses watched the leading waves falling prone in regular lines. One inexperienced officer asked excitedly, "Why do they stop?"

"They are dead," was the quiet reply.

It was true. In a matter of minutes and with appalling ease over 2000 of these magnificent British regulars had been scythed down. "I have never seen such a slaughter in my life," recalled one member of the 10th Canadians. "They were lined up—I can see it still—in a long line—straight up and the Hun opened up on them with machine guns. They were just raked down. It was pathetic."[6]

On the left the Warwickshires pressed on in small groups regardless. "The German machine guns were busy now, and sent sprays of bullets flicking up the grounds all round us," Bairnsfather noted. "Lying behind a slight fold in the ground we saw them whisking through the grass, three or four inches over our heads . . . Dawn had come now, and in the cold grey light I saw our men out in front of me advancing in short rushes towards a large wood in front. The Germans were firing star shells into the air in pretty large numbers, why, I couldn't make out, as there was quite enough light now to see by."[7]

To the attackers it seemed there was no artillery support at all. This was not the case. The three Canadian batteries were called upon several times that morning to hit various targets. As St. Julien was still thought to be occupied by Canadians, several fierce concentrations were layed down on any German troops seen advancing on the village, although St. Julien itself was not hit. Then at 10:40, after the truth had been discovered, 960 rounds were fired into the ruins in fifteen minutes — 60 rounds per gun. Thus Brigadier Hull reported, "The artillery fire was good, but there was not enough of it to seriously damage the enemy who were entrenched in a very strong position."

The 7th Argylls, the only non-regular soldiers in the 10th Brigade, were ordered to support the Seaforths and Warwickshires. They were exhorted by the Brigade Major, twice wounded, to "Stick it out, Argylls."[8] They did that and lost 425 men and twelve officers that morning.

Nowhere did the attackers reach their objectives and come to grips with the enemy. Brigadier General Hull, realizing this, attempted one last gamble to salvage something. At 6:15 he ordered the 7th Battalion of the Northumberland Fusiliers to support the attack on St. Julien. They met a similar fate when they ran into large numbers of Germans advancing towards them under cover of heavy fire from the village.

In the meantime those trapped in the open fields underwent a hell unspeakable. Bairnsfather had carried out a wounded Canadian officer and had deposited him in a dressing station at Mouse Trap Farm. This was in all probability the one operated by Captain Francis Scrimger, M.O. of the 14th Royal Montreals. "Shells were crashing into the roof of the farm and exploding round it in great profusion. Every minute one heard the swishing rush overhead, the momentary pause, saw the cloud of red dust, then 'Crumph!' That farm was going to be extinguished, I could plainly see."[9]

The young 2nd Lieutenant made his way back to his machine gun section. "As I went I heard the enormous ponderous, gurgling, rotating sound of large shells coming. I looked to my left. Four columns of black smoke and earth shot up a hundred feet into the air, not eighty yards away. Then four mighty reverberating explosions that rent the air. A row of four 'Jack Johnsons' had landed not a hundred yards away, right amongst the lines of men, lying out firing in extended order . . . The shelling of the farm continued; I ran past it between two explosions and raced along the old gully we had first come up . . . As I was on the sloping bank of the gully I heard a colossal rushing swish in the air, and then didn't hear the resultant crash . . . I lay in a filthy stagnant ditch covered with mud and slime from head to foot. I suddenly started to tremble all over. I couldn't grasp where I was. I lay and trembled. I had been blown up by a shell."[10]

Bairnsfather was merely one of 2,419 10th Brigade casualties which occurred in those two hours. In all, British casualties during the attack were over 3,000. A few hours later in a distant part of the world another attack would be launched which was to go down in history as one of the great military disasters—the landings at Gallipoli. Yet the casualties sustained there in capturing the beaches were less than those suffered by Hull's men who failed to even come to grips with the enemy. General Hull now ordered the shocked survivors to dig in where they lay.

The situation unfolding at General Alderson's Headquarters that morning appeared to be vastly improved over yesterday despite the disastrous results of the assault. The survivors of the attack had begun to dig in along the Haanebeek thus closing one of the gaps of last night.

An erroneous report by an airman that British trenches extended from St. Julien to Locality C lifted another burden from General Alderson's mind. It can only be imagined what Alderson would have felt like if he had known the truth—that the trenches were indeed there but they were filled with Germans. Alderson assumed, as he had reason to do, that this line was occupied by his own 1st Brigade which his emissary, Gordon-Hall, had ordered up.

Another comforting, but erroneous belief was that General Bulfin's 28th Imperial Division had been busy since last evening constructing a 'switch-line' along the Fortuin-Gravenstafel Road. Despite Bulfin's repeated orders to dig this line, almost nothing had been achieved. This was primarily due to Lt. Col. Lipsett's moving appeals for reinforcements. As soon as the work parties had appeared, they had been spirited by Lipsett and Tuxford into the gap behind the 2nd Brigade. Thus, little actual construction had been done on the switch line.

The situation regarding reserves also looked comparatively rosy. Alderson still had three fresh battalions of the Northumberland Fusiliers (4th, 5th, and 6th of 149th Brigade). In the Corps reserve under General Snow were three more Territorial battalions, the 6th, 7th and 9th Durham Light Infantry, plus one regular battalion, the 1st Welsh Regiment. In addition, V Corps had informed him that the Lahore Division and the 11th Brigade were on their way. As a result, at 11:50, Alderson sent the encouraging news to his brigades, "that strong reinforcements are coming up to our assistance."

On the other side of no man's land there was also enormous suffering amongst the common soldiers and consternation amongst the staff. Duke Albrecht's main blow that day was to have been launched from Kitcheners' Wood and St. Julien. It was here that his main force had been concentrated in readiness to launch the overwhelming attack. So when the British force had materialized out of the wakening dawn it had been a total surprise. The results had been disastrous for both sides. Hall's 10th Brigade had attacked opposite the main body of enemy whose small arms fire had completely overwhelmed them. On the other hand, the rather skimpy British-Canadian artillery bombardment had caused unprecedented casualties in the crowded forming-up areas. The German Official History later revealed, "Not until 7 a.m. could the hostile attack, delivered in great strength and carried out by successive waves, finally be brought to a standstill. But the striking power of the now greatly weakened German troops was also worn out in the doing."

The German's subsidiary attack near Broodseinde was also slow in developing. At nine o'clock the preliminary bombardment began. The target was the stretch of trench held by the British 84th and 85th Brigades. All morning the screaming rush of shells and their shattering explosions rocked the 28th Imperial Division's two brigades. Parapets were destroyed and many men were rendered almost helpless by the large number of gas shells included in the German barrage. From the village of Passchendaele the 244th Reserve Infantry Regiment moved southwest into their jumping-off positions around eleven o'clock. But it was not until 1:00 p.m. that the long-awaited assault began.

From only 70 yards away the Germans poured across no man's land into a section of trench held by the 3rd Battalion, The East Surrey Regiment. Vicious hand-to-hand fighting surged back and forth. The support company of the 8th Middlesex came up in the center of the sector and helped to drive off the Germans. On the right the East Surreys killed their intruders except for one officer and 28 men of the 244th Reserve Regiment whom they captured. On the left, however, all the British officers were killed and the hand-to-hand fight swung in favour of the Germans. Finally only the *feldgrau* remained in this section of trench for the East Surreys were too depleted to dislodge them. It was not until midnight that Lt. Col. Bridgford was able to organize attempts to retake the trench, and both of these failed.

The Germans had also attacked the Royal Fusiliers between the East Surreys and 'Tuxford's Dandies.' Here no man's land was over 200 yards wide, however, and no *feldgrau* reached the British trenches.

The G.H.Q. Line received a continuous bombardment Sunday. The tension here could be felt, and nerves were nearing the breaking point after days of heavy action and constant shelling. In one of the "forts" an officer lost his reason and ordered his men to fire on the troops defending the line in front of him. "Fortunately," records one historian, "a German bullet put him temporarily out of action before any harm was done."[11]

The expected German attack never materialized, and things quietened down somewhat during mid-afternoon. Later that day however the enemy zeroed in on Mouse Trap Farm which housed 3rd Brigade Headquarters and an aid station. The first salvo was

right on target and the straw in the courtyard started a raging inferno. General Turner and his staff were forced out as were the occupants of the hospital. Captains Haywood and Scrimger, two
M.O.'s, ignored enemy fire and returned time and again to rescue
all the wounded. This was made most difficult by the fact that there
was a moat around the place with only one narrow roadway as entry;
thus it was easily sealed off by the German artillery. Those able,
swam the moat, and within minutes all but one of the wounded were
evacuated.

Captain Harold MacDonald, a staff captain with the 3rd
Brigade, remained, badly injured, being literally filled with shell
splinters. Scrimger returned and dressed his wounds, protecting
MacDonald with his own body, then during a comparative lull, carried the officer out of the blazing building on his back. There was no
shelter in sight so Scrimger laid the man upon the ground and
shielded him with his own body until help arrived sometime later.

Farther to the rear things were quieter. Near Potizje where the
9th Battery was situated Lieutenant Lovelace wrote in his diary, "As
I wandered about not too far away from our guns, there were a few
unburied about—here and there, and I saw little services where
Padres were sitting on trench-edge or funk holes with a grateful
group of soldiers round about listening to their message."

The reverses of Saturday had created a new apex. Sunday's
apex was in an even more precarious situation than those of the
previous days. Defensive positions were almost non-existent—first
there was the remains of the original line along the Stroombeek, but
it was entirely in the air on the left. Behind it lay a make-shift
second line which connected up, more or less, with the remainder of
the Allied line on the left where the breakthrough had occurred.
This second line however was in no position to support the first as it
lay on Gravenstafel Ridge 1000 yards to the rear. Its left too was
under heavy enfilade fire, while its right did not connect up with the
neighbouring 28th Imperial Division. The 'switch line' ordered to be
constructed last night which would have joined the two lines, had
hardly even been started. Thus it can be seen that Brigadier Currie
had a most unusual and difficult situation to handle.

As every minute passed, the pressure on the front line increased. The shelling and machine gun fire raked the trenches without cease and the enemy infantry made several sorties with grenade and bayonet. D Company of the 'Little Black Devils' beat off an attack launched from a sap dug out the night before from the German line only 200 yards away. Some time later a bombing attack hit the Durhams' open left flank while another was launched across a second-growth turnip patch against D Company. The latter assault was driven off but the bombing attack against the green British troops began to have effect. Bit by bit the Durhams gave way, but not before their own B Company was called forward to reinforce them. The company made good progress till it emerged from a hedge near its objective. A cascade of fire descended upon it from that point and the survivors retreated.

This small reverse movement gave rise to many rumours amongst observers in the rear, and the word spread that the 8th Durhams were in full retreat. But all this while the two front line companies and D Company of the 'Little Black Devils' hung on despite the worsening situation. Not only was their left flank surrounded on three sides, but British artillery fire was now falling on their disintegrating trenches.

Under somewhat less pressure, were the two companies to their right. These were B and A of the 5th Western Cavalry. Next to them were two platoons of the 3rd Battalion, Royal Fusiliers of the 28th Imperial Division which carried the original front line on southwards.

The second line had been established by the miscellaneous British companies coaxed there the night previously by Lipsett and augmented by the remaining men of the 8th Battalion. But this line's rear was also enfiladed by the Germans on the left. Since nine o'clock that morning both lines had been pounded unmercifully by all calibres and from all directions. There was nothing the poorly entrenched troops could do except endure.

Shortly after noon the bombardment increased its intensity. A number of the green troops in the second line along the Gravenstafel Ridge broke and fled in disorder. "I gathered them in," wrote Lt. Col. George Tuxford, "and placed them in the trenches with instructions to pick up and use the rifles that were lying around. Raw troops as they were, rushed into the midst of a veritable inferno, they had more than bravely borne themselves throughout that long morning's bombardment, until the strain became more than human men could stand."

Distant observers from both the 28th and 5th Imperial Divisions had spotted this retirement, but interpreted it as a German breakthrough on Gravenstafel Ridge—the *second* line. General Alderson back at Divisional Headquarters was informed of this supposed development. He immediately requested General Snow, still in command of reserves, to order the remaining three battalions of the 151st (D.L.I.) Brigade to the 'switch line' he believed had been dug last night by the 28th Imperial Division. Snow replied by sending one battalion (9th D.L.I.) forward only a distance of several hundred yards. Thus the confusion in the rear continued to escalate.

It was at the same time (1:00 p.m.) that the retreat of these troops occurred that Brigadier Currie discovered that his brigade was isolated. Having expected the 1st Brigade to fill in the gap as had been ordered by Colonel Gordon-Hall, he was amazed to eventually locate the Brigade south of St. Julien. It was also at this time that Currie learned of the failure of the 10th Brigade's attack. The true gravity of his command's position was now clear to him.

Currie, now at 5th Battalion Headquarters, received late in the afternoon two messages relayed from Division. The first stated that the Germans were "attacking in long columns" northwest of Locality C and Boetleer Farm. This was tantamount to saying that his brigade was being surrounded, particularly as he was under the impression that the 8th Durhams had earlier given way entirely. The second message informed him that the reinforcements Currie had been expecting (the 151st (D.L.I.) Brigade), were ordered to dig in well *behind* his position on Gravenstafel Ridge. It appeared to Currie that his Brigade's position had already been given up as hopeless by higher authorities. Therefore, shortly after five he ordered an immediate withdrawal.

"But sir," Tuxford objected, "It is impossible to retire in daylight."

Currie was adamant, "Our position has been adjudged hopeless."[12]

"He wrote out the order to me," Tuxford recalled, "and Captain Hilliam, the Adjutant, wrote the orders to the two Companies in the front line to retire, and I signed it.

"Hilliam started to take the message, when Major Dyer stepped forward and holding out his hand, demanded the message, claiming that it was his right to deliver it. These two—old men—they will forgive me for so calling them, but they were both old in years, commenced arguing who should have the privilege of bearing this message that courted almost certain death. To end the discussion, I duplicated the message, and giving one to each, instructed them to deliver one to the right and the other to the left Company in the line."

By a stroke of luck, as runners for the other battalions set out, both Lipsett and Major Odlum appeared on the scene. They too were briefed on their roles in this difficult operation. The troops in the front line were to withdraw down a slope, cross the Stroombeek, then move up and over Gravenstafel Ridge and down its southern slope—all this under enfilade fire in broad daylight.

For those in the second line the situation was the same except that they had to travel only half the distance. Sergeant Bagshaw, Orderly Room Sergeant of the 5th Western Cavalry, wrote in his diary as he waited to move out, "Ordered to retire at once in daylight. God help us all. It is madness to go before dark. We say goodbye to each other and part."[13]

The first to withdraw were the men in the second line. Lipsett and Tuxford persuaded Brigadier Currie to go back to his Brigade Headquarters, and he ran the gauntlet of fire with a runner. Then Lipsett moved left to bring out his three companies. "The din of bursting shells and the noise of battle were bewildering," recalled Tuxford. "It looked like a forgone case, so I got together my maps and papers, and going out alone behind one of the buildings, buried them deep with a spade . . . The remnants of the 8th Battalion—and they now comprised also men from the 5th, 7th, and 10th—now came straggling over the rise from the left. All cohesion had vanished, and they blindly obeyed the order to retire. It was pitiful to see these men, who had come from the very jaws of hell, staggering along absolutely dazed, gassed, hungry, and parched with thirst. I directed them down the road . . . It was then time to send my Staff off, and I instructed them to assemble at a point near the Zonnebeke Road. One by one they went, Captain Nash, the Signalling Officer, Sergeant-Major Mackie, the Battalion Sergeant-Major; Sergeant Bagshaw, the Orderly Room Sergeant, and Corporal Meikle of the Orderly Room, dodging and doubling down the hill, for the whole slope was being searched with shrapnel. I watched Bagshaw roll head over heels and thought, 'There goes Bagshaw!' But he had only missed his footing and was up again. I was now by myself for some twenty minutes. Bricks were flying in all directions and a shell took the telephone board off the side of the house.

"Watching the 250 men of the 8th in their progress, I saw them reach and pass over the brook where they were to dig in and head down the Zonnebeke Road. Grabbing a rifle — and it was the third Ross rifle I picked up before I found one in which the bolt was not jammed — I ran after them and caught them up on the road."

The situation in the first line by now was desperate. At 5:00 the three company commanders (A and D of the 8th D.L.I., and D of the 'Little Black Devils') had consulted behind the broken walls of Supply Farm which constituted the centre of their portion of the line. They had decided to request permission to withdraw, but their message never reached Headquarters. After awaiting a reply in vain, they sent several parties of wounded back but these were cut down before they reached the crest of Gravenstafel Ridge. It was then decided to seize a house on the extreme left thereby denying it to the enemy while the retirement took place. Led by a young subaltern, a platoon of Durhams advanced carefully on the house. But upon crawling into a field of beets they found themselves suddenly surrounded by a large party of Germans which had been hidden there waiting for the moment to attack.

Now the dwindling garrison moved down their trench to the right but the pressure increased from front, left, and left rear. Captain Northwood of the 'Little Black Devils' ordered Sergeant Knobel to lead a party to the rear. This party was the last to escape. The remaining men fought on to the bitter end. All but one of the machine guns had been knocked out. On the right, Sergeant Alldritt continued to fire, inflicting enormous losses on the swarms of Germans approaching from all sides.

Back in the front line it was seven o'clock when Captain Northwood discovered that B Company of the 5th had begun to retire. "Daddy" Dyer had gotten through! The elderly farmer from Manitoba had carried his copy of the message to the front line. Both he and Captain Hilliam — also a farmer, but from B.C. — had somehow made it to a hedge within a few hundred yards of the front line.

"Upon stepping out of the cover of the hedge, Hilliam was shot through the chest immediately," Colonel Tuxford wrote. "A moment later, Dyer was shot within an inch of the heart. Pulling himself together, this man of iron half scrambled, half dragged himself, until he dropped some few yards short of the trench, into which he was immediately dragged and the message was delivered."

These two companies of the 5th had been firing steadily at the enemy all afternoon encouraged by their C.O.'s, Major Edgar on the left and Major Tenaille on the right. The latter was a Corsican and a colorful personality, strangely out of character for a prairie battalion. He had spent the day as usual cursing in broken English and exhorting his men, "Shoot, shoot! Damn zem! Come on, Boche, We feex you!"[14]

Now that a written order to withdraw had arrived the 5th had no choice; they sullenly began their retirement. It was disciplined and orderly. "In their midst was 'Daddy' Dyer, carried with the utmost care by his men. Several stopped to pick up Hilliam but found only a piece of board with a message written upon it in mud, "I have crawled home."

On their left however Currie's orders had not reached the survivors of the 'Little Black Devils' and the Durhams. A withdrawal was now impossible for them. Sergeant Alldritt had been overpowered and thus their last machine gun silenced. From all sides came the grey-clad enemy in a final rush and then it was all over. Few escaped back to Gravenstafel Ridge — of 32 machine gunners seven returned while D Company of the 8th lost every officer and 139 men. The apex was destroyed once more.

While these events were taking place other developments were unfolding farther to the rear. Lt. Col. Lipsett had by now discovered on his battalion's arrival at the Langemarck-Zonnebeke Road that the battalions of the 28th Imperial Division had not retired, but were still in place both to right and left. Although the companies of the Cheshires and Northumberland Fusiliers had withdrawn according to Brigadier Currie's order, the other independent companies had not. Lt. Col. Turnbull of the 8th Durhams was in doubt as to whose command he was under so he and his last company remained on Gravenstafel Ridge defending Boetleer Farm as did the companies of the Monmouth and the Middlesex regiments. Lipsett, who like Tuxford had opposed the withdrawal from the first, put his small command into some degree of order and turned around. The men obeyed silently, and, without a word, crossed that gauntlet of fire again.

Tuxford had by this time arrived, assembled what was left of his C Company which had been mixed in with the 'Little Black Devils,' and had turned them around. He was desperately anxious to cover the withdrawal of his two forward companies now that he had some troops under his command.

Back across the open field they walked. Particularly troublesome was machine gun fire coming from the left at a range of only 600 yards. It was the same machine gun which had bothered Tuxford's headquarters for the last two days, situated as it was in the old farm house to his left rear. "When we had got two-thirds up the hill this machine gun fire ceased, and looking backwards I saw that the farm house was badly dismantled, having palpably been hit by shell fire."

RSM Mackie, a former horse artilleryman, had found a British battery on the right. He had explained the situation to the battery commander and they had calculated the position on a map, the house not being in sight. At that moment a shell made a direct hit on the battery. The wounded Battery Commander, now lying on the ground, shouted out his fire orders. The remaining guns scored direct hits on the target, and the advancing troops finally obtained some respite from the enfilading fire.

"During the journey up the hill, which was swept with machine gun and artillery fire, I remember seeing the Battalion Cook, Purvis, a bright young fellow, who always appeared to be in the best of spirits, plodding steadily along, with his cap stuck jauntily on one side of his head, and the man looking across, actually winked at me," remarked the colonel.

Through the maelstrom they trudged, too exhausted to run. At last they crossed the crest of Gravenstafel Ridge and dropped into a line of shallow reserve trenches. "Retiring towards us up the slope in open skirmishing order as quietly as though it were a practice retirement, came the two Companies. In their rear was a howling mob of Germans, yelling and blowing horns, . . . I never saw a man quicken his pace . . . . Upon my passing the order down the line to fix bayonets, a Sergeant called to me, as he snapped his bayonet home with a click, 'Tell us what to do, sir, and we'll do it.' "

The advancing Germans were stopped by the fusillade which now crashed down upon them. "We let go, and they must have thought the whole Canadian Army was at the back of it," declared A.H. Fisher of the 8th. "It was an absolute surprise to them."[15]

The two companies saved from the front line now took their places in a new front line. By this time the 3rd Royal Fusiliers, the next battalion to the right, had established a switch line of sorts back to a road behind Berlin Wood, and fifty of these fusiliers joined in to fire on the Germans' flank.

The Germans had suffered heavily in their advance, for the westerners had retired in such good order that they had picked off many pursuers. One, Sergeant Bowie, accounted for fourteen *feldgrau*. But the Canadians too had suffered. Lipsett's batman was shot at his side and was carried out by the colonel who returned with a bullet hole through his cap. Tuxford instinctively ducked a shell only to have it explode on the lip of a trench above him. His battalion listed 124 casualties, while the 8th's D Company had been wiped out.

That evening the infantry of the Canadian Division was ordered into reserve. As the weary troops trudged towards the rear the shelling continued with almost diabolical accuracy throughout the night. These men from the front line witnessed some terrible scenes that night in the rear areas.

"Here one saw a limber with a six horse team, all lying dead in the traces as the shell had struck them," wrote the former cavalryman, George Tuxford. "There were the remains of a motor bicycle, with two arms — all that was left of the rider — still grimly clinging to the handle bars; and again, a little knot of bodies, gone down at one fell swoop."

The 5th turned into St. Jean. At the main crossroads a little ahead of them sat a motor ambulance. All at once it erupted into a blinding flash as a shell scored a direct hit. Of all the occupants only one emerged, a sheet of living flame. The ghastly figure ran blindly down the road until it dropped and lay still. The flames flared for several moments longer then flickered out. The infantrymen horrified, detoured past the corner, found their billets and collapsed. It was 4:00 Monday morning.

The remainder of the 2nd Brigade, the 7th and 10th Battalions, less than 300 strong, had not received the orders to withdraw from their scratch trenches facing Locality C. They and a company of the 1st Suffolks had remained, outflanked on both sides, till well after midnight. In the darkness, Major Odlum, their senior officer, returning from Currie's headquarters, had been unable to find them. He eventually retired with a handful of stragglers to the new headquarters near St. Jean. Meanwhile, the balance of the two battalions remained in position. In the grey of the morning, under cover of a heavy mist, these units succeeded in withdrawing silently to their left.

The 10th was now commanded by Major Guthrie, a former New Brunswick politician. Three days ago he had been at Divisional Headquarters on a legal matter from England. On hearing of the plight of the 10th after their midnight attack he had requested a transfer to that battalion. "I'll go as a lieutenant, of course,"[16] and as such he was transferred. Now as the senior surviving officer, he became the 10th Canadians' fourth Commanding Officer in three days.

Around Boetleer Farm a small island of resistance still held out. What was left of the 8th Durham Light Infantry along with an assortment of Tommies and Canucks clung to their meagre shelter. On each side of them were large gaps—half a mile to the right and an even larger one to the left. These fresh-faced youths, absolute rookies only hours ago, held an impossibly exposed position; they were far in advance of the "line" and had either flank uncovered. Both the Monmouth and Middlesex companies had now received orders to rejoin their units, but it was not until four o'clock that Lt. Col. Turnbull's Durhams fell back. By that time large numbers of the enemy had again and again pressed in upon Boetleer Farm despite having been repeatedly driven off. Now at four the Durhams retired in good order as another German attack broke upon the farm. Steadily these young soldiers withdrew to Gravenstafel Ridge, but the enemy did not press them. Boetleer Farm had at last fallen.

The valiant Durhams had lost 19 officers and 574 men in the 24 hours since they had first marched wide-eyed into the trenches on Stroombeek Ridge. The exhausted survivors of a battalion were now reorganized into a company of 140 men and 6 officers.

On the other side of no man's land exhaustion was also setting in. Patrolling must have been almost non-existent for the Germans failed to discover or exploit either of the two enormous gaps in the Allied line. Duke Albrecht himself had become disillusioned by this time as shown by his order: "The Corps must be satisfied with what it had gained . . . The aim of the (Fourth) Army operation was for the present to lop off the pocket east of Ypres."

That evening at St. Omer Sir John French had a visitor. It was General Smith-Dorrien who had motored over to speak with his superior in person. He pleaded with his Chief not to order any further attacks and pointed out that despite Foch's promises, the French effort to date had been minimal. The need to reorganize after the morning's disastrous attacks was also stressed by Smith-Dorrien. Sir John's reply to these pleas was recorded by Smith-Dorrien in a letter to the former written only five days later:

"You did not want to surrender any ground if it could possibly be avoided, but unless the French regained the ground they had lost, or a great deal of it, you realized that it might become impossible to retain our present very salient position in front of Ypres. It was essential, though that the situation should be cleared up, and the area quieted down as soon as possible, even if I had to withdraw to a more retired line, so that you might be able to continue your offensive elsewhere. You felt sure I should not take a retired line until all hope of the French recovering ground had vanished. You did not wish me to have any more heavy casualties, as you thought the French had got us into the difficulty and ought to pull us out of it.

"You mentioned that in any combined attack I was to be careful to see that our troops did not get ahead of the French."[17]

Smith-Dorrien must have been somewhat depressed and confused as he returned to his own headquarters. Sir John had more or less agreed with his own assessment — which was hopeful — but seemed completely unwilling to take the initiative in dealing with Foch or to order a withdrawal. The French, according to Sir John, were about to make "a big effort" tomorrow and he intended to support them to the fullest, even to throwing in his last available infantry division.

On Sir Horace's return journey he passed near Ouderdom where soldiers of the Lahore Division stood about miserably in the mud. This Division was the last major unit remaining in reserve. The men were mostly veterans although one battalion of Pathans had arrived direct from Hong Kong only eighteen days ago. None of these men knew that they were already scheduled to go "over the top" at 5 p.m. tomorrow.

Some time after Sir Horace's return to Second Army Headquarters he received copies of Putz's orders. They revealed that the French attack was not to be the "big effort" spoken of by Sir John, but was to be made by one division less a brigade. Immediately afterwards another message arrived announcing that the time of attack had been advanced three hours! Smith-Dorrien was horrified and promptly got onto the telephone to the Field Marshal. He protested that the French attack was obviously too light to have any effect and it would once again involve British troops making an exhausting night-long march prior to launching an attack. Sir John was not impressed by these protests and he ordered his subordinate to proceed according to previous instructions. Tomorrow the Lahore Division must attack.

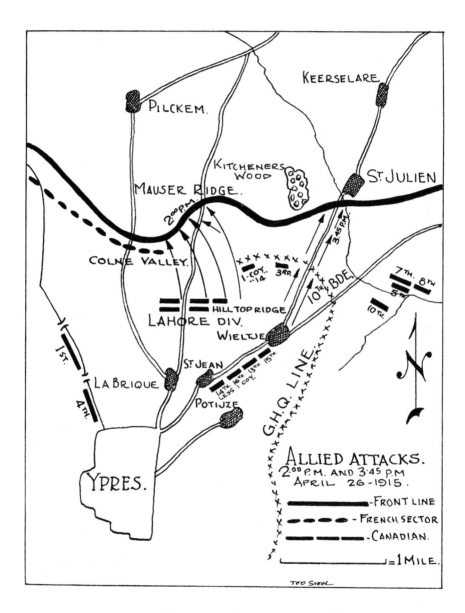

PILCKEM.

KEERSELARE

KITCHENERS WOOD

MAUSER RIDGE.

St JULIEN

2:00 P.M.

3:45 P.M.

COLNE VALLEY.

X X X X X X X X X
1-COY. 3RD.
-14.

7TH. 8TH

10TH. BDE.

5TH.

HILLTOP RIDGE

10 TH.

LAHORE DIV.

WIELTJE

1ST.

St JEAN

14TH. 16TH 13TH. 15TH.
LESS COY.

La BRIQUE

4TH.

POTIJZE

G.H.Q. LINE.

N

YPRES.

ALLIED ATTACKS.
2:00 P.M. AND 3:45 P.M
APRIL 26 -1915.

———— -FRONT LINE
- - - - - FRENCH SECTOR
– – – – -CANADIAN.
——————=1 MILE.

TED STEEL

Chapter Thirteen

Lambs to the Slaughter
(Monday, 26 April, 1915)

"He is brought as a lamb to the slaughter."
Isaiah LIII, 7

U nder a tarpaulin, in a field south of Brielen Brigadier General Turner V.C. was sound asleep as dawn broke that Monday morning. This was Turner's first opportunity for a nap in over seventy hours and he was totally exhausted. No less so were the remnants of his 3rd Brigade, scattered around him in the grassy field. They were out of the Salient at last.

"I had not been in the Land of Nod half an hour when I roused by the trample of a horse and the voice of a horseman enquiring for me," wrote Colonel Currie of the 15th. "I was up in an instant and found a staff officer looking for General Turner. I refused at first to waken him unless the matter was urgent, but when I was assured that it was, I roused him and he opened his message. It was an order to take the brigade back immediately to La Brique to go into support of the Lahore Division . . . which was to attack that afternoon."[1]

In minutes the troops, unbelievably weary, were on the road east once more, lurching back into the Salient in the last stages of exhaustion. By this time it was broad daylight and the enemy artillery enjoyed a field day shelling the shambling little column. Only their paltry numbers prevented an enormous loss of life. As it was, several direct hits blasted gaping holes in the straggling line, but onward they trudged, and none looked back.

Deeper in the Salient at Wieltje the 2nd Brigade too was being assembled in pathetic little companies to march back towards their old line. A breakthrough had been reported on the right flank of Brigadier Hasler's 11 Brigade which had only hours earlier moved into position south of Gravenstafel Ridge. Again the 2nd Brigade

181

was unlucky: they marched into the German's preliminary bombardment. "This movement was carried out under extremely heavy shell fire, the heaviest yet experienced," reported General Currie. The battered Canadians arrived to find their march in vain. The valiant 11th had not been broken, so they dug in once again behind the British troops.

But it had been a near thing. Both the 11th and the neighbouring 85th Brigade had been under severe pressure since midnight. The 1st Hampshires of the 11th Brigade held the position adjoining the new apex where their trench lay at right angles to the Berlin Wood still held by the Royal Fusiliers of the 85th Brigade. The latter had extended its line by forming an arc around the northern end of the wood, but between the two battalions lay a 400 yard gap. Into this, under cover of the heavy mist, a large group of Germans had advanced calling out, "We are the Royal Fusiliers." A Hampshire patrol had in this way been fooled and captured, but a company commander who had detected an unusual accent amongst the avowed Londers had ordered his men to open fire. This had dispersed the attackers until dawn. Since then the British line had been deluged with shell fire.

To the left of the Hampshires at Otto Farm lay a composite force known as "Auld's Detachment." This party of Suffolks, Northumberland Fusiliers, Cheshires, and Canadians had been under the command of Major Moulton-Barrett of the Cheshires until he had been wounded during the withdrawal to this point. Now the force was commanded by Captain Auld, the 2nd Northumberland Fusiliers' adjutant.

Several hundred yards away, on the northeast side of Gravenstafel Ridge the men of Sturmbrigade Schmieden were preparing to administer the *coup de grâce*. The defenders consisted of one company of the 8th Middlesex and Lt. Col. Turnbull's 8th Durham Light Infantry. These youngsters fought tenaciously along with a handful of Canadians to hold a line just east of Boetleer Farm. Outflanked on both sides, and all but overwhelmed from the front, they began their withdrawl, swinging to the south in line with the mixed British units on the Zonnebeke Ridge. The History of the Regiment Heygendorf records for 26 April, "Hand to hand fighting at Gravenstafel. The crest of the ridge taken and the new line consolidated. One Canadian officer and two men captured." By 4:30

that morning Gravenstafel Ridge was in the hands of Sturmbrigade Schmieden.

Shortly thereafter the 5th Matrosen Regiment began its assault from Locality C. They progressed down the southern slope and across the shallow Haanebeek, and by 6:30 reported themselves to be in possession of Bombarded Crossroads. This advance had been made into one of the wide gaps in the allied front, but the Matrosen Regiment had halted 700 yards from the thin line of British companies scattered almost helter-skelter between Zonnebeke Ridge and Berlin Wood. It was not a very impressive *"coup de grâce,"* but as things turned out, it was the final German advance of the April battles.

Duke Albrecht's Fourth Army had shot its bolt. All reserves had been committed and the majority of his front line troops were unspeakably weary. The allied line had been pushed back toward Ypres, and the Salient was now even more difficult for the Allies to defend, but their line was still intact and the big breakthrough had never materialized. Without further reserves Albrecht had no option but to dig in and forget about offensive action.

Two French attacks had been expected yesterday but these had both fallen through. The Territorial troops west of Lizerne had been too exhausted to move, and so much time had been expended in reorganizing the command structure that no assault had been launched. Further south and on the east side of the canal, Colonel Mordacq's *zouaves* had moved forward momentarily at noon, but this attack had been short-lived. An hour later an even less effective attempt had been made. The strength of these attacks can best be judged by their literary results—The French Official History devoted five half-lines to them, and Mordacq does not even mention them. Although Foch still spoke of massive French reinforcements, it had become evident that these would not be committed Monday—or possibly ever.

Nevertheless, the allied plan was "to press the offensive with the greatest vigour and without intermission."[2] The French were to seize Lizerne, Steenstraat and Het Sas, cross the canal, and advance on Bixchoote. Farther to the south and on the east side of the canal elements of General Joppé's 152nd Division would take Pilckem thus allowing Quiquandon to recross the Yser Canal at Boesinghe. To the right, the Lahore Division was to attack through the positions held by the Canadian Division. The former division's objective was Langemarck. To reach this the battalions must sweep over Mauser Ridge at the same spot where Geddes' Detachment and the 1st and 4th Canadians had been almost wiped out three days earlier.

There was to be no attempt at deception—just a straight-forward frontal attack on an entrenched enemy in broad daylight. The advance to the start-line would have to be carried out in plain view of the enemy who had been much strengthened in artillery. This fact had already been discovered by the exhausted men of the 2nd and 3rd Canadian Brigades that had been ordered forward after dawn. The Germans had had three days in which to bring their artillery into the captured area, dig it in, and establish order, and they had made ample use of it.

The allied artillery on the other hand was in a disorganized state. Despite the fact that more guns were available than at any other time in the past four days, the chance of successful artillery support was almost nil. The batteries most closely involved during the last few days were mixed in a wild array: of the 12 Canadian batteries, only seven were now together as units. The guns of the newly-arrived Lahore Division were still on the west side of the canal. They would have to be hurriedly sited with little attention to cover, and there was not time enough to run lines to forward observation officers. It was also impossible for these batteries to register on likely targets before the actual barrage.

It appears that only one general opposed the planned operation. Smith-Dorrien, already out of favour with Sir John French, had tried to prevent the attack from taking place. But to the generals and staff officers in the drawing rooms of exquisite chateaux thirty miles from the screaming shells, these plans looked perfectly reasonable on a map. Besides, Sir John French felt that it was necessary to appear to view matters optimistically and accept General Foch's assurances at face value. Yet his Chief of Staff, "Wully" Robertson, advised Smith-Dorrien at ten, "Attack same time as French. Secretly keep in mind not to attack before them."[3] Does this suggest that even Sir John did not expect great results from this hasty "offensive"?

At Ouderdam, four miles northwest of Ypres, the head of the

Lahore Division under Major-General H.D'U. Keary was lodged in hutments. The division had distinguished itself since the early days of the war, particularly in the hard fighting at Neuve Chapelle the previous October. The three brigades were not numbered, but bore the names of their home stations—Jullundur, Sirhind, and Ferozepore. Originally each had consisted of one British and three Indian battalions, but recently a British Territorial battalion had been added to beef up their dwindling numbers. The division had lost heavily, and because supplying reinforcements had proven difficult, the Indian battalions were well below fighting strength. Transportation too was a serious problem. Having left their own specialized mountain transport in India, the division had been forced to make do with a skimpy share of the transport available in France.

The first formation to move off for the Salient was the Ferozepore Brigade consisting of the Connaught Rangers—a battalion of wild western Irishmen—the 9th Bhopal Infantry, the 57th Wilde's Rifles, the 129th Duke of Connaught's Own Baluchis, and the 4th City of London Battalion. At 5:30 these units were *en route* to St. Jean by way of Vlamertinghe. The Ferozepore Brigade soon came under heavy artillery fire although it was fortunate and suffered few casualties.

It was not till 7:00 that the Jullundur Brigade moved off on its route along Ypres' ancient canal and thence to Wieltje. Here too the bombardment was intense, but most of the shells detonated harmlessly amongst the acres of rubble. The marching men cheered each time a shell exploded in the moat shooting up a momentary tower of sparkling water. For the 40th Pathans the sound of the "Wipers Express," as the German 'heavies' were dubbed, was a novel experience. The 40th had just arrived from Hong Kong eighteen days earlier. The Pathans had astonished citizens of Marseilles that morning by marching through the busy city headed by their band of shrill reedpipes and thumping *dhols* wailing *Les Marseilles*. Now they were marching to grimmer music through a more forbidding city.

By eleven that morning all three brigades were in place—the Ferozepore at St. Jean, the Jullundur at Wieltje, and the Sirhind in reserve southeast of St. Jean. However, the men had almost lost their Divisional Commander. General Keary's car, while threading its way through the rubble, corpses, and dead animals, had nearly been hit by a German shell. It had exploded so close that all of Keary's kit had been blasted off the roof of the vehicle. Somewhat shaken, the General made it safely to St. Jean, his advanced headquarters.

Across no man's land, 1,500 yards away atop Mauser Ridge, things were much quieter. German infantrymen made last minute preparations for the expected assault, while some rested, and others composed letters. One optimistic *feldgrau* wrote, "Very probably we are going to settle the hash of the wicked English. We are making use of a new means of fighting, against which they are simply defenceless."[4]

At 12:30 the Jullundur and Ferozepore Brigades moved out to their positions of deployment. By this time they were under steady artillery fire directed from the German scout planes circling above. Their own batteries had become easy targets for the well-hidden German guns. All ranks realized that this was going to be a very unequal artillery duel.

Farther to the west men of the 4th Moroccan Brigade had begun to cross the canal at bridges 4 and 5. They made a colorful sight in their baggy *pantalons,* blue jackets, and jaunty fezzes. This brigade, under Colonel Savy, consisted of only two regiments — the 1st Moroccan Infantry and the 8th Tirailleurs de Marche. They advanced into position behind the thin line of trenches held by a British unit, the 4th Battalion, The Rifle Brigade.

On the other side of the canal west of Lizerne and Het Sas one brigade of the 18th Division was moving into position. It also consisted of only two line regiments.

Frantic last minute activity was going on behind the allied lines. For some reason there had been a serious delay in issuing orders for the attack. Somewhere along the allied chain of command the staff work had broken down. Two examples will suffice: Brigadier Burstall, in charge of all Canadian artillery, did not receive his orders until eleven minutes after the assault had begun! Fortunately for the Lahore Division, one of their own staff officers had shown him a copy of the orders and Burstall instructed the

Canadian batteries — still just behind the line — to give close support.

The other example was much more tragic. At 1:30 that afternoon Brigadier J.F. Riddell of the 149th (Northumberland) Brigade received the following brief order from General Alderson:

"The Northumbrian (sic 'Northumberland') Brigade will attack St. Julien and advance astride of Wieltje-St. Julien road at same time as Lahore Division moves forward."

That was all — there were no instructions as to supporting fire, boundaries, or the like. What was even worse, the order arrived ten minutes *after* the preliminary bombardment had begun. Riddel had earlier that day supplied one of his battalions, the 5th Northumberland Fusiliers, to the 10th Brigade, but he hastily deployed his three remaining battalions, the 4th, 6th, and 7th battalions of the same regiment. By 1:50 they had begun moving forward along the Wieltje-St. Julien Road on a frontage of 600 yards. Although they were uninformed of the fact, the G.H.Q. Line lay a few hundred yards ahead of them with its barbed wire entanglements still intact. The main assault was to begin in ten minutes and they were still 1500 yards behind the start line with a stretch of barbed-wire to cross in the meantime.

The preliminary bombardment crashed out exactly at 1:20 p.m. and lasted forty minutes. Then at two o'clock, the moment chosen for the infantry assault to begin, all guns commenced rapid fire on the German trenches. This continued for only five minutes then lifted to form a barrage 200 yards behind the enemy line. The two Lahore Brigades had been assigned three batteries of 18 pounders and two 4.5 howitzer batteries as close support. Unfortunately the two Canadian batteries had not yet received their orders with the result that they were to do little or nothing to help the infantry during the hours that followed.

At the same moment French troops advanced to the attack in two areas — on the west side of the canal near Lizerne, and in the sector adjacent to the Lahore Divison. The northern attack by the French 153rd Division was supported by elements of the 18th Division and a battalion of Belgians.

Theirs was a long afternoon of pounding during which the Germans were pushed back a few yards although still retaining their bridgehead over the Yser Canal. At the northern tip of the Salient savage fighting by the Belgians and French eventually gained half the destroyed village of Lizerne. One hundred and fifty prisoners and five machine guns fell to the *poilus* thus raising morale somewhat. Farther south there was less progress for a small wood encircling a farm just outside of Het Sas had been so well fortified by the enemy that all attempts to capture it failed. Here the attack had been delayed till 3:00 due to problems in providing artillery support. Het Sas itself also remained in German hands.

At 2:00 east of the canal the 4th Moroccan Brigade under Colonel Savy scrambled from its trenches and advanced towards Mauser Ridge. The 1st Moroccan Infantry led the advance under a heavy barrage and a hail of machine gun bullets. The 8th Tirailleurs de Marche were echeloned to the left and slightly behind the Moroccans.

Sharp at 2:00 p.m. the Lahore Division was off. On its extreme left flank adjacent to the 4th Moroccan Brigade were the Connaught Rangers, "The Devil's Own" as they were often known. Beside them the 57th Wilde's Rifles advanced. The Frontier Force Battalion had a brilliant record as a fighting regiment stretching from the Mutiny when they stormed the Sikandarabagh, through the Afghan War, Waziristan, and the Boxer Rebellion to the 1st Battle of Ypres. On the left of the Ferozepore Brigade were the men of the 129th Baluchis. This regiment of mountaineers from the northwest frontier had been the first Indian regiment to attack the Germans, and a detachment had later held Hollebeke to the last man—one badly wounded sepoy survived to be awarded the Victoria Cross. The 129th also bore the distinction of being the only Empire unit ever to have served in Japan.

The Ferozepore Brigade pressed steadily forward up the first slope. It was moving over ground less than 1,000 yards east of the route followed by the 1st and 4th Canadian battalions three days previously and in the same area that Geddes' Detachment had attacked. Up the slope to the top of Hill Top Ridge the men strode under severe shelling. "When the troops reached the crest," wrote the Indian Corps historian, "they came under a perfect inferno of fire of all kinds, machine gun, rifle, and every variety of shell, many of which were filled with gas."[5]

Ahead lay another slope devoid of cover and stretching 500

yards, then a long glacis-like slope extended to the German trenches on the summit of Mauser Ridge. The Connaught Rangers were impeded by a series of hedges which could only be penetrated at irregular gaps. This kept the battalion back and they suffered even more severely than most when the supporting bombardment ceased. "The Devil's Own" lost their C.O., Lt. Col. Murray, and fifteen other officers before they were finally stopped 120 yards from the German line.

Beside the Irishmen Wilde's Rifles advanced steadily. Losses had been light before they crossed that fateful ridge; thereafter casualties mounted appallingly. The battalion lost 17 officers and 258 men in the assault. Captain Banks' Sikh orderly, Bahn Singh, although severely wounded in the face, had followed him faithfully. "On seeing Captain Banks fall, Bhan Singh's one thought was to bring him back, alive or dead. Weak as he was from his wound, he staggered along under appalling fire, carrying the body, until he fell from exhaustion and was forced to give up the attempt, contriving, however, to bring in the dead officer's accoutrements."[6]

The right battalion of the brigade, the 129th Baluchis, advanced slowly, but was hampered when its neighbors in the Jullundur Brigade began to bear left into its own line of attack. Soon the entire division had begun to angle towards the left. The 129th was severely mauled after they crested Hill Top Ridge, but they eventually reached the road beyond Canadian Farm 300 yards from the enemy.

The Jullundur Brigade was also suffering severely. In fact its left battalion incurred more casualties by proportion to its strength than any other that day. The 47th Sikhs, mentioned in Parliament for their valour at Neuve Chapelle, were stopped only 70 yards short of the enemy line. By that time the battalion was under command of a subaltern of only five years service, Lieutenant A.E. Drysdale. In those few moments the 47th had become a mere shadow of a battalion.

The 40th Pathans, wild and reckless Afridis from the northwest frontier, were in the centre of the Jullundur Brigade. Although recent arrivals, the "40 Thieves" as they had always been known, swung into action like veterans. Over Hill Top Ridge they swept, moving rapidly to take advantage of the supporting barrage. But on crossing the ridge they ran into a hail of bullets likened by one who went through it to "a scythe being drawn across the legs of the troops as they advanced. At one moment they were moving forward as if nothing could stop them; the next second they had simply collapsed."[7]

The "40 Thieves" machine gun detachment reached the small brook at the bottom of the slope only eight-strong. All those carrying the guns had been hit. Sepoy Muktiara volunteered to return across this bullet-swept slope to bring back one of the guns. He retrieved one by crossing 250 yards of open ground each way. Muktiara, aided by another Pathan sepoy, Haidar Ali, set the gun up and opened fire, but to their dismay they found the gun to be useless. It repeatedly jammed as a result of being immersed in a stream where the original carrier had fallen.

Meanwhile the 40th's depleted companies had pushed on by short rushes and were close to the enemy. Probably the man nearest the enemy that day was Lieutenant Thornton, the Pathans' Bombing Officer. He fell wounded forty yards from the German trench and, unable to move, was forced to lie there behind one of the many manure piles for six hours. Colonel Rennick had been mortally wounded, so Lt. Col. Hill assumed command. He bore a charmed life although saved on two occasions by a hair's breadth — one bullet cut his revolver case off his belt, and a second went through a notebook in his breast pocket — from left to right.

That battalion on the right flank of the attack was the 1st Manchester Regiment. The men moved forward in the most orderly style although within minutes most of the officers had become casualties. By the time the Manchesters were stopped, 60 yards from the enemy, most platoons and companies were under the command of Sergeants or Privates.

The front had narrowed drastically, due partly to the Jullundur Brigade's loss of direction whereby it had swung more to the left, and partly because of the extreme losses. The units were now so thin that bunching up had become inevitable. But individuals and small groups attempted desperately to come to grips with the faceless enemy on Mauser Ridge.

Lieutenant Brunskill of the 47th Sikhs spotted a group of the enemy in their round "pork-pie" hats bolting from a section of trench. He rushed forward with two privates, one a Connaught and one a Manchester. Immediately they were followed by a small party of men from various battalions.

"Between our firing line and the Germans was a ditch which Lieutenant Brunskill managed to reach in one rush," recorded one historian. "In his second rush he got forward to within a very short distance of the enemy who had now been reinforced by a new regiment wearing *pickelhaubes* (spiked leather helmets) instead of the round caps which the men who bolted were wearing. Here practically the whole party were knocked over."[8]

These masses of men advancing in broad daylight across open fields provided marvellous targets for the German gunners. The howitzers were especially effective, knocking over groups of men with each shot. The three batteries of the Guard Cavalry Division alone fired over 2,000 rounds at the Lahore Division's two brigades. The German gunners did not have it all their own way however. Situated as they were in front of Langemarck, they were enfiladed by the allied artillery at Boesinghe and lost several ammunition wagons to spectacular direct hits. Despite this inconvenience they kept up a heavy fire all afternoon, their 5.9's knocking over entire platoons of Indians and British with a single shell.

In those first twenty minutes all three brigades had gone through hell, but much worse was to come. At 2:20 men of the 4th Moroccan Brigade saw what looked like the nozzles of fire hoses being pushed over the sandbags of the German parapets a few yards away. Small puffs of white "smoke" erupted from them, but almost immediately changed to yellowish-green as the vapours billowed out.

All realized the awful truth—gas! The German infantry had begun to lose their steadiness, shaken by the ordeal of the past days and by the sight of new waves of attackers advancing relentlessly. In desperation, local commanders had ordered the gas released from a few F Batteries at this critical moment. In some cases, the enlisted men of Pionierregiment 35 had opened the valves on their own initiative. The light wind did the rest, carrying the deadly fumes across the Moroccans' front toward the battered battalions of the Lahore Division.

As that six foot high wall of death rolled towards them, men made frantic last-ditch attempts to protect themselves. Some had handkerchiefs on which they poured their precious water; others began to unwind their pagris in order to cover their faces, many were only able to press their faces into the earth and pray. Inexorably the cruel cloud rolled on. It silently engulfed the Moroccans on the left and billowed over the mixed Irish, Sikhs, Pathans and English on the slope of Mauser Ridge.

In a few minutes that slope was littered with the bodies of scores of men writhing in unspeakable torture, their faces turning first a saffron color and finally purplish as slow suffocation claimed them. The Germans, encouraged by the success of the chlorine gas, redoubled their rifle and machine gun fire as the vapour rolled on down the slope.

The allied line was forced to give way. Mixed in hopeless confusion, the soldiers from far distant corners of the earth streamed down the slope. Blue and red mixed with khaki and colorful turbans. Many stopped at the first bit of shelter they found and steadfastly remained there, but most ran, stumbling and gasping, to La Brique before it was possible to rally them.

At least one small party—only one hundred or so of all units—refused to move. Major Deacon of "The Devil's Own" remained with this collection of courageous remnants who had survived everything. The Germans surged down upon this tiny band. The fighting was vicious and at close quarters as Deacon's men, facing enormous odds, were slowly pushed down the slope. After eighty yards of this unequal retrograde struggle the Germans withdrew up the slope to their trenches. The small groups of survivors stopped right there and dug themselves in. They were to hold this exposed position in spite of repeated German attacks for another twelve hours, and they only withdrew when they were relieved.

At another spot Jemadar Mir Dast of the 57th, a veteran of the northwest frontier and holder of the Indian Order of Merit, remained in position despite the chlorine gas. His officers all having become casualties, the Jemadar collected a number of men—many of them wounded or slightly gassed—and rallied them into a defensive force which hung on till nightfall. As he listened to the terrible cries of his wounded comrades he resolved as soon as darkness fell to venture out once more and rescue them.

The Ferozepore and Jullundur Brigades had been smashed into a bloody pulp in one hour, an hour which could not be dignified with the term "battle." The slaughter had claimed 1,943 veteran British and Indian troops and had achieved nothing. Although the soldiers had suffered with incredible courage they had inflicted no losses upon their opponents and had gained no ground which could be held. Famous regiments had been all wiped out. The 47th Sikh Regiment, commended earlier in the House of Commons, now consisted of two young lieutenants and 92 sepoys. The 40th Pathans after only 18 days in France had lost twenty of their officers and 300 dusky mountain warriors in that hour. The Connaught Rangers, the wild "Devil's Own," had lost 376 men — the list went on and on.

The Moroccans too had suffered though not as severely. The three battalions of Moroccan Infantry lost two officers and fourteen killed with seven officers and 102 native soldiers being wounded. However when a count was made, another 109 men were missing. A portion of these had undoubtedly vanished behind the lines when the troops had fled, even abandoning the trenches from which they had launched their attack. Despite the obvious disorder and confusion — even panic in some cases — the Germans atop Mauser Ridge made no move to take advantage of it by advancing or even reoccupying Turco Farm.

While these terrible scenes were being enacted on the slopes of Mauser Ridge, the men of the 149th (Northumberland) Brigade were hurrying toward their start line. At approximately zero hour they filed through the handful of narrow gaps in the G.H.Q. Line. Once again they formed up in attack formation, this time under heavy shelling, and resumed their advance on St. Julien. Their route followed the Wieltje-St. Julien Road which crossed in front of the German position before Kitcheners' Wood and eventually converged with it in St. Julien. Thus they were obliged to advance in plain view *across* the enemy's front.

Although their artillery support had ceased over a quarter of an hour before, the two lines of platoons advanced gallantly. These men from the villages of Northumberland realized that theirs was the first Territorial brigade ever to attack the enemy, and they were determined to set a high standard for those who followed. At 2:45 they crossed the decimated 10th Brigade's shallow trenches and stepped into no man's land.

The three battalions of the Northumberland Fusiliers advanced with complete disregard for danger. Their ranks were cut down in swaths by machine gun fire from the buildings of St. Julien. All the while shells mushroomed viciously against the gaping ranks. These valiant Territorials never reached the enemy. Those who had escaped death dug in, forming a line of shallow rifle pits several hundred yards from the enemy. By 3:15 Brigadier Riddell erroneously reported his troops to be occupying St. Julien. He was not given the opportunity to correct this message for within minutes he was shot through the head near Vanheule Farm, almost in the front line.

The 149th Northumberland Brigade had lost in those two hours 42 officers (including their Brigadier) and 1,912 other ranks.[9] They had achieved nothing, although scores of Northumberland villages would never forget that afternoon nor the men for whom it was the last.

Along the G.H.Q. line a motley crew of Tommies and Canucks endured. There had been no further German attacks that Monday, but the incessant shelling continued. That plus the tension of waiting for another massive German attack wore down men already exhausted from days of effort, fear, and privation.

Then there occurred one of those humorous incidents which eased the strain for all. Someone chanced to look to the rear and gasped as he discovered an amazing sight. Every man in the line was soon craning his neck in silent astonishment, for mincing towards them was "a bevy of fashionable ladies and gentlemen, dressed in all sorts of finery, the former stepping daintily over ditches assisted by their companions. There were couples arm in arm, gracefully bowing to each other and to the troops, each person, lady or gentleman, carrying a pail."[10]

There was a sudden outburst of laughter as the troops began to recognize some of the stubbly, grimy faces under the finery. It was the water party of the 16th Canadian Scottish. The men had been sent back to St. Jean to try to find water for the parched troops. In that they had been unsuccessful, but they had returned with something even more welcome; each carried a pail of washy Belgian beer.

In the meantime steps had been taken to retrieve the Moroccan Brigade's lost trenches. By late afternoon the 4th Chasseurs (from Mordacq's force) had retaken Turco Farm without difficulty. The 4th Moroccan Brigade was then ordered to exploit this success by advancing once again and seizing their abandoned trenches. This time all three battalions of the 8th Tirailleurs (Algerian) would carry out the attack. The Lahore Division therefore made preparations to co-operate. Because the Jullundur Brigade had suffered so heavily, three battalions were brought up from the Sirhind Brigade—the 1st Highland Light Infantry, the 1st Battalion, 4th Gurkha Rifles, and the 15th Ludhiana Sikhs. The latter battalion, the first Indian troops ever to set foot in France, advanced on the left. To their right the 4th Gurkha Rifles moved quietly forward. "Streams of wounded and gassed men were encountered on the way, the blackened and swollen faces and protruding eyes of the latter giving evidence of the torture to which they had been subjected,"[11] wrote the Corps historian. Overhead could be heard the screaming, roaring sound of numerous "Wipers Express" hurtling towards the ruins of Ypres.

So at seven the Tirailleurs advanced "with such noise and shouting that they drew early fire."[12] The dusky warriors continued on till they came nearly abreast of the Lahore Division's remnants. "When our troops approached the enemy trenches new clouds of chlorine descended upon them and stopped our forward movement," reported their war diary. "The wind, stronger than in the afternoon, and having changed direction, caused the gas to be carried towards the southwest and affected our troops less enabling them to remain in all their positions."[13]

Consequently, by nightfall, the allied line was back where it had begun the day. But darkness was the chance to relieve the exhausted and to regain the initiative. With this in mind, the three Sirhind battalions stole across the corpse-strewn valley of death. The Ludhiana Sikhs, the 4th Gurkhas, and the famous Highland Light Infantry were advancing up Mauser Ridge to the attack.

"The night was fine and clear, but by this time it was quite dark, and the air was sickly with the smell of chlorine from the German gas, the effects of which were felt as far as Poperinghe, seven miles west of Ypres. Communication from the front line had been so scanty, owing to telephone wires being continually cut by shells, that even at this late period of the day the position of the enemy was not known to the regiments not actually engaged in the attack.

"After much wandering in the dark, the Sikhs and Gurkhas under Lt. Col. J. Hill, D.S.O., arrived at a point on the right of the French, who had by this time been reinforced. Inquiry was then made from the officer commanding the French, but even he was unable to give any information.

"The attack was halted, and officers went forward to attempt to ascertain the situation. At last a man of the Manchesters was met, who led Colonel Hill to a trench where he found the battered remnants of the gallant little body of men under Major Deacon, still holding on amidst their dead and wounded."[14]

When Hill learned the true state of affairs he reported to Brigadier Egerton of the Ferozepore Brigade. It was decided that the planned night attack through the uncut German wire was not feasible. Therefore Hill's men dug in to the right of Major Deacon's survivors with the assistance of the 34th Sikh Pioneers, the divisional labour force. At 2:30 in the morning a part of the Highland Light Infantry under Captain Tarrant relieved Deacon's mixed force. All through that night a precarious trench line was being scraped out on the slopes of Mauser Ridge.

Meanwhile, nightfall had enabled scores of shadowy figures — in small knots and singly — to slip out upon the grim hillside on errands of mercy. They willingly took their lives in their hands, for the jittery enemy shot up a constant volley of flares, flooding no man's land with their pale glare. Every movement attracted a nervous burst of machine gun fire. One of these shadowy figures was Jemadar Mir Dast of the 57th who left the small section of trench he had earlier organized as a defensive position. During that long night of suffering the Jemadar brought in eight wounded officers, British and Indian both, although during one of these forays he was himself wounded. Among those he found unconscious from the effects of gas was Havildar (Sergeant) Mangal Singh. On recovering consciousness, this hardy Sikh, despite intense suffering from the gas, returned time and time again to bring in other wounded men all the while under enemy fire.

There were others out that night on the slopes of Mauser Ridge. Two Royal Engineers, Captain E.H. Kisch and Captain F.P. Nosworthy moved cautiously across the face of the enemy line, freezing motionless each time a German flare shot up to dazzle the night. While the machine guns searched the interminable slopes of no man's land these two crawled to within a few yards of the German trenches to draw sketch maps of their position. Nosworthy had already been gassed and badly shaken by a shell but he stayed out almost till dawn to complete his work. When Kisch returned that morning he was found to be wounded. Nevertheless, he remained on duty till the next night.

On the other side of the corpse-strewn swath of no man's land the *feldgrau* were almost on the verge of collapse. On several occasions that afternoon troops had even fled in the face of advancing allied troops. The obvious fact that the French and British were suffering much worse, did not alleviate their own suffering nor raise their spirits. After the French had retaken part of Lizerne that afternoon the 204th Reserve Infantry Regiment was ordered to counter attack and recapture the ruins. The regiment refused even to attempt it. "The infantry again evidently lacks the right offensive spirit," lamented the XXIII Reserve Corps' War Diary—no doubt compiled by some staff officer, safe and comfortable, miles from the Salient.

Meanwhile, for the front-line soldiers, the hours of darkness brought stealthy movement and strenuous work. Rudolph Binding spent Monday night retrieving three guns not more than five hundred yards from the allied line. "We were all night on the job, constantly interrupted by furious bursts of fire and by the Verey lights, which obliged us to lie flat as long as they were burning. Before dawn we got all three guns into safety, together with their limbers and ammunition. One of my men was shot through the heart because he tried to bring back a sucking-pig which he found squeaking in its lonely pen. He sat on top of one of the limbers, while his comrades put their shoulders to the wheels. Suddenly he fell lifeless between the wheels, still holding the little pig in the grip of death.

"After fresh attacks a sleeping army lies in front of one of our brigades; they rest in good order, man by man, and will never wake again—Canadian divisions (sic). The enemy's losses are enormous."[15]

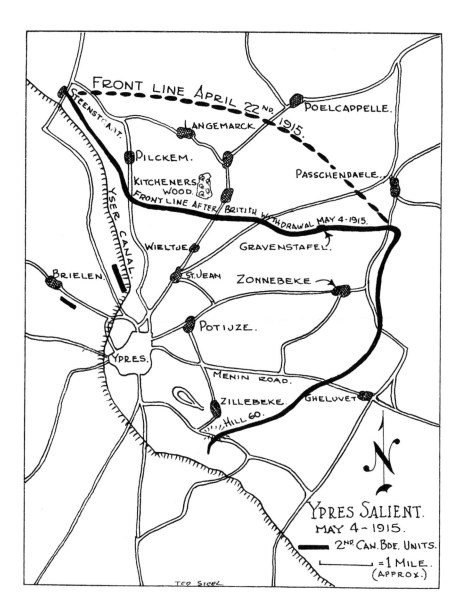

FRONT LINE APRIL 22ND. 1915.

POELCAPPELLE.

STEENSTRAAT.

LANGEMARCK.

PILCKEM.

PASSCHENDAELE.

KITCHENERS WOOD.

FRONT LINE AFTER BRITISH WITHDRAWAL MAY 4-1915.

YSER CANAL.

WIELTJE.

GRAVENSTAFEL.

BRIELEN.

ST. JEAN.

ZONNEBEKE.

POTIJZE.

YPRES.

MENIN ROAD.

ZILLEBEKE.

GHELUVET.

HILL 60.

N

YPRES SALIENT.
MAY 4 - 1915.
2ND. CAN. BDE. UNITS.
⊢──────⊣ = 1 MILE.
(APPROX.)

TED STEEL

Chapter Fourteen

A Cry from the Wilderness
(Tuesday, 27 April, 1915)

*"The voice of him that crieth in the
wilderness."*

Isaiah XL, 3

L ate Tuesday morning, Sir Horace Smith-Dorrien sat down
to write a long letter to Sir John French's Chief of Staff. It
was, in the words of his biographer, "a thoroughly competent, professional assessment of some very hard facts." Smith-Dorrien had
the night before received a copy of General Putz's orders for the
repetition of yesterday's tragic attack. He was "horrified to see" the
light weight of the French attack. Despite Foch's talk of divisions,
only three additional battalions were actually to be engaged:

"I need hardly say that I at once represented the matter pretty
strongly to General Putz, but I want the Chief to know this as I do
not think he must expect that the French are going to do anything
very great—in fact although I have ordered the Lahore Division to
co-operate when the French attack at 1:15 p.m., I am pretty sure
that our line tonight will not be in advance of where it is at present
moment.

"I fear the Lahore Division have had heavy casualties and so,
they tell me, have the Northumbrians, and I am doubtful whether it
is worth losing any more men to regain this French ground unless
the French do something really big.

"Now, if you look at the map, you will find the line the French
and ourselves are now on allows the Germans to approach so close
with their guns that the area East of Ypres will be very difficult to
hold, chiefly because the roads approaching it from the west are
swept by shell-fire, and were all yesterday and are being today . . .

"If the French are not going to make a big push, the only line

199

we can hold permanently and have a fair chance of keeping supplied would be that passing just East of Wieljie (sic) and Potijze (the G.H.Q. Line) to join our present line about 1,000 yards North East of Hill 60.

"This, of course, means the surrendering of a great deal of trench line, but any intermediate line, short of that, will be extremely difficult to hold."

While Smith-Dorrien waited for a reply to this telling argument against proceeding with the attack, events moved inexorably on.

The plan for the renewed allied attack was identical in outline to the previous day's. The only changes were in personnel: the shattered battalions from the previous day had been replaced by fresher ones, albeit there were fewer of them today. The Lahore Division was to advance over the same ground as before, the Sirhind Brigade in touch with the French right and the Ferozepore Brigade prolonging the line to the east. West of the Ypres-Pilckem Road General Joppé's mixed force was to advance with the 4th Moroccan Brigade beside the Sirhind, a brigade from the 18th Division in the centre, and Mordacq's *zouaves* on the left beside the canal.

At 12:40 the allied bombardment opened up. The Ferozepore Brigade which had endured the same thing yesterday, was situated well to the right rear of the Sirhind Brigade. Therefore they moved off immediately so as to arrive in line with the later brigade by 1:15 at which time the guns would lift onto the Germans' second line.

However, Brigadier Walker, commanding the Sirhind Brigade, ordered his battalions to advance at the same time thus putting his men well in advance of the allied attack line. To Walker it seemed better to face the risk of outdistancing the troops on his flanks than to run out of artillery support at the critical moment.

Well to the front of the Sirhind Brigade, only 100 yards from the enemy was B Company of the Highland Light Infantry under Captain Tarrant. They still occupied the exposed position held since yesterday afternoon by Major Deacon's mixed force.

The Sirhind Brigade moved forward over the ground littered with the dead of the Jullundur Brigade. On the left next to the French the 1st Battalion 1st (King George's Own) Gurkha Rifles advanced under Lt. Col. W.C. Anderson. Beside them came another

Gurkha battalion, the 1st Battalion, 4th Gurkha Rifles commanded by Major Brodhurst who was killed almost immediately. The Gurkhas were favourite comrades of the British soldier. Small, sturdy mountaineers from Nepal, they were known for their incredible courage and never-failing good humour. Their favourite weapon was the *kukri*, a broad curved knife, about which a host of legends had already accumulated. Behind the Gurkhas, in support, were the remaining companies of the Highland Light Infantry, the 15th Ludhiana Sikhs and the 4th Special Reserve Battalion, The King's Regiment (Liverpool).

Thus, on a two battalion front the Sirhind Brigade advanced towards Hill Top Ridge and the inferno beyond. One who watched them was Lieutenant Stan Lovelace of the 9th Canadian Battery. He had been serving as a forward observation officer in a farm since early morning. "I witnessed a very exciting charge by the Gurkha troops," he wrote in his diary. "They started from somewhere near my observing station and moved quickly in groups of about a dozen to rush forward then drop. Then a rush to the right or the left and on about 500 yards over a slight ridge. What wonderful little men!"

Over the crest of Hill Top Ridge went the Gurkhas and immediately a severe frontal crossfire opened upon them from several directions. The German artillery had registered on every likely spot of cover and their shells rained down with devastating accuracy.

On the left, the 1st Gurkha Rifles had by now passed a battery of French guns abandoned almost five days ago. These were later recovered during the hours of darkness—possibly the only success achieved by Tuesday's attack. Despite the courage of the little mountaineers only thirty, under three officers, reached Canadian Farm at the bottom of Mauser Ridge. The remainder of the Sirhind's attackers lay dead, wounded, or pinned down along the deadly slope before the German line.

Reduced to 38 British officers and only 1,648 men, the Brigade now equalled less than two battalions. The three Indian battalions together totalled only 688 rifles. Today the battalion on the right was the 9th Bhopal Infantry, the "Bo-Peeps" to their comrades. This unit had already lost heavily during its service in France, and as it had no linked battalion from which to draw reserves, the 9th was badly depleted.

The 4th City of London Regiment made up the left of the line.

In support, the battered Connaught Rangers followed 400 yards behind the Bhopals. The Ferozepore's two other battalions, the 57th Wilde's Rifles and the 129th Baluchis Regiment were in Brigade Reserve, mere skeletons as a result of yesterday's attack.

Both of Ferozepore's front line battalions suffered badly in those few minutes. The Bhopals lost 122 men, and one company of the 4th Londons was reduced to a mere thirty men. The Londons' machine gun section was so badly hit that only one gun reached the front line and that was handled by the Machine Gun Officer, 2nd Lieutenant Pyper.

Meanwhile there seemed to be little activity west of the Ypres-Pilckem Road. The French troops did not begin their advance till 2:00. By now General Joppé had under his command a very mixed force. Next to the Lahore Division was his own 4th Moroccan Brigade with the 8th Tirailleurs in front supported by the 1st Moroccan Infantry. In the centre he had a brigade from the 18th Division—the 66th Infantry Regiment supported by the 32nd. Joppé's left was made up of the 2nd and 7th Zouaves (45th Algerian Division) from Mordacq's Detachment. Attempts to co-ordinate this jury-built operation with such a motley force were almost futile.

What really took place that afternoon will probably never be satisfactorily explained. The War Diary of Joppé's 152nd Division records: "After a strong preparation by the artillery, the Moroccan Brigade at 2:00 advanced to the attack, but it was stopped and even gave way like the left of the Lahore Division (English) and the right of Mordacq's Detachment, due to the release of asphyxiating gas. The troops were driven back, regaining the trenches which they had left."[1] However, the history of the Lahore Division makes no mention of gas at this time, and certainly it did not "give way" as stated by Joppé.

The diary of the 4th Moroccan Brigade clouds the picture even further. "After a violent bombardment of the enemy trenches, the battalions of the first line advanced by infiltrating *(en s'enfiltrant)* towards the enemy. The advance was difficult and very slow due to the presence of German machine gun fire which beat all over the ground in front."[2] No other entry appears till 5:30 and there is no mention of gas or of a retreat. Yet the entry certainly does not suggest an advance of any significance.

The British Official History dismisses the French portion of the early afternoon attack almost unconsciously in one sentence: "The French pinned to the ground by a heavy barrage put down on their infantry in its position of assembly did not make an attack."[3] Certainly, if there was a French attack towards Mauser Ridge at 2:00 that afternoon, it made no impression, either on friend or on foe.

The attack had come to a standstill well short of its objectives and after a tragic loss of life. Once more, the valley between Hill Top and Mauser Ridges echoed to the screams and moans of torn, wounded men, suffering to no purpose.

Shortly after the assault had commenced Smith-Dorrien had received a telephone call. It was Sir John French's reply to his letter of that morning and the speaker was the C.G.S., "Wully" Robertson. The message, annotated at 2:15 p.m., was tersely recorded by Robertson in his own handwriting:

"Chief does not regard situation nearly so unfavourable as your letter represents. He thinks you have abundance of troops and especially notes the large reserves you have. He wishes you to act vigorously with the full means available in co-operation with and assisting the French attack having due regard to his previous instructions that the combined attack should be simultaneous. The French possession of Lizerne and general situation on Canal seems to remove anxiety as to your left flank.

Letter follows by Staff Officer."

Reluctantly following these telephoned instructions (the letter mentioned above was never sent), Smith-Dorrien was forced to order his friend "Daddy" Plumer, to press the attack with vigour.

Plumer faced a very difficult decision. He had no infantry formations left so he had been forced to create a scratch force of decimated British battalions by scraping together all of his V Corps' reserve units. This "brigade" which had been put under command of the senior colonel was now given orders to attack at 6:30 that evening.

In the meantime the French had at last recaptured Lizerne, the farthest west position held by the Germans. General Codet, the commander in that sector had achieved this with various units, none of which were from his own 45th Algerian Division. A total of 100 Germans had become prisoners and one machine gun and one "bomb thrower" had been taken by the *poilus*. It was not much, but it was the first encouraging sign in a day of tragedy. It buoyed up the ever-optimistic Foch to the point that at four he sent a wildly optimistic (if not downright dishonest) report to Joffre. After listing the modest booty taken — both Monday's and Tuesday's — he blandly stated, "To the north of Mooslede Farm [there was no such place — possibly he was refering to Turco Farm which the French referred to as Mortleje Farm] on the west of the Ypres-Langemarck Road, the attack is reported to have advanced several hundred metres, and to be moving forward. The English are reported to have got into Bois des Cuisiniers [Kitcheners' Wood]."[4]

At this very moment the Sirhind Brigade's last reserves were being thrown in to get the attack moving once more. Behind the remnants of the 4th Gurkhas, now pinned down by deadly fire, the 4th King's Liverpools were advancing in short rushes, taking advantage of every suggestion of cover. These reservists were cut down in writhing heaps. Only one small party under Major Beall managed to get within two hundred yards of the enemy line. Here they discovered that the German barbed wire was still intact; there was no way to come to grips with the enemy. The Liverpools' heroic but futile gesture had cost 383 casualties.

By this time Colonel H.D. Tuson of the 2nd Duke of Cornwall's Light Infantry had moved forward to discover if there was sufficient space between the German lines and the survivors of the Lahore Division to allow for preliminary bombardment before his scratch "brigade" made its attack. At 4:25 a report arrived from the Sirhind Brigade announcing that a bombardment was feasible. In the meantime, Tuson's "brigade" was being brought together behind him. It was a sorry assault force — 260 men from his own 2nd D.C.L.I., 280 from the 1st York and Lancasters, 400 from the 5th King's Own, and the 350 men who now constituted the 2nd Duke of Wellington's Regiment. This scratch force of 1,290 battered and weary warriors was to be thrown against Mauser Ridge. Without a staff, or any ancillary troops, without a plan or any reconnaisance, Tuson was ordered to lead these men in an attack on a position which had in two afternoons destroyed an entire division.

As these final tragic preparations were being completed a telegraphed message arrived at Smith-Dorrien's Headquarters. It had been sent *en clair,* meaning that all operators who heard it in transmission now knew its contents. Its message was brutal and blunt:

"Chief directs you to hand over forthwith to General Plumer the command of all troops engaged in the present operations about Ypres."

This message was staggering, but Smith-Dorrien's humiliation was not yet complete. He was also ordered to turn over his staff to Plumer, who was instructed to deal directly with Sir John in future.

At 5:30 the preliminary bombardment opened up once more upon Mauser Ridge. Two battalions of the Sirhind Brigade, not waiting for Tuson's composite force, pressed forward to the attack under cover of the fire. The Highland Light Infantry advanced steadily to relieve its B Company still in position 100 yards from the German line. It was feared that Captain Tarrant's men must have been overwhelmed by now, but this was not the case. Despite the terrible ordeal which they had gone through all that day, the highlanders had refused to give up their isolated outpost even when Tarrant himself was killed.

The 15th Ludhiana Sikhs were also on the move. They had managed to assemble behind a strong earthwork which had once sheltered a battery of French guns. The moment the Sikhs broke from this cover an incredible crossfire caught them and shrapnel rained down with increased fury. In moments the battalion was reduced to less than 400 men.

On the left General Joppé's native infantry had already commenced their assault. Great holes were torn in the lines of colorfully-garbed North Africans as they moved towards Mauser Ridge. When their ragged waves neared the objective a deluge of gas shells burst amongst them. Panic tore the force asunder, and "in the mysterious way that bad news travels in battle"[5] word flashed along the line. "Gas! The Turcos are running away!" These rumours were almost immediately verified by the terrible spectacle which ensued on the banks of the canal. Mobs of Colonials easily identified by their flamboyant uniforms could be seen and heard screeching and wailing as they desperately fought their way across the canal bridges. In vain their officers attempted to stem the tide of fugitives.

It is difficult to determine how the rout ended. The War Diary of the 4th Moroccan Brigade ignores the facts by blandly stating: "The troops were obliged to regain their first line trenches under enemy machine gun fire,"[6] The French Official History admits that the asphyxiating gas "forced them to withdraw to the south of the jumping off place. The situation was re-established by the intervention of local reserves." The British Official History goes a step or two further. It states that General Putz appealed to V Corps for a brigade of British cavalry "to stem their flight.'"[7] Rumour, as may be expected, was much less reticent and told of looting and raping behind the lines and of the murder of officers who tried to halt the rabble.

Whatever the truth, the result was clear. Too much had been asked of too few for too long. Exhausted and demoralized as they were, ordered to attack without adequate support and in the absence of cover, the men of several lands had, each in his own manner, at last refused to throw their lives away to no purpose. The entire attack collapsed, as even the British and Indians went to ground to await darkness.

That night while wounded Gurkhas, Englishmen, Scots, Sikhs, Frenchmen, Moroccans, and Algerians were being carried off the slopes of Mauser Ridge, a German soldier was writing in his diary:

"The Battlefield is fearful. One is overcome by a peculiar sour, heavy, and penetrating smell of corpses. Rising over a plank bridge you find that its middle is supported only by the body of a long-dead horse. Men that were killed last October lie half in swamp and half in yellow sprouting beet-fields. The legs of an Englishman, still encased in puttees, stick out into a trench, the corpse being built into the parapet; a soldier hangs his rifle on them. A little brook runs through the trench, and everyone uses the water for drinking and washing; it is the only water they have. Nobody minds the pale Englishman who is rotting away a few steps farther up. In Langemarck cemetery a hecatomb had been piled up; for the dead must have lain above ground level. German shells falling into it started a horrible resurrection. At one point I saw twenty-two dead horses, still harnessed, accompanied by a few dead drivers. Cattle and pigs lie about, half-rotten; broken trees, avenues razed to the ground; crater upon crater in the roads and in the fields."[8]

That evening the troops who had first stemmed the tide were finally withdrawn. The Canadian Division was ordered back into reserve after six days of constant fighting and shelling, and twelve days in the front line. The Division, now only 5,000 strong, had become world famous in those few days. When 22 April had dawned the Canadians had been thought of as undisciplined and unsoldierly; now they were on their way to achieving a reputation second to none. As the infantry trudged silently to the rear, senior officers noted that many of the men no longer carried Ross rifles. A later count revealed that 1,452 of those who survived had armed themselves with discarded Lee-Enfields.

As the pathetic columns trickled eastward the men were astounded by the scenes of destruction. The last time they had seen Ypres it had been a bustling city of cafes, historic buildings, and colorful uniforms. "What a change from the place we had marched through a week before," noted Tom Drummond of the Little Black Devils. "Whole rows of houses were flattened, bodies of the citizens, women and children as well as men, lay where they had fallen, some still clutching their few pitiful possessions with which they had attempted to flee. Holes large enough to hold a couple of Greyhound buses were in many of the streets. Everywhere, it seemed, there were dead and wounded awaiting attention. Troops were passing to and fro and a few civilians were still about, carting their possessions on baby carriages, barrows, dog-carts, or carrying them on their shoulders. These became thicker as the outskirts were again reached and the roads for miles beyond were black with humanity; troops going forward, civilians going back. A regiment of French *currasiers* in the ancient uniform of breastplate and red trousers lined the road at one place. It was evident that the bottom of the manpower barrel had been reached."

And so Tuesday, 27 April, 1915, passed into history. The chance for either side to gain any kind of victory out of the battle passed with it. Gone too were the young men in field-grey, in blue, and in khaki—the best manhood of many lands. For years to come, the name "Ypres" would echo with a proud melancholy in far away corners of the earth — in the mountains of Nepal; the Punjabi plains; the rugged Hindu Kush; the Algerian deserts; and the endless frontiers of Canada. The Second Battle of Ypres continued officially till 31 May, 1915, but its outcome had already been decided by these young men and the generals who had led and misled them.

Epilogue

The Whirlwind

*"They have sown the wind and they shall reap
the whirlwind."*

Hosea VIII, 7

For future historians, at least, the Second Battle of Ypres was now over, though it would drag on without decision till the end of May when it finally passed into legend. The Germans had lost their chance for victory as early as the third day. The Allies, after avoiding almost certain defeat, had in turn thrown away their chances of regaining the lost ground.

By 27 April Foch had lost interest in the Salient. He no longer promised reinforcements but insisted that the forces on the spot were sufficient "to proceed with the affair and to resolve it." He had long planned an offensive near Arras, and now this new prospect of success had pushed the sad affair of the Salient into the background.

Sir John French, for his part, issued preliminary orders for a withdrawal less than eighteen hours after he had relieved Smith-Dorrien, ostensibly for suggesting that very thing.

During the next six days Sir John and Foch held many meetings. Foch made a daily promise of major French attacks although none ever materialized. Sir John continued to talk of withdrawal without actually withdrawing. Foch hoped to keep the British, if not in constant attack, then at least in a threatening attitude till 6 May when his own grand offensive near Arras would have begun. He confided in a letter to his superior, Joffre, "In my memo to the Field Marshal I have painted the picture of the consequences of withdrawal blacker than they appear to me — because the fact is that the enemy is not very noxious except with his gas — and we know all about that now."

Five nights after the Lahore Division's final assault the British withdrew up to 4,500 yards. The retirement was not a text-book affair; it was clumsy and costly. The new line was something of a compromise and thus had many faults. Smith-Dorrien and others had hoped for a withdrawal all the way back to the canal, thereby eliminating the Salient completely; Foch, of course, was opposed on principal to any withdrawal. The resulting contraction was in the words of one historian, "a miserably cramped and shallow bulge, dug in on the reverse slopes of ridges that gave the Germans perfect observation of the whole area and 'a permanent target for artillery practice for the next three years.' "[1]

All this time Sir Horace Smith-Dorrien, a spectator commanding a solitary corps, watched as his recommendations were carried out in an indecisive and costly manner. Although he was the senior Army Commander, almost all of his force was now under the command of his subordinate and had been designated "Plumer's Force" by Sir John. The situation embarrassed his two old friends, 'Daddy' Plumer and 'Wully' Robertson, and not least of all himself. On 6 May Sir Horace suggested that he be transferred to another command as he evidently did not have the confidence of his Commander-in-Chief. That night he was visited by Sir John's Chief of Staff, the awkwardly blunt 'Wully' Robertson. His old friend took him aside and gruffly blurted out, " 'Orace, you're for 'ome."[2]

Sir John French had at last gotten rid of the man whom he had most resented, the one man, incidentally, who had tried to prevent the destruction of so many fine battalions in the hopeless attacks of the last week.

In later years many questions were asked about the conduct of the Second Battle of Ypres, as it was officially designated. Probably the most searching were those asked by the historian, Captain Basil Liddell-Hart. His first crucial query was, "Why did the gas come as so complete a surprise?"[3] Only one general, Ferry, whose 11th French Division had captured the two deserters, accepted the deserters' stories at face value. The others considered him a credulous fool and ignored other ever more convincing evidence. Why?

The answers will never be fully known but several points seem quite obvious. Ferry was the general who would have been most involved had the attack not been postponed due to lack of a favourable wind. To him, any threat to his troops had to be taken in deadly earnest. To those above him, ensconced in luxury far from the front, attack by poison gas appeared to be a fantasy, the unfounded alarms of a panicky subordinate. Besides, using poison gas as a weapon would not be at all sporting. The fact that Ferry's division was a rather sloppy and unimpressive formation (as judged by their trench conditions, discipline, and morale) also spoke against him. That no other divisional commander accepted the evidence seems to be the result of years of training. Superiors, no matter how mediocre, were treated as being almost omniscient. If Foch and Sir John found nothing to be alarmed about there seemed little cause for concern by their subordinates.

In retrospect it is always easy to find fault, yet the generals' complete blanking out process seems incredible. By 16 April several interlocking pieces of evidence had corroborated one another—Lucieto's espionage coup; the two deserters' stories; their gas masks; the three red flares on 13 April; and the Belgian agent's warning to expect the attack on 16 April *providing the wind was favourable.** The wind was not favourable, but this fact was not a military secret; it was obvious to soldiers on both sides of the line. Why then was no further attention paid to this startling chain of information and evidence? What harm could possibly have been done to the allied cause by heeding it even it if had been a clever German ruse? The primitive gas masks carried by the deserters were not investigated or copied by any allied general from the Commanders-in-Chief down to brigadier. Gauze or cotton waste was easily obtained yet no general made a move to provide such protection for his troops although it was obvious the enemy already had done so.

Probably the most convincing argument against an imminent attack was the obvious lack of preparation by the Germans. After all, who had ever heard of a major attack without huge reinforcements and a massive artillery preparation? Allied air reconnaissance had revealed that the enemy had not been bringing up the extra divisions usually required to launch an offensive. Therefore, reasoned the generals, there was obviously no possibility of an attack. This, plus the attitude that one's superior knows best, prevented the Allies from taking preventive measures.

---

* Authors' italics.

What preventive measures could have been employed in any case? General Ferry's orders to shell the German line in an attempt to break open the gas cylinders was the first step. The second would have been his order to thin out the defenders in the front line by taking the bulk of the troops back to reserve positions. Another expedient would have been to equip the troops, or at least those remaining in the front line, with "gas masks" patterned on those taken from the two deserters. The latter step would have involved some simple laboratory testing such as might be done in any high school today. This could have been difficult to carry out in the circumstances of the times and the place, yet it would have been entirely possible if judged urgent. *After* the attack British Headquarters acted efficiently, and by 26 April, while the Jullundur and Ferozepore brigades were being cut to pieces, an experimental laboratory was being put together at G.H.Q. Within three days it had been staffed with chemists.

Was it known beforehand that the poison gas was chlorine? It is difficult to believe that "the French Ace," Lucieto, would risk his life to report something as vague as "poison gas," particularly as he was at the time working in the centre where the chlorine was produced. Therefore it seems reasonable to assume that the French, at least, had been informed of the nature of the gas cloud. Consequently, defensive measures would have become comparatively simple. It was relatively common knowledge that chlorine gas is water soluble. Therefore, reasonable protection could have been provided for at least the nose, mouth and lungs by a wet cloth. However, the failure of allied intelligence assessments to tie together Charles Lucieto's reports on the gas manufactured in Mannheim with front line reports of possible German attacks employing gas nullified a fairly simple, if temporary, solution.

Liddell-Hart's second crucial question is equally thought-provoking: "Why did the Germans fail to exploit such a surprise?"[4] Tactically, the German operations suffered, at least in the initial stages, from the men's lack of confidence in the chlorine gas cloud. On 22 April the troops had not followed close behind the gas cloud and they had underestimated the catastrophic effect it had had on the 45th Algerian and the 87th Territorial Divisions. Due to the lateness of the attack, caused by the nature of the gas cloud itself, failing light had prevented the attacking units from realizing the true situation. Thus after an almost effortless advance of over two miles they had stopped in front of an enormous gap and dug in to repel an attack from non-existent allied troops. All ranks had, of course, become conditioned to defensive tactics, and little aggressive patrolling had been carried out to tear away the veils of night.

On each succeeding day the Germans' chances of success had dwindled. During the first evening Ypres had been theirs for the taking; on the second day a fast assault through the scattered companies of British and Canadians would have taken the old city; on the third day the Germans attempted to swing more to the east and take St. Julien — this they achieved but only after the bitterest struggle. After that savage Saturday, Duke Albrecht's men had lost any real hope of taking Ypres, let alone of cutting through to the Channel ports as their purpose was believed to have been. The latter threat was the great fear of the defenders although it never seems to have entered German thinking at all. Certainly such a success would have overturned the war situation completely, giving the Germans a better bargaining position if peace negotiations could be held.

However, the net result of the German effort — besides enormous casualties and untold suffering — was a smaller Salient. In the first *hour* of the attack they had achieved over two miles and had created a four mile hole in the Allies' line at its most delicate spot — the junction of three allied armies. Ypres had been within sight from Turco Farm, a two mile stroll across deserted fields. Yet ten days later although they had advanced a few hundred yards farther on their left flank, Ypres itself was not a yard closer.

The German tactics were basically centuries-old siege tactics. Short advances were made after very careful preparation to a predetermined line. Each of these steps resulted in a new parallel and a contracted enemy perimeter. Possibly Duke Albrecht and his subordinates felt this cautious approach was necessary due to the low numbers and indifferent morale of their men. Success in such a siege operation inevitably depends on the artillery, and in this, the Germans certainly held an enormous advantage. On each and every day of the battle the Allies had faced their opponents' artillery with rifles — and in the Canadians' case, with rifles which were almost useless. As the British Official History points out, the Allies "were driven back by overwhelming artillery fire, with the *assistance* from time to time of further discharges of gas, although shell fire was throughout the determining force."[5] The gas cloud had been used merely to trigger the operation; after that first success it had failed to affect the outcome of the struggle.

From a strategic point of view the failure of the German thrust had been almost assured by the lack of reserves. This lack meant that the attack was bound to run out of steam quite early although not nearly so soon as it actually did. Ironically, the failure to exploit the success of the gas cloud was based on the nature of the gas cloud itself. Falkenhayn was certainly justified in not banking too much upon the attack because any reserves allotted for the operation would have had to wait for days, possibly even weeks, for the right wind. Such reserves could not have been long hidden from the Allies and would have in all probability suffered enormous casualties from artillery fire, without an attack ever having taken place.

Because of previous failures in using gas the German High Command had lost faith in their new weapon. These failures had been caused by the use of ineffective gasses developed by the scientists. They had wasted thousands of precious artillery shells resulting in a decision to cease discharging gas by means of shells. This decision had taken place at about the same time that Fritz Haber had developed an effective asphyxiating agent. Thus at the moment chlorine gas shells would have given them overwhelming superiority, the Germans were employing the relatively inefficent cloud form while shooting over the unsuccessful xylyl bromide in "T" shells.

The German scientists themselves however had made a colossal blunder. They had overlooked the fact that prevailing winds along the front were westerly and blew from the allied lines *across the German lines*. In the words of Liddell-Hart, "the Germans thus offered a hostage to fortune. Disclosing their new weapon prematurely and for a paltry prize, they gave their opponents the advantage in retaliation."[6]

The final of Liddell-Hart's three questions is the most difficult to answer. "Why did the British escape disaster when taken unawares by the French collapse and yet suffer so disproportionately when the Germans had forfeited their advantage?"[7]

The answer to the first part of that question is simple enough. The British somehow escaped disaster because of the incredible courage and determination of the common soldier — Canadian, and later, British. From the vantage point of seventy-odd years it is difficult to comprehend the reverence for "duty" felt by these men. It was, they believed, their duty to hold on, even if death was the inevitable result; their duty was simple and they would do it whatever the cost. Yet these ordinary fellows, recent civilians from the unsophisticated cities of Canada and its lonely frontiers, were embarrassed to talk of duty and courage. "We mustn't boast much because it wasn't heroism that made us stay there and fight through that battle. We just did not know how to get out," said Major Odlum much later. "We were out at the end of the Salient. Everything was happening and we couldn't get information. The only thing to do as far as we could see was just stay where we were. And we did."[8] Said another, "No one had any idea of getting out. We didn't know enough about it to know that we were licked. We went in there and we were going to stay there, and that was that."[9] No general and few colonels had anything to do with the magnificent stand. Second Ypres will endure as a monument to the sublime courage of the common man.

British casualties had been heavy during the first three days while the problem had been crucial, yet the bulk of their casualties had been suffered in fruitless counterattacks on the succeeding days—*after* the danger of the German breakthrough had all but vanished. Of six such counterattacks only one had succeeded in coming to close quarters with the enemy. That was the first attempt, the midnight attack by the 10th Canadians and the 16th Canadian Scottish. It, of course, had failed despite the soldier's victory over his German counterpart. After driving out the enemy by sheer determination, the Canadians had discovered that the tactical position made it impossible for them to hold on to their gains.

In every succeeding attack conditions were the same—no preparation, poor coordination between units and commanders, and lack of artillery support. Only one circumstance differed—visiblity. The first attack was made in darkness which shrouded German eyes and nullified their preponderance in firepower. The other five were made in broad daylight, and in these, allied troops failed even to reach the German position. The possibilities of anything except disaster were remote under such circumstances. Yet in each repeat performance the only change in method had been to throw in a larger number of victims.

This appallingly poor tactical performance on the part of the Allies had been caused by pressure from above. Those commanders in charge of strategy had been totally out of touch with the reality of the Salient and had made impossible demands upon their subordinates. At the highest levels the governing idea had been that the French must restore the portion of the line lost by them and that the British should only assist. After the first day or so it became obvious that this concept was an illusion. It was an illusion because General Foch was unwilling to commit troops in the numbers required to retake the lost ground. He had talked to his British counterpart of massive reinforcements but had ordered his subordinate, Putz, to carry out the attacks without anything approaching the strength required, in either infantry or artillery. Thus none of the French counterattacks had the slightest chance of success.

Sir John French, for his part, had co-operated fully with an uncharacteristic gullible acceptance of Foch's promises. It had soon become evident that the roles had become reversed; the British were now expected to retake the lost ground assisted by the French. Sir John had evidently begun to realize this and had even opposed the idea. Yet every time he had met with the bombastic Foch he had come away committed to yet another hasty and ill-prepared attack.

Experience learned the hard way at Neuve Chapelle the previous month had shown that nothing but a carefully prepared offensive — after weeks of planning — could possibly dislodge the enemy once they had several days to fortify an area. Yet Sir John ordered attack after attack with no preparation whatsoever. Could he possibly have been incompetent to such a degree that he had not realized the obvious consequences? Could he possibly have been so gullible as to have believed Foch's promises time after time? And what of Ferdinand Foch? Why had he egged on his ally with false promises of co-operation? Why had he caused his ally to fritter away the bulk of his strategic reserve when (even if they had been successful) Foch's own lack of co-operative action would have doomed that ally to ultimate defeat? Who can understand two such commanders?

To have retrieved the lost ground in the Salient would have required a massive operation. Would it have been worthwhile even if successful? Strategically there would be no benefit, but politically the loss of one of the remaining small segments of Belgium would have been disheartening to the Belgians. But was such a minor consideration worth the price paid? The natural defensive line was one along the canal, eliminating the Salient entirely. This shortening of the line would have freed troops and left the Germans with a small piece of shattered landscaped paid for at a terrible price. When it is also considered that the Allies had been organizing a large offensive in Artois, and that the British had just embarked on the very ambitious Dardanelles campaign, it seems completely inexcusable to have incurred such costly losses holding the Salient.

For better or for worse, the price had been paid, but the merchandise received was a smaller, easily dominated Salient. As Liddell-Hart points out, "to throw good money after bad is foolish. But to throw away men's lives where there is no reasonable chance of advantage is criminal . . . For such manslaughter, whether it springs from ignorance, a false conception of war, or a want of moral courage, commanders should be held accountable to the nation."[10]

What did fate have in store for the commanders of Second Ypres? Foch, in April, 1918, was appointed Commander-in-Chief of all allied armies on the Western Front. He became a Marshal of France and oversaw the final victories of the Last Hundred Days. General Putz, by October, 1918, had become the Assistant Inspector General of the French Army. Jean Mordacq became a General and chief military aide to Clemenceau. He later commanded the French Occupation Forces in Germany after the war. Mordacq died on 12 April, 1943, during the German occupation of Paris. His body was found in the Seine, and the Vichy government reported his death as suicide. General Ferry paid the penalty for being right when his superiors were wrong. His warnings of the impending gas attack were rewarded by years of obscurity.

What happened to some of the less exalted soldiers of France? "Mr. Moroc," the Algerian who had attached himself to the 16th Canadian Scottish, eventually was ordered to return to his unit. This he did reluctantly. He had become very popular, and his departure was sorrowful, but he cut a remarkable figure as he marched away in his kilt and highland bonnet. Many other 'Turcos' had attached themselves to Empire units and had earned loyal friends and proud memories. The last known Algerian to serve with a British unit died on 8 May with the Northumberland Fusiliers. Blinded by a severe wound, he clambered onto the parapet where he stood hurling his defiance at the enemy till he was shot down.

Sir John French was removed from command in December, but was created an earl. He had the effrontery to choose as his title, "Earl of Ypres." Lord French next became Lord Lieutenant of Ireland from 1918 to 1921, in time, appropriately enough, to supervise the downfall of British rule there. Sir Horace Smith-Dorrien—possibly the ablest of all British generals—never received another military command although after being employed for some time he was appointed Governor of Gibraltar. He died in an automobile accident in 1930. General Plumer commanded the Second Army for the duration and engineered several victories including the notable Messines affair of 1917. He later served as Governor of Malta and High Commissioner for Palestine. "Wully" Robertson climaxed his rise from Private by being made Field Marshal in 1920. By that time he had served as Chief of the Imperial General Staff for three years and later as Commander in Chief British Army of Occupation in Germany. General Alderson rose to become first commander of the Canadian Corps and eventually Inspector General of Canadian Forces in England. General Snow later commanded the VII Corps. Hull rose to command a division, but the unfortunate Colonel Geddes was killed by shell-fire in the act of breaking up the makeshift 'Geddes' Detachment' on 28 April.

Several of the Canadians also earned promotions to positions of authority. This is an interesting development because Canadian officers, before Ypres, were generally considered by their British counterparts to be almost useless. It will be noted that during the entire course of the Second Battle of Ypres, no British troops were ever put under control of a Canadian. (General Alderson, it will be remembered was a British general.) One striking example will suffice: On 23 April, Brigadier Mercer of the 1st Brigade had been left with two battalions and his entire headquarters staff, yet in his area seven British battalions were placed under a British colonel (Geddes) who had no headquarters staff. Despite this attitude, these Canadian militia officers had begun to make their marks: Currie (O.C. 2nd Brigade) eventually commanded the Canadian Corps, after Alderson and Julian Byng; Turner and McNaughton served as Chiefs of the General Staff; while Mercer, Loomis, Watson, Lipsett, and Burstall rose to command divisions; Tuxford, Hayter, Hughes,

Leckie, Rennied, Dyer, Hilliam, Ormond, and Odlum all became Brigadier Generals.

There were no immediate changes in the German High Command. Falkenhayn's summer offensive in Galicia was a great success, but had not knocked Russia out of the war. His next big operation was the attack on Verdun. This, of course, became a bloodbath of unprecedented proportion, and Falkenhayn was relieved as Chief of the General Staff in 1916. He did however continue to serve in various lesser capacities till his resignation in June, 1919. Duke Albrecht of Württemberg remained in command of the Fourth Army with reasonable success till the war's end. Fritz Haber, the German Jew who has often been labelled the "Father of Chemical Warfare," was awarded the Nobel Prize for Chemistry in 1918. It is ironic that in 1933 after the rise to power of the former Corporal, Adolf Hitler, Haber was forced to escape German anti-semitism by fleeing to England.

One other humbler German also endured a fate less than pleasant. The deserter, August Jaeger, was sentenced to ten years in the penitentiary for desertion and betrayal by the Reich Supreme Court on 17 December, 1932. His activities had finally come to light when his name was revealed by General Ferry in a 1930 magazine article.

In the final analysis any battle must be judged by its far-reaching effects. In the case of the Second Battle of Ypres, these long-range results were infinitely more important than were those perceived at the time. The French left the Salient to their British allies for the remainder of the war. Foch's much anticipated Artois offensive has gone unremarked into the background of military history. Although not attributable to the Ypres battle alone, the French Army began to modernize; within months "horizon blue," an attempt to combine tradition with the need for camouflage, had replaced the dashing blue, white, and red uniforms of the French infantry.

The British took over the defense of the Salient, and despite numerous reverses, held it for the rest of the war. So tenaciously did they cling to the dogma of its importance that a Third Battle of Ypres was fought in 1917. To history it is best remembered as Passchendaele—a lasting symbol of mindless folly and waste of life. The British—despite assurances to the contrary by Haber and other German scientists—soon outdistanced the Germans in the employment of gas. Their Gas Brigade rapidly developed the most terrifying and lethal forms of gas, and discharged them in a variety of ways—by cloud gas, shells, and projectors.

For Canadians the Second Battle of Ypres had come as an enormous shock. Canadian newspapers had been trumpeting the heroic stand of their division and had been warning for days that casualties might go as high as 1,000. On 3 May the true figures hit the headlines—at least 6,000 casualties, with 2,536 missing. One battalion, the 15th (48th Highlanders) had alone lost 691 men. It was this shock which at last made clear the facts of war to the fledgling nation. A surge of nationalism soon made up the losses however, as thousands of young men rushed to volunteer. Eventually four frontline divisions formed a Canadian Corps, and the spirit born at Ypres carried them on through the Somme, Vimy Ridge, Hill 70, Passchendaele and the glorious Last Hundred Days. By that time these colonials, who had been considered too undisciplined, too free and easy to make good soldiers, had become a reliable striking force for the Allies—praised by friend and foe alike. That proud reputation had been founded during April, 1915, in the Ypres Salient.

The confused struggle had glaringly highlighted the Allies' weakness in command structure, communications, and intelligence. The Canadians led the way in making administrative changes to facilitate the control of large forces and to prevent the terrible muddles of April, 1915, from repeating themselves.

The results to the Germans were other than they had planned. Two dramatic blunders on the part of their scientists soon produced horrendous results for the German war effort. First was the failure to note the direction of the prevailing winds, and second was the assumption that Britain would never be able to produce an effective system of chemical warfare. According to the records available,* the Germans launched a total of 24 cloud gas attacks (including phosgene), but they were the recipients of several Russian, 20-odd

---

* All the following figures are taken from *Gas Brigade,* by Maj.-Gen. C. H. Foulkes.

French, and 150 British cloud gas attacks. Thus German troops suffered nearly ten times more attacks than did the Allies.

The most far-reaching effect of Second Ypres was the development of gas warfare from the primitive chlorine cloud gas to a host of far more lethal gasses delivered by projectors. In this field German science fell so far behind that if the war had lasted into 1919 as expected, the Allies would have achieved an absolutely overwhelming superiority. As it was, the British alone launched 768 successful gas operations during the war. German records do not show how many they launched themselves, but at best it was only a fraction of the above.

Total British casualties from gas after May, 1915, were 181, 053. This figure includes even very slight cases. Of the above total 6,109 were fatal. No figures were kept for the Second Battle of Ypres, but the usually accepted estimate is 3,000. Thus it appears that the Germans' greatest success with gas was its first use. After that the tables were turned dramatically.

The German High Command made a systematic attempt to cover up their blunder by not revealing the enormity of their casualties due to allied gas operations. Gas casualties were listed only as wounded or killed with no mention of the cause. Even long after the war German historians released no figures, and, in fact, claimed that none existed, although for a handful of British attacks which were not successful figures miraculously appeared. Interrogation of German prisoners also revealed that they had been instructed not to talk about gas or gas casualties.

After the war numerous German Regimental Histories were published, but all skirted around the topic of gas casualties. Many even denied the use of gas by the Germans and claimed their successes to be without the use of gas.*

The official view was probably best illustrated by von Falkenhayn in his memoirs. Here he described the Second Battle of Ypres as merely one of several operations "to cloak the transportation of troops to Galicia . . . One such undertaking in the area of the Fourth Army before Ypres developed into a serious attack because

---

* The History of Regiment Reussner quoted previously recorded for 24 April, "Again let it be emphatically declared that no gas cloud was released, that Regiment Reussner was only supported by artillery." see Duguid, p. 326, Appendix 706d.

the gas weapon, which was used for the first time on a large scale, supplied the opportunity. Its surprise effect was very great. Unfortunately we were not in a position to exploit it to the full. The necessary reserves were not ready. The success achieved, however, was considerable."[10]

With this bland statement von Falkenhayn dismissed the Second Battle of Ypres.

In the final analysis the German Command had failed to make worthwhile use of their new secret weapon. But worse than that, in failing, they had unleashed upon their own troops a form of warfare so terrible that a conspiracy of silence was convened to erase it from their history.

The Second Battle of Ypres was a miniature of the entire First World War. In it were seen all the elements of war — the heroism, the atrocities, the total destruction of a way of life and the achievements of centuries, the terrible toll in maimed and killed, the missed opportunities, the callousness of the leaders towards those they led. But there is also that ultimate horror so characteristic of the "War to End War" — so many had died to achieve nothing.

Appendix One

Order of Battle

1st Canadian Division: Lieutenant General E.A.H. Alderson

1st Canadian Brigade. Brigadier General M.S. Mercer
  1st Battalion, Western Ontario Regiment
  2nd Battalion, Eastern Ontario Regiment
  3rd Battalion, Toronto Regiment
  4th Battalion, Central Ontario Regiment

2nd Canadian Brigade. Brigadier General A.W. Currie
  5th Battalion, Western Cavalry
  7th Battalion, 1st British Columbia
  8th Battalion, 90th Rifles
  10th Battalion, Canadians

3rd Canadian Brigade. Brigadier General R.E.W. Turner, V.C.
  13th Battalion, Royal Highlanders of Canada
  14th Battalion, Royal Montreal Regiment
  15th Battalion, 48th Highlanders of Canada
  16th Battalion, The Canadian Scottish

1st Canadian Divisional Artillery. Brigadier General H.E. Burstall
  1st Brigade, C.F.A. (1st, 2nd, 3rd, 4th Batteries)
    4 gun batteries
  2nd Brigade, C.F.A. (5th, 6th, 7th, 8th Batteries)
    4 gun batteries
  3rd Brigade, C.F.A. (9th, 10th, 11th, 12th Batteries)
    4 gun batteries
  118th (Howitzer) Brigade, R.F.A. (458th, 459th Batteries)

Field Companies, Canadian Engineers
  1st, 2nd, 3rd

Mounted Troops
  Special Service Squadron, 19th Alberta Dragoons
  1st Canadian Divisional Cyclist Company

British Divisions (Infantry)

4th Division: Major General H.F.M. Wilson

10th Brigade. Brigadier General C.P.A. Hull
    1st Battalion, The Royal Warwickshire Regiment
    2nd Battalion, Seaforth Highlanders
    1st Battalion, Princess Victoria's (Royal Irish Fusiliers)
    2nd Battalion, The Royal Dublin Fusiliers
    7th Battalion, Princess Louise's (Argyll and Sutherland Highlanders)
        (Territorial)

11th Brigade. Brigadier General Hasler
    1st Battalion, Prince Albert's (Somerset Light Infantry)
    1st Battalion, The East Lancashire Regiment
    1st Battalion, The Hampshire Regiment
    1st Battalion, The Rifle Brigade
    5th Battalion, The London Regiment (London Rifle Brigade)
        (Territorial)

12th Brigade. Brigadier General F.G. Anley
    1st Battalion, The King's Own (Royal Lancaster Regiment)
    2nd Battalion, The Royal Irish Regiment
    2nd Battalion, The Lancashire Fusiliers
    2nd Battalion, The Essex Regiment
    5th Battalion, The Prince of Wales' Volunteers (South Lancashire
        Regiment) (Territorial)
    2nd Battalion, The Monmouthshire Regiment (Territorial)

5th Division: Major General T.L.N. Morland

13th Brigade. Brigadier General R. Wanless O'Gowan
    2nd Battalion, The King's Own Scottish Borderers
    2nd Battalion, The Duke of Wellington's (West Riding Regiment)
    1st Battalion, The Queen's Own (Royal West Kent Regiment)
    2nd Battalion, The King's Own (Yorkshire Light Infantry)
    9th Battalion, The London Regiment (Queen Victoria's Rifles)
        (Territorial)

14th Brigade. Brigadier General G.H. Thesiger
    1st Battalion, The Devonshire Regiment
    1st Battalion, The East Surrey Regiment

1st Battalion, The Duke of Cornwall's Light Infantry
2nd Battalion, The Manchester Regiment
5th Battalion, The Cheshire Regiment (Territorial)

15th Brigade. Brigadier General E. Northey
1st Battalion, The Norfolk Regiment
1st Battalion, The Bedfordshire Regiment
1st Battalion, The Cheshire Regiment
1st Battalion, The Dorsetshire Regiment
6th Battalion, The King's Liverpool Regiment (Territorial)

27th Division: Major General T.D'O. Snow

80th Brigade. Brigadier General W.E.B. Smith
2nd Battalion, The King's Shropshire Light Infantry
3rd Battalion, King's Royal Rifle Corps
4th Battalion, King's Royal Rifle Corps
4th Battalion, The Rifle Brigade
Princess Patricia's Canadian Light Infantry

81st Brigade. Brigadier General H.L. Croker
1st Battalion, The Royal Scots
2nd Battalion, The Gloucestershire Regiment
2nd Battalion, The Queen's Own Cameron Highlanders
1st Battalion, Princess Louise's (Argyll and Sutherland Highlanders)
9th Battalion, The Royal Scots (Territorial)
9th Battalion, Princess Louise's (Argyll and Sutherland Highlanders)
(Territorial)

82nd Brigade. Brigadier General J.R. Longley
1st Battalion, The Royal Irish Regiment
2nd Battalion, The Duke of Cornwall's Light Infantry
2nd Battalion, Princess Victoria's (Royal Irish Fusiliers)
1st Battalion, The Prince of Wales' Leinster Regiment
1st Battalion, The Cambridgeshire Regiment (Territorial)

28th Division: Major General E.S. Bulfin

83rd Brigade. Brigadier General R.C. Boyle
2nd Battalion, The King's Own (Royal Lancaster Regiment)
2nd Battalion, The East Yorkshire Regiment
1st Battalion, The King's Own (Yorkshire Light Infantry)

1st Battalion, The York and Lancaster Regiment
5th Battalion, The King's Own (Royal Lancaster Regiment)
    (Territorial)
3rd Battalion, The Monmouthshire Regiment (Territorial)

84th Brigade. Brigadier General L.J. Bols
2nd Battalion, The Northumberland Fusiliers
1st Battalion, The Suffolk Regiment
2nd Battalion, The Cheshire Regiment
1st Battalion, The Welsh Regiment
12th Battalion, The London Regiment (The Rangers) (Territorial)

85th Brigade. Brigadier General A.J. Chapman
2nd Battalion, The Buffs (East Kent Regiment)
3rd Battalion, The Royal Fusiliers (City of London Regiment)
2nd Battalion, The East Surrey Regiment
3rd Battalion, The Duke of Cambridge's Own (Middlesex Regiment)
8th Battalion, The Duke of Cambridge's Own (Middlesex Regiment)
    (Territorial)

50th (1st Northumbrian) Division (Territorial):
Major-General Sir W.F.L. Lindsay

149th Brigade (1st Northumberland). Brigadier General J.F. Riddell
4th Battalion, The Northumberland Fusiliers
5th Battalion, The Northumberland Fusiliers
6th Battalion, The Northumberland Fusiliers
7th Battalion, The Northumberland Fusiliers

150th Brigade (1st York and Durham). Brigadier General J.E. Bush
4th Battalion, The East Yorkshire Regiment
4th Battalion, Alexandra, Princess of Wales' Own
    (Yorkshire Regiment)
5th Battalion, Alexandra, Princess of Wales' Own
    (Yorkshire Regiment)
5th Battalion, The Durham Light Infantry

151st Brigade (1st Durham Light Infantry). Brigadier General H. Martin
6th Battalion, The Durham Light Infantry
7th Battalion, The Durham Light Infantry
8th Battalion, The Durham Light Infantry
9th Battalion, The Durham Light Infantry

Lahore Division (Indian Army): Major General H.D'U. Keary

Ferozepore Brigade. Brigadier General R.G. Egerton
    Connaught Rangers
    9th Bhopal Infantry
    57th Wilde's Rifles
    129th Duke of Connaught's Own Baluchis
    4th Battalion, The London Regiment (Royal Fusiliers) (Territorial)

Jullundur Brigade. Brigadier General E.P. Strickland
    1st Battalion, The Manchester Regiment
    40th Pathans
    47th Sikhs
    59th Scinde Rifles
    4th Battalion, The Suffolk Regiment (Territorial)

Sirhind Brigade. Brigadier General W.G. Walker, V.C.
    1st Battalion, The Highland Light Infantry
    15th Ludhiana Sikhs
    1st Battalion, 1st King George's Own Gurkha Rifles
        (The Malaun Regiment)
    1st Battalion, 4th Gurkha Rifles
    4th Battalion, The King's Liverpool Regiment

Détachement d'Armée de Belgique, General Putz

18th Division: General Lefevre

35th Brigade. General de Cugnac
    32nd Infantry Regiment
    66th Infantry Regiment

36th Brigade
    77th Infantry Regiment
    135th Infantry Regiment

45th Division: General Quiquandon

90th Brigade. Colonel Mordacq
    2nd *bis* Zouaves de marche
    1st Tirailleurs de marche

1st Battalion d'Afrique
3rd Battalion d'Afrique

91st Brigade. General Codet
7th Zouaves de marche
3rd *bis* Zouaves

152nd Division: General Joppé

304th Brigade
268th Infantry Regiment
290th Infantry Regiment

4th Moroccan Brigade. Colonel Savy
1st Moroccan Infantry
8th Tirailleurs de marche

153rd Division: General Deligny

306th Brigade
418th Infantry Regiment
2nd Battalion Chasseurs à pied
4th Battalion Chasseurs à pied

3rd Moroccan Brigade. General Cherrier
1st mixte Zouaves et Tirailleurs
9th Zouaves de marche

87th Territorial Divison: General Roy

73rd Brigade
73rd Territorial Regiment
74th Territorial Regiment

174th Brigade
76th Territorial Regiment
79th Territorial Regiment
80th Territorial Regiment

186th Brigade. Colonel Marcieu
100th Territorial Regiment
102nd Territorial Regiment

German

Fourth Army: General Duke Albrecht of Württemberg

XXII Reserve Corps. General von Falkenhayn

43rd Reserve Division:

85th Reserve Brigade
201st Reserve Infantry Regiment
202nd Reserve Infantry Regiment

86th Reserve Brigade
203rd Reserve Infantry Regiment
204th Reserve Infantry Regiment

44th Reserve Division:
207th Reserve Infantry Regiment of the 88th Reserve Brigade

XXVI Reserve Corps: General von Hugel

51st Reserve Division:

101st Reserve Brigade
233rd Reserve Infantry Regiment
234th Reserve Infantry Regiment

102nd Reserve Brigade
235th Reserve Infantry Regiment
236th Reserve Infantry Regiment
23rd Reserve Jaeger Battalion

52nd Reserve Division:

103rd Reserve Brigade
237th Reserve Infantry Regiment
238th Reserve Infantry Regiment

104th Reserve Brigade
239th Reserve Infantry Regiment
240th Reserve Infantry Regiment
24th Reserve Jaeger Battalion

Attached Formations:

4th Naval Brigade
     4th and 5th Naval Regiments

37th Landwehr Brigade
     73rd and 74th Landwehr Infantry Regiments

2nd Reserve Ersatz Brigade
     3rd Reserve Ersatz Infantry Regiment. (33rd, 34th, and 35th
          Reserve Ersatz Battalions)
     4th Reserve Ersatz Infantry Regiment. (36th, 37th, and 38th
          Reserve Ersatz Battalions)
Composite Brigade of the 43rd Reserve Division (XXII Reserve Corps)

XXVII Reserve Corps: General von Carlowitz

53rd Reserve Division:

105th Reserve Brigade
     241st Reserve Infantry Regiment
     242nd Reserve Infantry Regiment

106th Reserve Brigade
     243rd Reserve Infantry Regiment
     244th Reserve Infantry Regiment
     25th Reserve Jaeger Battalion

54th Reserve Division:

107th Reserve Brigade
     245th Reserve Infantry Regiment
     246th Reserve Infantry Regiment

108th Reserve Brigade
     247th Reserve Infantry Regiment
     248th Reserve Infantry Regiment
     28th Reserve Jaeger Battalion

Attached formation:

38th Landwehr Brigade
    77th Landwehr Regiment
    78th Landwehr Regiment

Sturmbrigade Schmieden:
(temporary formation with the XXVII Reserve Corps)

Regiment Wilhelmi
    II/78 Landwehr Infantry Regiment (38th Landwehr Brigade)
    III/78 L.I.R. (38th Landwehr Brigade)
    II/244 R.I.R. (106th Reserve Brigade, 53rd Reserve Division)

Regiment Reussner
    II/241 R.I.R. (105th R.B., 53rd R.D.)
    III/241 R.I.R. (105th R.B., 53rd R.D.)
    II/242 R.I.R. (105th R.B. 53rd R.D.)

Regiment Heygendorff
    III/245th R.I.R. (107th R.B., 54th R.D.)
    II/247th R.I.R. (108th R.B., 54th R.D.)

Appendix Two

Victoria Cross Winners
Ypres, 22-27 April, 1915

Fisher, Corporal Fred. 13th Battalion, Canadian Expeditionary Force. 23 April, 1915 (posthumous).

Hall, Sergeant Major Frederick William. 8th Battalion, Canadian Expeditionary Force. 24 April, 1915 (posthumous).

Bellew, Lieutenant Edward Donald. 7th Battalion, Canadian Expeditionary Force. 24 April, 1915.

Scrimger, Captain Francis Alexander Caron. Canadian Army Medical Corps (attached to 14th Battalion, C.E.F.). 25 April, 1915.

Dast, Jemedar Mir. 57th Wilde's Rifles, Indian Army Corps. 26 April, 1915.

Rhodes-Moorehouse, 2nd Lieutenant William Barnard. Special Reserve, Royal Flying Corps. 26 April, 1915 (posthumous).

Smith, A/Corporal Issy. 1st Battalion Manchester Regiment, Indian Army Corps. 26 April, 1915.

Notes

Chapter One

1   Ferry,General Edmond, "Ce qui s'est passé sur l'Yser," *La Revue Des Vivants*, Paris, Juillet 1930, pp. 899, 900.
2   Ibid.
3   Clark, Alan, *The Donkeys*, New York, Award Books, 1965, pp. 80.
5   Edmonds, Brigadier J.E. and Wynne, Captain G.C., *History of the Great War: Military Operations France and Belgium, 1915*, Volume 1 London, Macmillan, 1927, pp. 164. (Hereinafter referred to as B.O.H.)
6   V. Corps War Diary, 15 April, 1915. Quoted by Duguid, Colonel Fortescue, *History of the Canadian Forces*, 1914-19, Volume 2, Ottawa, Department of National Defence, 1938, pp. 232 appendix 323. Italics are authors'.
7   *With the First Canadian Contingent*, Toronto, Hodder and Straughton, 1915. pp. 75.
8   Ferry, General Edmond, pp. 900.
9   Seth, Ronald, *Some of My Favourite Spies*, Chilton, Philadephia, 1968, pp. 78-9.
10 Foulkes, Major General C.H., *Gas! The Story of the Special Brigade*, Edinburgh, Blackwood and Sons Ltd, 1934, pp. 32.
11 *The Times History of the War*, 22 Volumes, The Times, London, 1914-19, Vol. 5 pp. 49-50.

Chapter Two

1   Trumpener, Ulrich, "The Road to Ypres: The Beginning of Gas Warfare in W.W.I" *Journal of Modern History*, Chicago, volume 47, No. 3, September, 1975, pp. 462-3.
2   Mordacq, Colonel J.J., *Le drame sur l'Yser*, pp. 245-6.
3   Trumpener, Ulrich, pp. 470-1.
4   *Reichsarchiv*, quoted in B.O.H., 1915, Vol. 1 pp. 188-90.
5   German Regimental History quoted in Duguid, vol. 2, pp. 325, appendix 706d.
6   Ibid.
7   Trumpener, Ulrich, pp. 474-5.

Chapter Three

1   *Letters From the Front*, 2 volumes, The Canadian Bank of Commerce, 1920, vol. 1, pp. 13.
2   Duguid, Col. Fortescue, vol. 2, pp. 86 appendix 111.
3   Ibid.
4   Mordacq, Colonel J.J., pp. 46-7.
5   Ibid, pp. 41-2.

6   Ibid, pp. 50.
7   Currie, Colonel J.A. *The Red Watch,* Toronto, McClelland, Goodchild and Stewart, 1916, pp. 213.

Chapter Four

1   Mordacq, pp. 49.
2   Bell, George V. Manuscript held in the Public Archives of Canada.
3   Currie, Col. J.A., pp. 214.

Chapter Five

1   *The Times History of the War,* vol. 5, pp. 56.
2   Mordacq, Colonel J.J., pp. 75.
3   Ibid, pp. 69.
4   Ibid, pp. 75-6.
6   From the CBC series "Flanders Fields" written and produced by J. Frank Willis and edited by Frank Lalor, Toronto, 1964, No. 5, pp. 4.
7   Canadian War Records, pp. 269.
8   CBC, No. 5, pp. 4.
9   Currie, Colonel J.A., pp. 219.
10 CBC, No. 5, pp. 5.
11 Swettenham, John, *McNaughton,* vol. 1, Toronto, Ryerson, 1968, pp. 44-5.
12 Ibid, pp. 45.
13 Duguid, Colonel Fortescue, vol. 2, pp. 320, appendix 706.
14 Trumpener, Ulrich, pp. 460.

Chapter Six

1   Mordacq, Colonel J.J., pp. 85-6.
2   Ibid, pp. 86-7.
3   Ibid, pp. 108.
4   Pollard, Hugh B.C., *The Story of Ypres,* London, McBride, Nast & Co., Ltd., 1917, pp. 53-4.
5   Urquhart, H.M., (Canadian Scottish) pp. 57.
6   Ibid, pp. 58.
7   *The Times History of the War,* vol. 5, pp. 61.
8   Ibid, pp. 62-3.
9   Urquhart, H.M., (Canadian Scottish) pp. 59.
10 Canadian War Records, pp. 244.
11 Peat, Harold R., *Private Peat,* Indianapolis, Bobbs-Merrill, 1917, pp. 153.
12 Fetherstonhaugh, R.C., *The Royal Montreal Regiment 14th Battalion C.E.F. 1914-1925,* Montreal, The Royal Montreal Regiment, 1927, pp. 41.
13 CBC, No. 5, pp. 6.
14 Canadian War Records, pp. 244.

Chapter Seven

1 *Fifty Amazing Stories of the Great War*, London, Odhams, 1936, pp. 428.
2 CBC, No. 5, pp. 11.
3 Peat, Harold R., pp. 157-62.
4 *Fifty Amazing Stories of the Great War,* pp. 428.
5 Mordacq, Colonel J.J. pp. 137.
6 *Trinity War Book,* Toronto, Trinity Methodist Church, 1921, pp. 45.
7 CBC, No. 5, pp. 11.
8 Duguid, Col. Fortescue, vol. 2, pp. 324, Appendix 706A.

Chapter Eight

1 Liddell Hart, Sir Basil H., *Reputations Ten Years After*, Boston, Little, Brown, and Co., 1928, pp. 161.
2 Clark, Alan, pp. 79.
3 Urquhart, H.M., (Canadian Scottish), pp. 62.
4 Chapman, Guy, *Vain Glory*, London, Cassell and Co., 1937, pp. 32.
5 Clark, Alan, pp. 77.
6 Chapman, Guy, pp. 31.
7 CBC, No. 5, pp. 13.
8 *Canada in the Great World War,* vol. 3, pp. 105.
9 Mordacq, Colonel J.J., pp. 135.
10 CBC, No. 5, pp. 14.
11 B.O.H., 1915, vol. 1, pp. 213.

Chapter Nine

1 CBC, No. 5, pp. 15.
2 Rae, Herbert, *Maple Leaves in Flanders Fields*, Toronto, Wm. Briggs, 1916, pp. 161-2.
3 CBC, No. 5, pp. 17.
4 Urquhart, H.M., (Canadian Scottish), pp. 65.
5 CBC, No. 5, pp. 17.
6 Ibid.
7 Ibid, pp. 16.
8 Ibid, pp. 27.
9 Ibid, pp. 18.
10 Ibid, pp. 17.
11 Ibid, pp. 17-18.
12 Ibid, pp. 18.
13 "Daily Province," Vancouver, 12 Nov., 1917.

Chapter Ten

1 Nicholson, Colonel G.W.L., *Canadian Expeditionary Force 1914–1919*, Ottawa, Queen's Printer, 1962, pp. 77.

2   Urquhart, H.M., *Arthur Currie,* Toronto, J.M. Dent and Sons, 1950, pp. 90.
3   Swettenham, John (McNaughton), pp. 45-6.
4   Ibid, pp. 46.
5   Chapman, Guy, pp. 33.
6   Ibid.
7   Ibid, pp. 33-4.
8   CBC, No. 5, pp. 19.
9   Ibid, pp. 20.
10 Ibid.
11 Chapman, Guy, pp. 34-5.
12 Ibid, pp. 35.

Chapter Eleven

1   Duguid, Colonel Fortescue, vol. 1, pp. 335.
2   Mordacq, Colonel J.J., pp. 116.
3   Ibid, pp. 178.
4   Foulkes, Major General C.H., pp. 306.
5   Mordacq, Colonel J.J., pp. 175-6.
6   Binding, R., *A Fatalist at War,* (translated by Ian F.D. Morrow) London, George Allen and Unwin Ltd., 1929, pp. 64.

Chapter Twelve

1   Bairnsfather, Bruce, *Bullets & Billets*, New York, G.P. Putnam's Sons, 1917, pp. 265.
2   Ibid, pp. 272.
3   CBC, No. 5, pp. 21.
4   Ibid, pp. 22.
5   Bairnsfather, Bruce, pp. 277.
6   CBC, No. 5, pp. 22.
7   Bairnsfather, Bruce, pp. 277.
8   Morrison, A.D., *The Great War, 1914—1918* (7th Battalion Argyll and Sutherland Highlanders), Alva, Cunningham, No date. Quoted from chapter titled "1915."
9   Bairnsfather, Bruce, pp. 280.
10 Ibid, pp. 283-4.
11 Urquhart, H.M., (Canadian Scottish) pp. 67.
12 Urquhart, H.M., (Arthur Currie) pp. 99.
13 CBC, No. 5, pp. 23.
14 Canada in the Great World War, vol. 3, pp. 171-2.
15 CBC, No. 5, pp. 23.
16 Aitken, Sir Max, *Canada in Flanders*, 3 volumes, London, Hodder and Stroughton, 1916-18, vol. 1, pp. 83.
17 Smithers, A.J., *The Man Who Disobeyed*, London, Leo Cooper, 1970, pp. 288-9.

Chapter Thirteen

1 Currie, Colonel J.A., The Red Watch, pp. 264.
2 Duguid, Colonel Fortescue, vol. 1, pp. 36.
3 Smithers, A.J., pp. 289.
4 *Times History of the War*, vol. 5, pp. 58.
5 Merewether, Lt. Colonel J.W.B. and Smith, Rt. Hon. Sir Frederick, *The Indian Corps in France,* New York, E.P. Dutton and Company, 1918, pp. 291.
6 Ibid, pp. 300.
7 Ibid, pp. 295.
8 Ibid, pp. 233.
9 Clark, Alan, *The Donkeys*, pp. 89.
10 Urquhart, H.M., (Canadian Scottish) pp. 68.
11 Merewether and Smith, pp. 308.
12 B.O.H., 1915, vol. 1, pp. 261.
13 War Diary, 4th Moroccan Brigade, 26 April, 191.
14 Merewether and Smith, pp. 308-9.
15 Binding, R., *A Fatalist at War,* pp. 65.

Chapter Fourteen

1 War Diary, French 152nd Infantry Division, 27 April, 1915.
2 War Diary, 4th Moroccan Brigade, 27 April, 1915.
3 B.O.H., 1915, vol. 1, pp. 273.
4 Ibid., pp. 274.
5 Ibid.
6 War Diary, 4th Moroccan Brigade, 27 April, 1915.
7 B.O.H., 1915, vol. 1, pp. 274.
8 Binding, R., pp. 65.

Epilogue

1 Clark, pp. 92.
2 Smithers, pp. 261.
3 Liddell Hart, B.H., *History of the Great War, 1914-1918,* Faber and Faber, 1936, pp. 245.
4 Ibid.
5 *British Official History,* pp. 210.
6 Liddell Hart, *History of the Great War,* pp. 247.
7 Ibid, pp. 245.
8 CBC, No. 5, pp. 27.
9 George Patrick, 2nd Battalion, CBC, No. 5, pp. 27.
10 Liddell Hart, *History of the Great War,* pp. 254.

Bibliography

1 Aitken, Sir Max (M.P.). *Canada in Flanders* 3 vols. London: Hodder and Stoughton, 1916.
2 Bairnsfather, Bruce. *Bullets and Billets.* New York: G.P. Putnam's Sons, 1917.
3 Banks, Arthur. *A Military Atlas of the First World War.* London: Purnell Book Services Ltd., 1975.
4 Beattie, Kim. *48th Highlanders of Canada 1891-1928.* Toronto: 48th Highlanders of Canada, 1932.
5 Binding, R. *A Fatalist at War* (translated by Ian F.D. Morrow). London: Geo. Allen & Unwin Ltd., 1929.
6 *Canada in the Great World War.* 6 vols. Toronto: United Publishers of Canada, Ltd., 1919.
7 Casson, Stanley. *Steady Drummer.* London: G. Bell and Sons Ltd., 1935.
8 Chapman, Guy. *Vain Glory.* London: Cassell and Co., 1937.
9 Clark, Allen. *The Donkeys.* New York: Award Books, 1965.
10 Currie, Col. J.A. (M.P.). *The Red Watch.* Toronto: McClelland, Goodchild and Stewart, 1916.
11 Duguid, Col. A. Fortescue. *Official History of the Canadian Forces in the Great War 1914-1919.* 2 vols. Ottawa: Minister of National Defence, 1938.
12 Edmonds, Brigadier J.E. and Wynne, Capt. G.C. *History of the Great War: Military Operations France and Belgium, 1915* (1). London: MacMillan, 1927.
13 Ferry, General. "Ce qui s'est passé sur l'Yser." *La Revue Des Vivants.* Paris: Juillet, 1930.
14 Fetherstonhaugh, R.C. *The 13th Battalion Royal, C.E.F., 1914-1925.* Montreal: The Royal Montreal Regiment, 1927.
1 6 *Fifty Amazing Stories of the Great War.* London: Odhams, 1936.
17 Fitzsimons, Bernard (ed.). *Tanks and Weapons of World War I.* New York: Beekman House, 1973.
18 Foulkes, Maj.-Gen. C.H. *Gas! The Story of the Special Brigade.* Edinburgh: Blackwood & Sons Ltd., 1934.
19 Goerlitz, Walter. *The German General Staff.* New York: Praeger, 1957.
20 Hahn, Major J.E. *The Intelligence Service Within the Canadian Corps* (Historical Resume by Gen. Sir Arthur Currie). Toronto: MacMillan, 1930.
21 Jackson, Major Donovan. *India's Army.* London: Samson Low, Marston & Co., 1938.
22 Lefebure, Victor. *The Riddle of the Rhine.* New York: The Chemical Foundation, Inc., 1923.
23 *Letters From the Front.* 2 vols. The Canadian Bank of Commerce, 1920.
24 MacPhail, Sir Andrew. *The Medical Services.* Ottawa: The King's Printer, 1925.
25 Malcolm, C.A. *The Piper in Peace and War.* London: John Murray, 1927.
26 McClung, Nellie L. *Three Times and Out.* Toronto: Thomas Allen, 1918.
27 Merewether, Lt. Col. C.I.E. and Smith, The Rt. Hon. Sir Frederick. *The Indian Corps in France.* New York: E.P. Dutton and Company, 1918.
28 Mordacq, Col. J.J.L. *Le drame sur l'Yser.* Paris: Édition des Portiques, 1933.
29 Murry, Col. W.W. OBE MC. *The History of the Second Canadian Battalion*

(East Ontario Regiment) Canadian Expeditionary Force. Ottawa: 1947.

30 Nicholson, Col. G.W.L. *Canadian Expeditionary Force 1914-1919.* Ottawa: Queen's Printer, 1962.

31 Nicholson, Col. G.W.L. *The Gunners of Canada* (vol. 1). Toronto: McClelland and Stewart Ltd., 1967.

32 Pollard, Hugh B.C. *The Story of Ypres.* London: McBride, Nast & Co., Ltd., 1917.

33 Purdom, C.B. (ed). *Everyman at War.* London: J.M. Dent & Sons, 1930.

34 Seth, Ronald. *Some of My Favourite Spies.* Philadelphia: Chilton, 1968.

35 Seton, Sir Bruce and Grant, Pipe Major John. *The Pipes of War.* Glasgow: Maclehose, Jackson & Co., 1920.

36 Smither, A.J. *The Man Who Disobeyed.* London: Leo Cooper, 1970.

37 Sixsmith, Maj.-Gen. E.K.G. *British Generalship in the Twentieth Century.* London: Arms and Armour Press, 1970.

38 Stewart, Charles. *Overseas: The Lineages and Insignia of the Canadian Expeditionary Force 1914-1919.* Toronto: Little and Stewart, 1971.

39 Swettenham, John. *McNaughton.* Vol. 1. Toronto: Ryerson, 1968.

40 Terraine, John. *Ordeal of Victory.* Philadelphia: J.B. Lippincott Co., 1963.

41 Trumpener, Ulrich "The Road to Ypres: The Beginning of Gas Warfare in World War I." *Journal of Modern History*, Chicago, Vol. 47, No. 3, September, 1975.

42 Urquhart, H.M. *Arthur Currie.* Toronto: J.M. Dent and Sons, 1950.

43 Urquhart, H.M. *The History of the 16th Battalion (Canadian Scottish) C.E.F.* Toronto: Macmillan, 1932.

44 Warren, Arnold. *Wait for the Wagon.* Toronto: McClelland and Stewart Ltd., 1961.

45 *With the First Canadian Contingent.* Toronto: Hodder and Stoughton Ltd., 1915.

Index

243

British Expeditionary Force battalions:

German units:

XXIII Reserve Corps, 26, 42, 87, 155.

XXVI Reserve Corps, 26, 42, 87, 101, 155.

XXVII Reserve Corps, 155, 156.

XXVIII Reserve Corps, 26.

45th Reserve Division, 26, 81, 87, 97.

46th Reserve Division, 26, 97, 150.

51st Reserve Division, 26, 87, 155-56, 161.

52nd Reserve Division, 87, 155.

2nd Reserve Ersatz Brigade, 36, 155.

38th Landwehr Brigade, 155.

204th Reserve Infantry Regiment, 197.

244th Reserve Infantry Regiment, 168.

Pionierregiment 35, 24-25, 155, 191.

Indian Army units:

Lahore Division, 90, 159, 179, 184, 186, 195.

Ferozepore Brigade, 185-86, 188, 200.

Jullundur Brigade, 185-86, 189, 190.

Sirhind Brigade, 185, 195, 200, 204.

Gurkha Rifles, 1st Bn., 1st Regiment, 200-01.

Gurkha Rifles, 1st Bn., 4th Regiment, 195, 201, 204.

Highland Light Infantry, 1st Bn., 195, 205.

Ludhiana Sikhs, 15th, 195, 205.

Manchester Regiment, 1st Bn., 190.

Pathans, 40th, (40 Thieves), 185, 189-90, 193.

Wilde's Rifles, 57th, 185, 189.

Photo Credits

The illustrations in this book came from the following sources:

Imperial War Museum:
Field Marshal Sir John French (Q28858)
General Sir Horace Smith-Dorrien (Q70054)
Lieut-General Sir Herbert Plumer (Q9228)
General Ferdinand Foch (Q48178)
Improvised Gas Alarm (Q56927)
Trench Conditions in the Ypres Salient (Q51195)
Indian Sikhs (Q49826, Q49827, Q49828, Q53344)

Public Archives Canada:
Road Near Fortuin (PA4643)
General View of ground after gas (PA4498)
Kitchener's Wood (PA4564)
Arthur Currie (PA1370)
8th Canadian Infantry Battalion (PA4705)
Capt. W.H. Hooper (PA107238)
Gas Cloud (PA84-12608)
The Second Battle of Ypres (C14145)
The Painting: The German Poison Belt (C3976)

Saskatchewan Archives Board:
"Sergeant Bill" (R-A 10, 210)
Brig. Gen. Geo. S. Tufford (R-A10, 224)

10 Battery Orderly Room:
St. Catharines Contingent

Drummond Family:
Pte. Tom Drummond

Somerville Family:
Gunner Linden Somerville

Cover Credit:
Men of the 2nd Argyll and Sutherland Highlanders wearing first pattern anti-gas respirators, late 1915
Imperial War Museum (Q48951)

Maps:
by Edward Steel